RICK **LOVERD** · HUANG **DANLAN** · MARCIO **MENYZ**

V E N U S ™

BOOM!
S T U D I O S

VENUS, October 2016. Published by BOOM! Studios, a division of Boom Entertainment, Inc. Venus is ™ & © 2016 Richard Loverd & Filip Sablik. Originally published in single magazine form as VENUS No. 1-4. ™ & © 2015, 2016 Richard Loverd & Filip Sablik. All rights reserved. BOOM! Studios™ and the BOOM! Studios logo are trademarks of Boom Entertainment, Inc., registered in various countries and categories. All characters, events, and institutions depicted herein are fictional. Any similarity between any of the names, characters, persons, events, and/or institutions in this publication to actual names, characters, and persons, whether living or dead, events, and/or institutions is unintended and purely coincidental. BOOM! Studios does not read or accept unsolicited submissions of ideas, stories, or artwork.

A catalog record of this book is available from OCLC and from the BOOM! Studios website, www.boom-studios.com, on the Librarians Page.

BOOM! Studios, 5670 Wilshire Boulevard, Suite 450, Los Angeles, CA 90036-5679. Printed in China. First Printing.

ISBN: 978-1-60886-904-6, eISBN: 978-1-61398-575-5

Aphelion
0.728213 AU
108939000 km

Perihelion
0.718440 AU
107477000 km

Semi-Major Axis
0.723332 AU
108208000 km

Eccentricity
0.0 67732

Orbital Period
224.701 Days
0.615198 Year
1.92 Venus Solar Day

Synodic Period
583.92 Days

Average Orbital Speed
35.02 km/s

Mean Anomaly
50.115°

Inclination
3.39458° to Ecliptic
3.86° to Sun's Equator
2.19° to Invariable Plane

Longitude of Ascending Node
76.678°

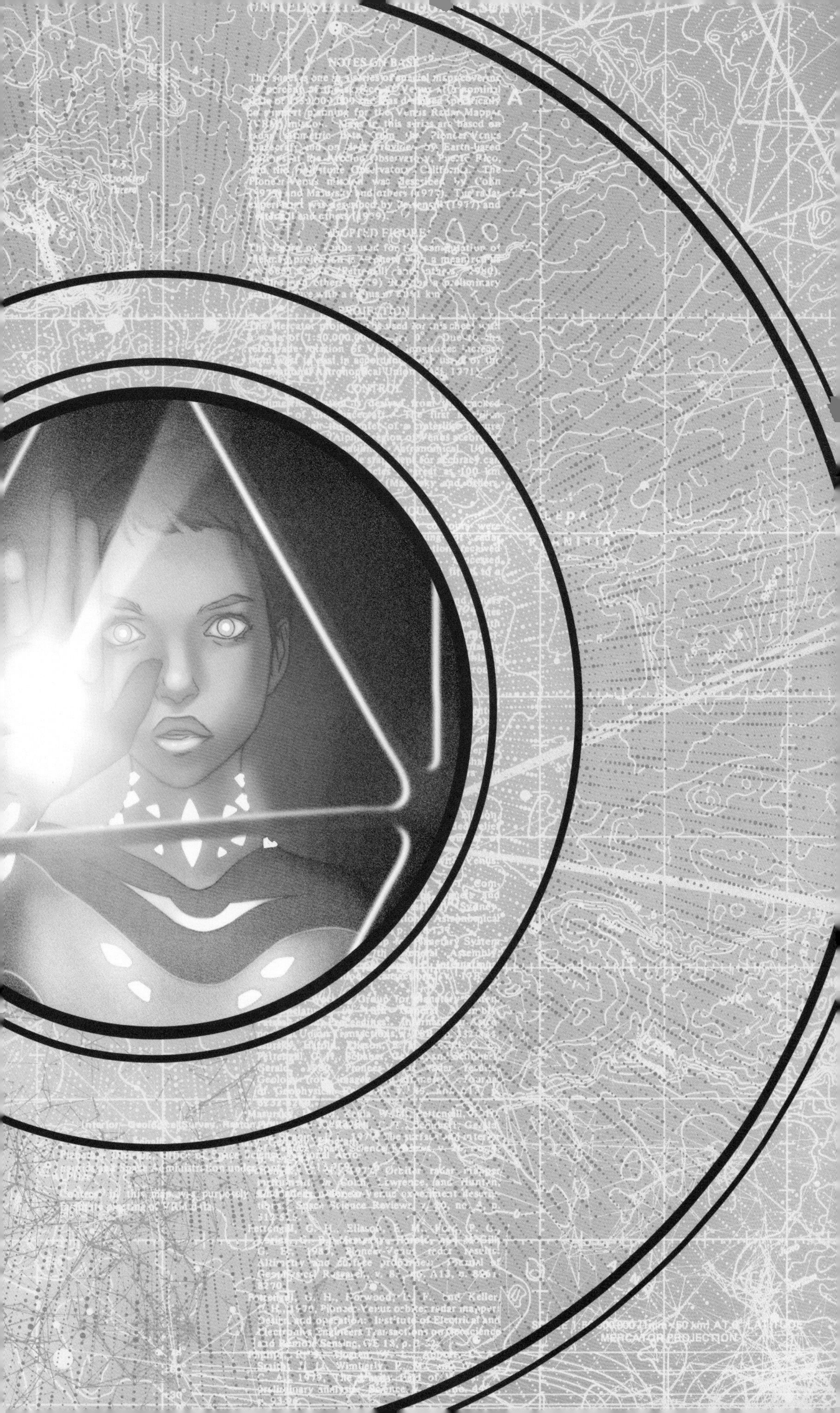
MERCATOR PROJECTION

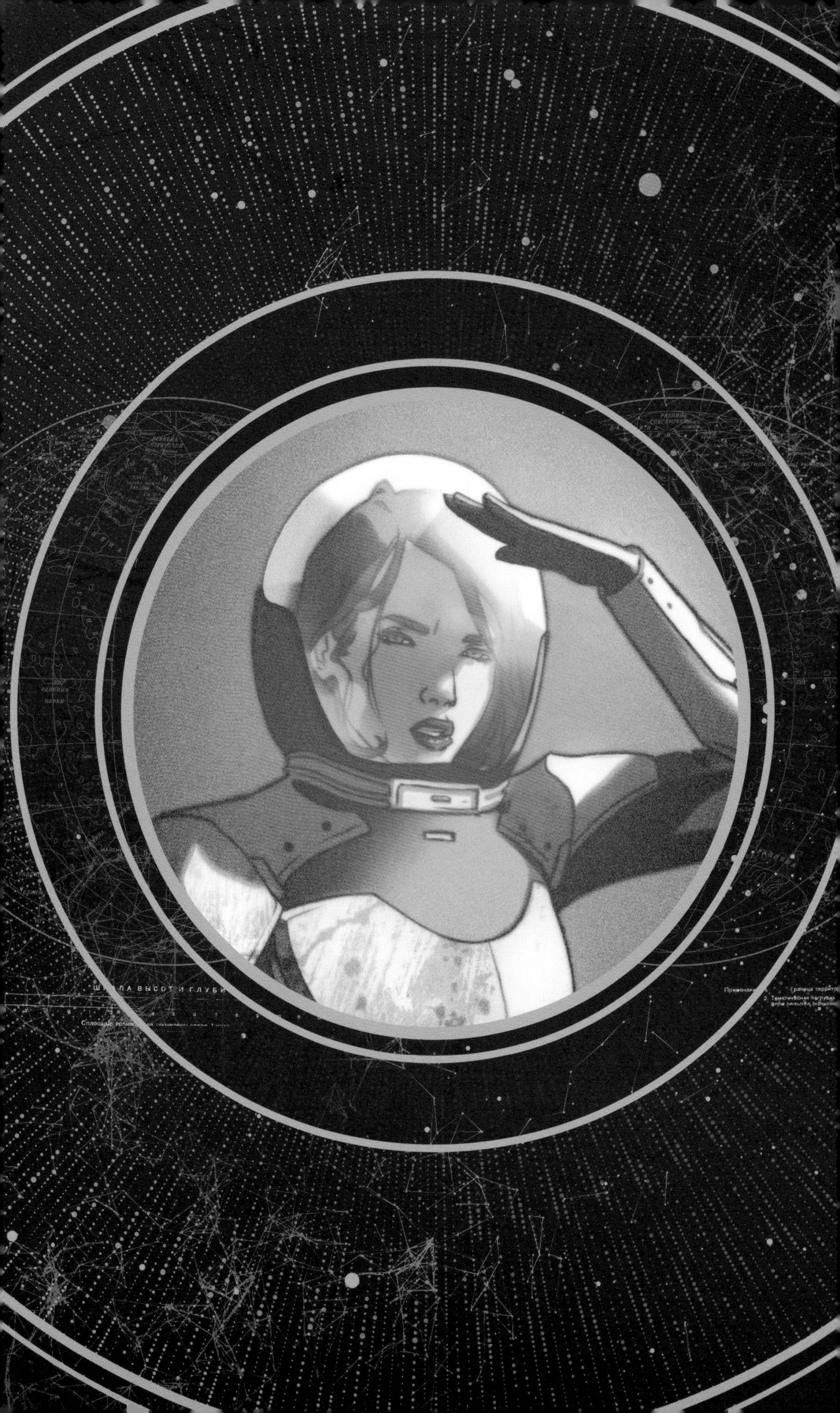

helion
28313 AU
39359000 km

rihelion
48440 AU
247000 km

Semi-Major Axis
0.723332 AU
108208000 km

Eccentricity
0.006773.33

Orbital Period
224.701 Days[2]
0.615198 Year
1.92 Venus Solar Day

Synodic Period
583.92 Days[2]

Average Orbital Speed
35.02 km/h

Mean Anomaly
50.115°

Inclination
3.39458° to Ecliptic
3.86° to Sun's Equator
2.19° to Invariable Plane[3]

Longitude of Ascending Node
76.678°

Argument of Perihelion
.86°

Written by
RICK LOVERD

Illustrated by
HUANG DANLAN

Colored by
MARCIO MENYZ

Lettered by
COLIN BELL

Cover by
W. SCOTT FORBES

Designer
SCOTT NEWMAN

Associate Editor
JASMINE AMIRI

Editor
ERIC HARBURN

VENUS™

Created by
RICK LOVERD & **FILIP SABLIK**

CHAPTER **ONE**

CREW OF THE MAYFLOWER VENUS EXPEDITION, THIS IS CAPTAIN KINCAID SPEAKING.

TOMORROW, MAY 15TH, 2150, A DAY HUMANITY WILL FOREVER REMEMBER.

I SPEAK TO YOU NOW NOT ONLY AS YOUR CAPTAIN, BUT AS AN ASTRONAUT FOLLOWING IN THE FOOTSTEPS OF NEIL ARMSTRONG, THE APOLLO MISSIONS, AND NASA ITSELF.

WE ALL KNOW THE STAKES. EIGHT YEARS AGO, THE PAN PACIFIC ALLIANCE CLAIMED MARS BY BUILDING THE LIWEI MINING COLONY.

"THEY DID IT TO GROW RICH DRILLING FOR RARE MINERALS ON ASTEROIDS.

"NOW IT'S TIME FOR AMERICA TO CUT A PATH TO THE FUTURE, TO ENSURE THAT OUR WAY OF LIFE ENDURES.

"ONE DAY THERE WILL BE CITIES ON VENUS, PEOPLE LIVING THE AMERICAN DREAM HERE."

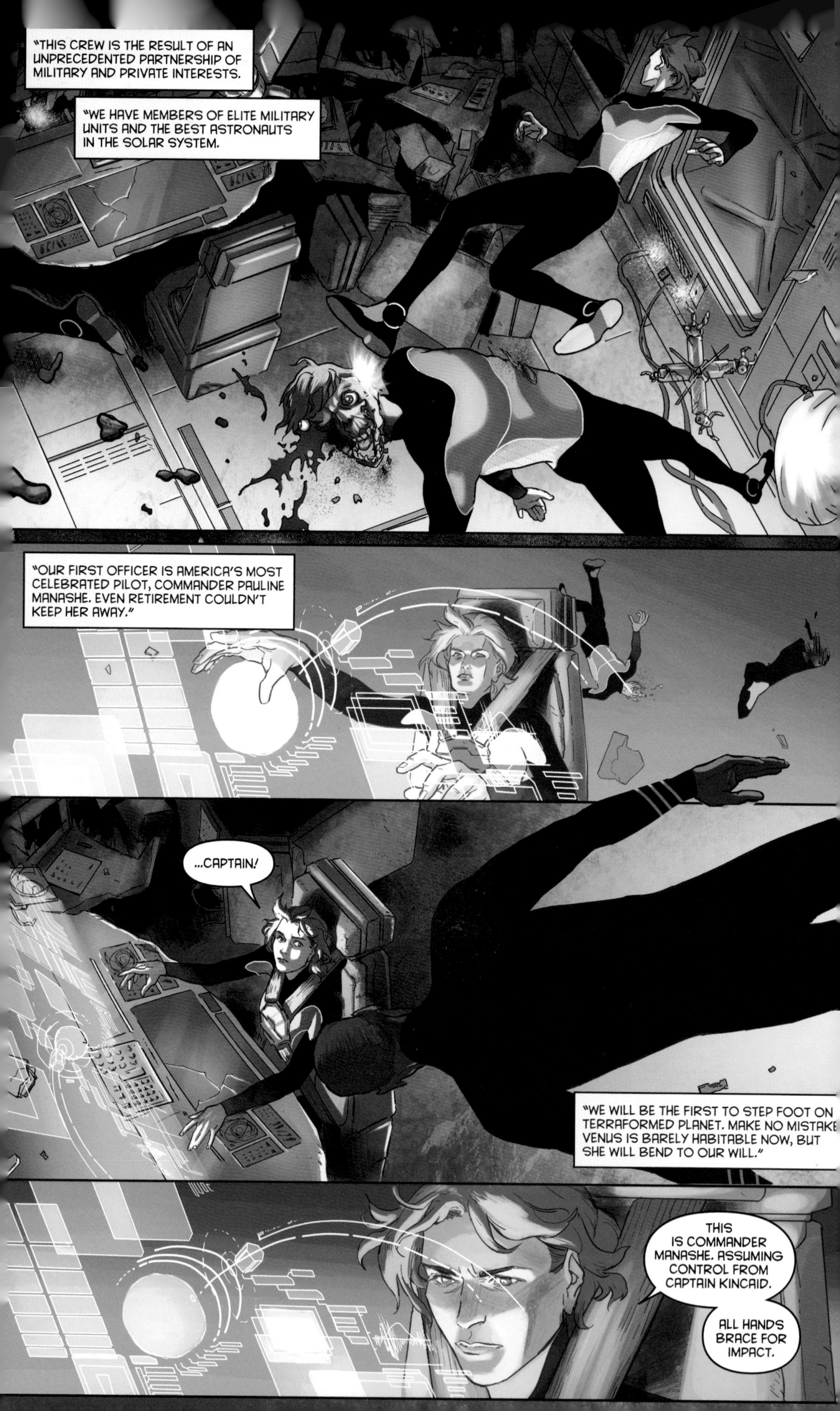

"THIS CREW IS THE RESULT OF AN UNPRECEDENTED PARTNERSHIP OF MILITARY AND PRIVATE INTERESTS.
"WE HAVE MEMBERS OF ELITE MILITARY UNITS AND THE BEST ASTRONAUTS IN THE SOLAR SYSTEM.
"OUR FIRST OFFICER IS AMERICA'S MOST CELEBRATED PILOT, COMMANDER PAULINE MANASHE. EVEN RETIREMENT COULDN'T KEEP HER AWAY."
...CAPTAIN!
"WE WILL BE THE FIRST TO STEP FOOT ON TERRAFORMED PLANET. MAKE NO MISTAKE VENUS IS BARELY HABITABLE NOW, BUT SHE WILL BEND TO OUR WILL."
THIS IS COMMANDER MANASHE. ASSUMING CONTROL FROM CAPTAIN KINCAID.
ALL HANDS BRACE FOR IMPACT.

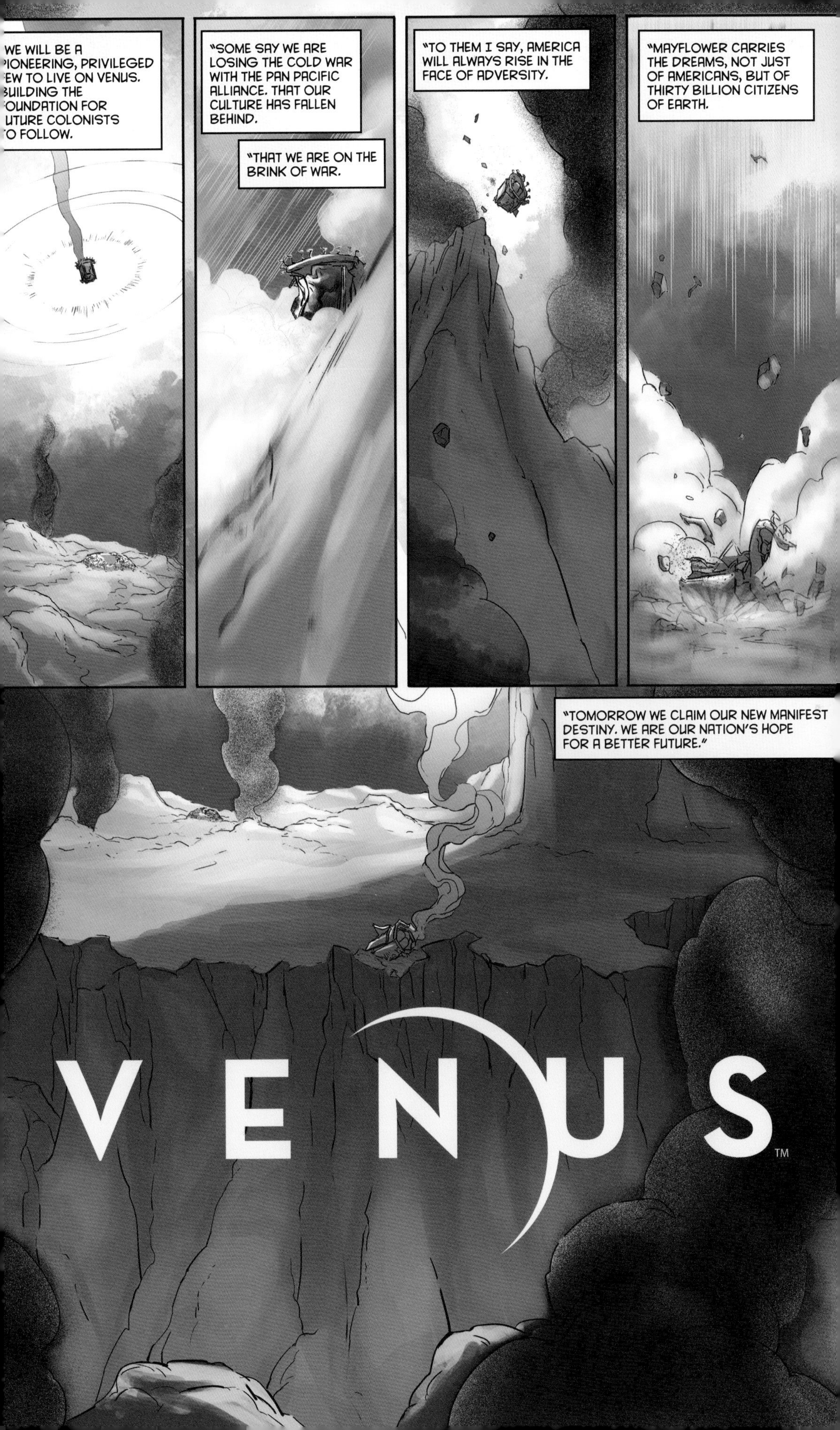
WE WILL BE A PIONEERING, PRIVILEGED FEW TO LIVE ON VENUS. BUILDING THE FOUNDATION FOR FUTURE COLONISTS TO FOLLOW.
"SOME SAY WE ARE LOSING THE COLD WAR WITH THE PAN PACIFIC ALLIANCE. THAT OUR CULTURE HAS FALLEN BEHIND.
"THAT WE ARE ON THE BRINK OF WAR.
"TO THEM I SAY, AMERICA WILL ALWAYS RISE IN THE FACE OF ADVERSITY.
"MAYFLOWER CARRIES THE DREAMS, NOT JUST OF AMERICANS, BUT OF THIRTY BILLION CITIZENS OF EARTH.
"TOMORROW WE CLAIM OUR NEW MANIFEST DESTINY. WE ARE OUR NATION'S HOPE FOR A BETTER FUTURE."
VENUS™

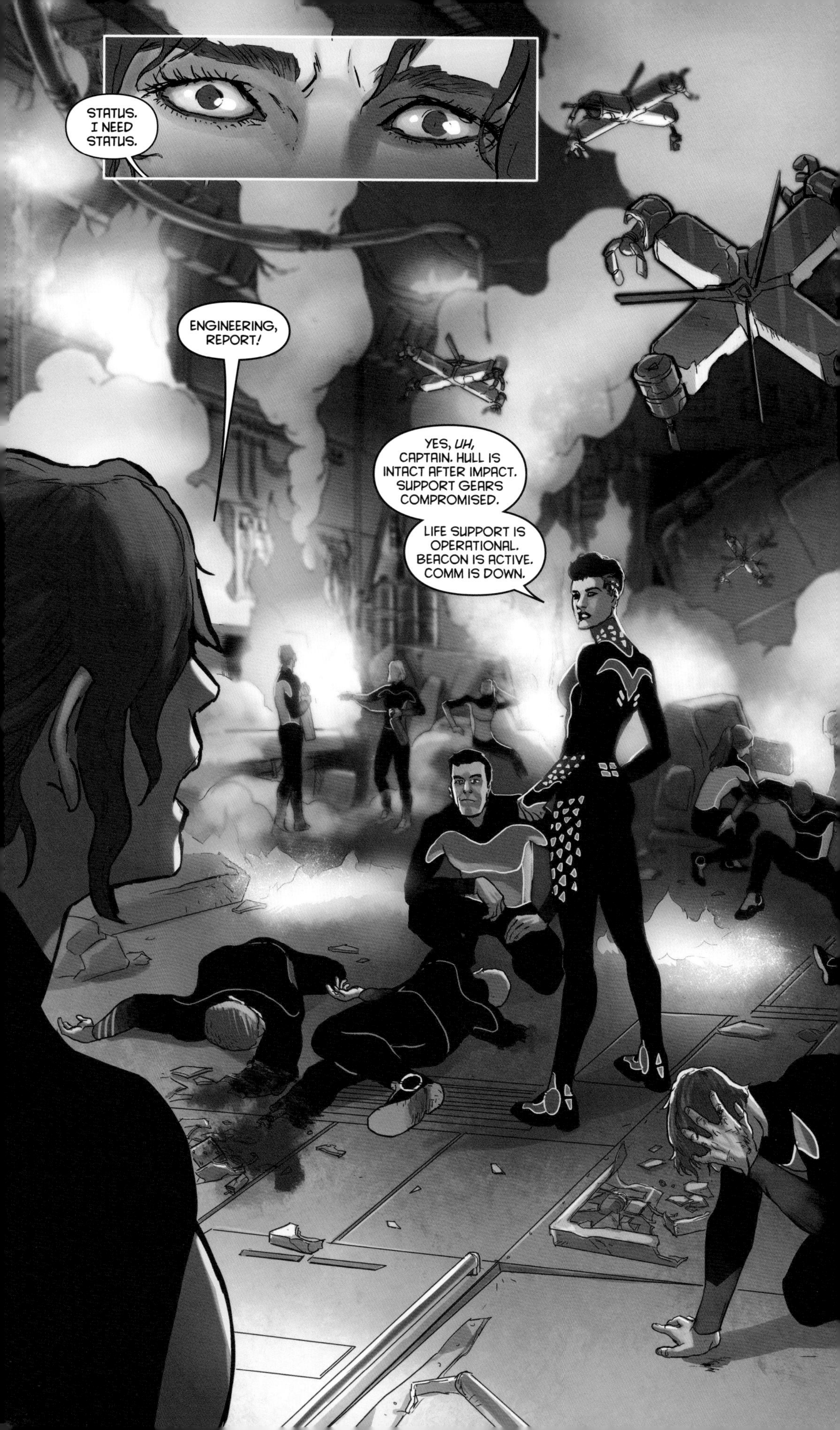
STATUS. I NEED STATUS.
ENGINEERING, REPORT!
YES, *UH*, CAPTAIN. HULL IS INTACT AFTER IMPACT. SUPPORT GEARS COMPROMISED.
LIFE SUPPORT IS OPERATIONAL. BEACON IS ACTIVE. COMM IS DOWN.

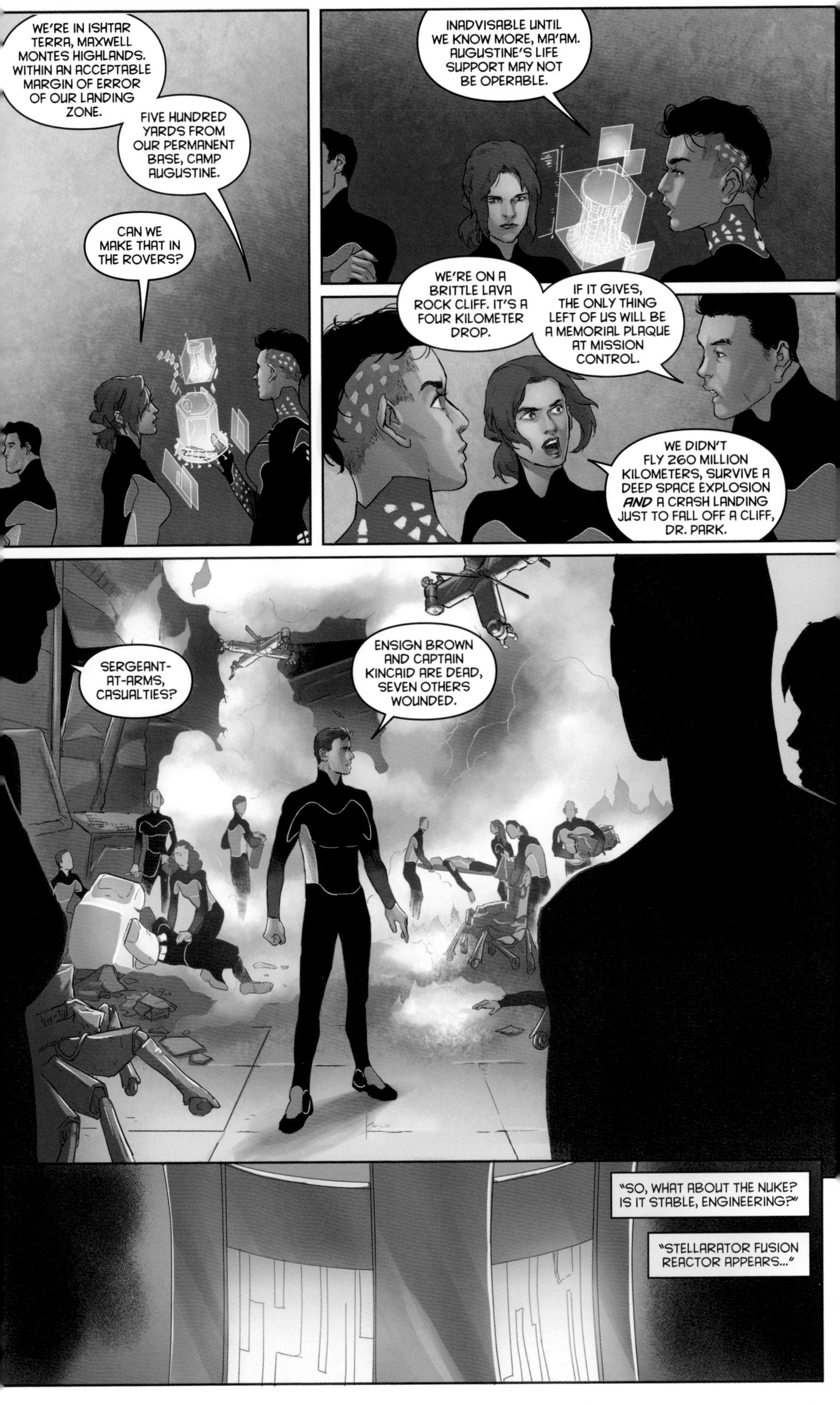

WE'RE IN ISHTAR TERRA, MAXWELL MONTES HIGHLANDS. WITHIN AN ACCEPTABLE MARGIN OF ERROR OF OUR LANDING ZONE.
FIVE HUNDRED YARDS FROM OUR PERMANENT BASE, CAMP AUGUSTINE.
CAN WE MAKE THAT IN THE ROVERS?
INADVISABLE UNTIL WE KNOW MORE, MA'AM. AUGUSTINE'S LIFE SUPPORT MAY NOT BE OPERABLE.
WE'RE ON A BRITTLE LAVA ROCK CLIFF. IT'S A FOUR KILOMETER DROP.
IF IT GIVES, THE ONLY THING LEFT OF US WILL BE A MEMORIAL PLAQUE AT MISSION CONTROL.
WE DIDN'T FLY 260 MILLION KILOMETERS, SURVIVE A DEEP SPACE EXPLOSION ***AND*** A CRASH LANDING JUST TO FALL OFF A CLIFF, DR. PARK.
SERGEANT-AT-ARMS, CASUALTIES?
ENSIGN BROWN AND CAPTAIN KINCAID ARE DEAD, SEVEN OTHERS WOUNDED.
"SO, WHAT ABOUT THE NUKE? IS IT STABLE, ENGINEERING?"
"STELLARATOR FUSION REACTOR APPEARS..."

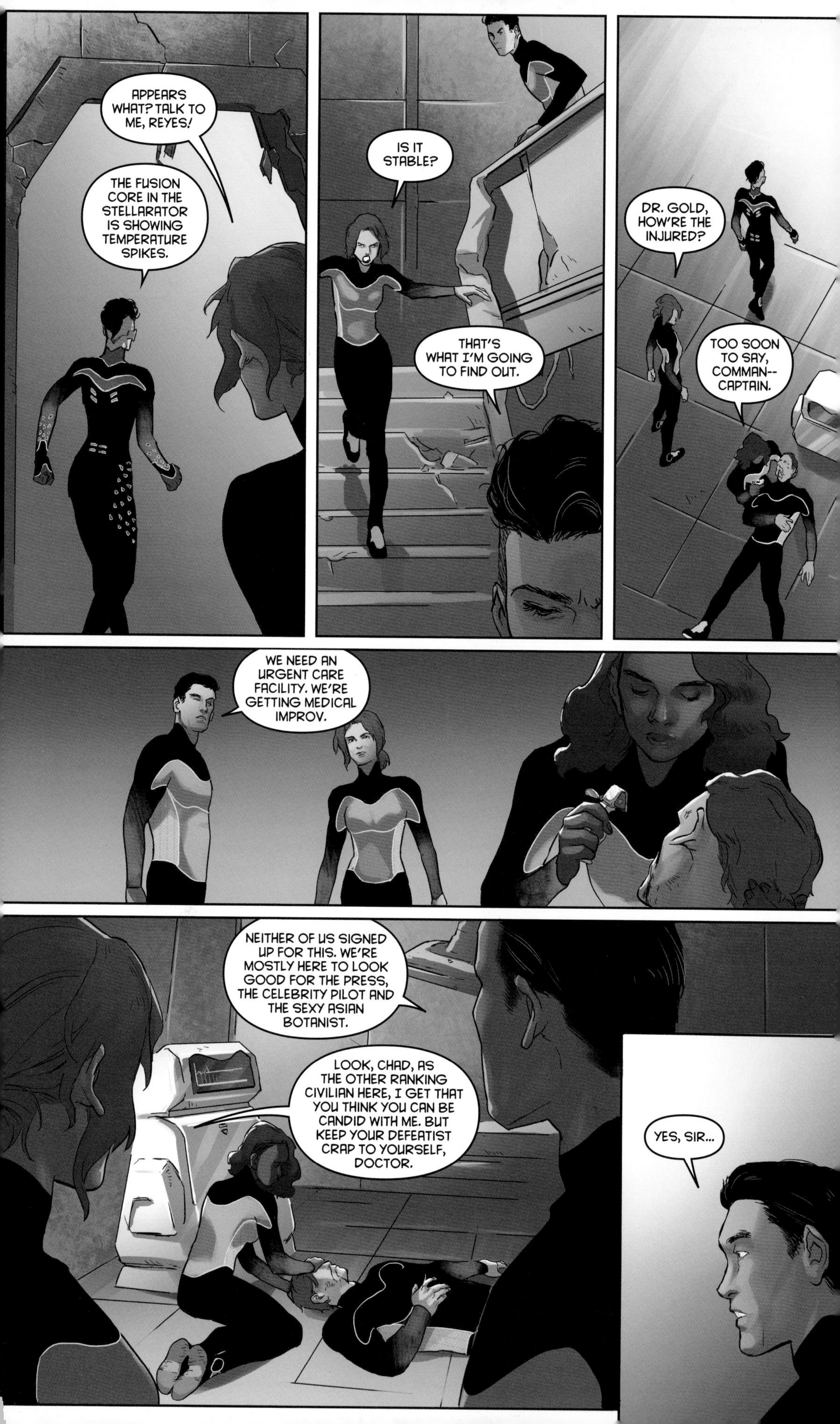
APPEARS WHAT? TALK TO ME, REYES!
THE FUSION CORE IN THE STELLARATOR IS SHOWING TEMPERATURE SPIKES.
IS IT STABLE?
THAT'S WHAT I'M GOING TO FIND OUT.
DR. GOLD, HOW'RE THE INJURED?
TOO SOON TO SAY, COMMAN-- CAPTAIN.
WE NEED AN URGENT CARE FACILITY. WE'RE GETTING MEDICAL IMPROV.
NEITHER OF US SIGNED UP FOR THIS. WE'RE MOSTLY HERE TO LOOK GOOD FOR THE PRESS, THE CELEBRITY PILOT AND THE SEXY ASIAN BOTANIST.
LOOK, CHAD, AS THE OTHER RANKING CIVILIAN HERE, I GET THAT YOU THINK YOU CAN BE CANDID WITH ME. BUT KEEP YOUR DEFEATIST CRAP TO YOURSELF, DOCTOR.
YES, SIR...

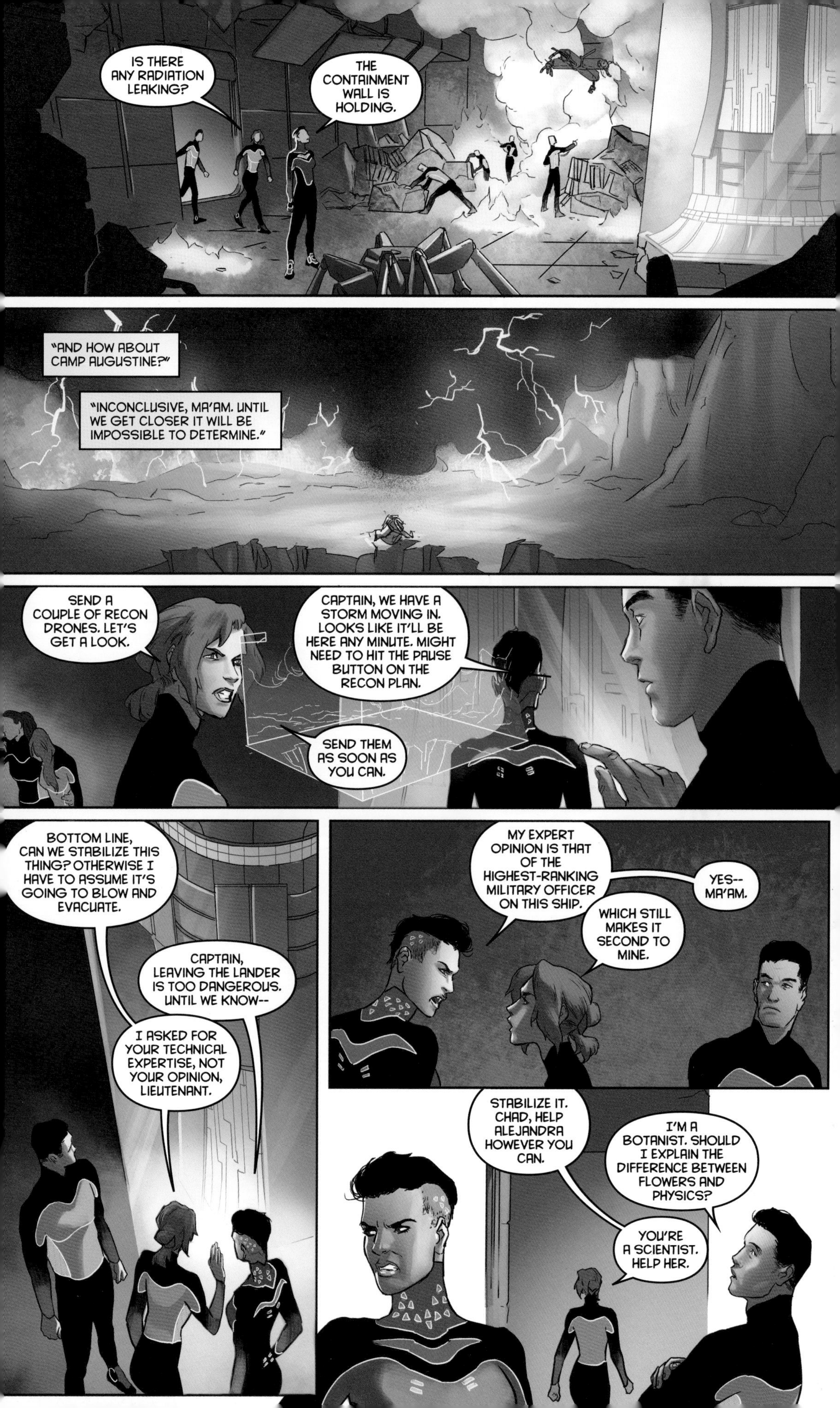
IS THERE ANY RADIATION LEAKING?
THE CONTAINMENT WALL IS HOLDING.
"AND HOW ABOUT CAMP AUGUSTINE?"
"INCONCLUSIVE, MA'AM. UNTIL WE GET CLOSER IT WILL BE IMPOSSIBLE TO DETERMINE."
SEND A COUPLE OF RECON DRONES. LET'S GET A LOOK.
CAPTAIN, WE HAVE A STORM MOVING IN. LOOKS LIKE IT'LL BE HERE ANY MINUTE. MIGHT NEED TO HIT THE PAUSE BUTTON ON THE RECON PLAN.
SEND THEM AS SOON AS YOU CAN.
BOTTOM LINE, CAN WE STABILIZE THIS THING? OTHERWISE I HAVE TO ASSUME IT'S GOING TO BLOW AND EVACUATE.
CAPTAIN, LEAVING THE LANDER IS TOO DANGEROUS. UNTIL WE KNOW--
I ASKED FOR YOUR TECHNICAL EXPERTISE, NOT YOUR OPINION, LIEUTENANT.
MY EXPERT OPINION IS THAT OF THE HIGHEST-RANKING MILITARY OFFICER ON THIS SHIP.
YES-- MA'AM.
WHICH STILL MAKES IT SECOND TO MINE.
STABILIZE IT. CHAD, HELP ALEJANDRA HOWEVER YOU CAN.
I'M A BOTANIST. SHOULD I EXPLAIN THE DIFFERENCE BETWEEN FLOWERS AND PHYSICS?
YOU'RE A SCIENTIST. HELP HER.

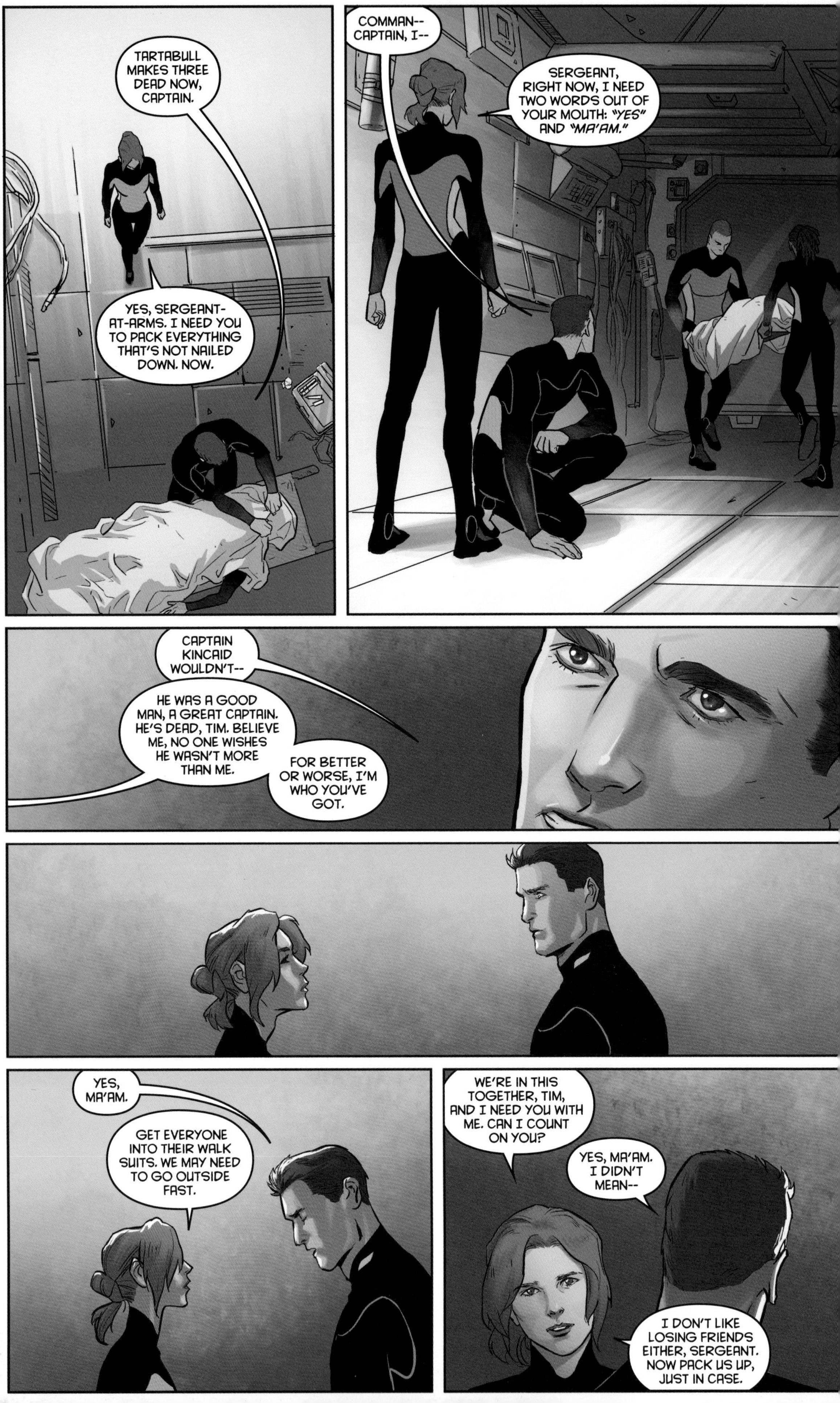

TARTABULL MAKES THREE DEAD NOW, CAPTAIN.
YES, SERGEANT-AT-ARMS. I NEED YOU TO PACK EVERYTHING THAT'S NOT NAILED DOWN. NOW.
COMMAN-- CAPTAIN, I--
SERGEANT, RIGHT NOW, I NEED TWO WORDS OUT OF YOUR MOUTH: "YES" AND "MA'AM."
CAPTAIN KINCAID WOULDN'T--
HE WAS A GOOD MAN, A GREAT CAPTAIN. HE'S DEAD, TIM. BELIEVE ME, NO ONE WISHES HE WASN'T MORE THAN ME.
FOR BETTER OR WORSE, I'M WHO YOU'VE GOT.
YES, MA'AM.
GET EVERYONE INTO THEIR WALK SUITS. WE MAY NEED TO GO OUTSIDE FAST.
WE'RE IN THIS TOGETHER, TIM, AND I NEED YOU WITH ME. CAN I COUNT ON YOU?
YES, MA'AM. I DIDN'T MEAN--
I DON'T LIKE LOSING FRIENDS EITHER, SERGEANT. NOW PACK US UP, JUST IN CASE.

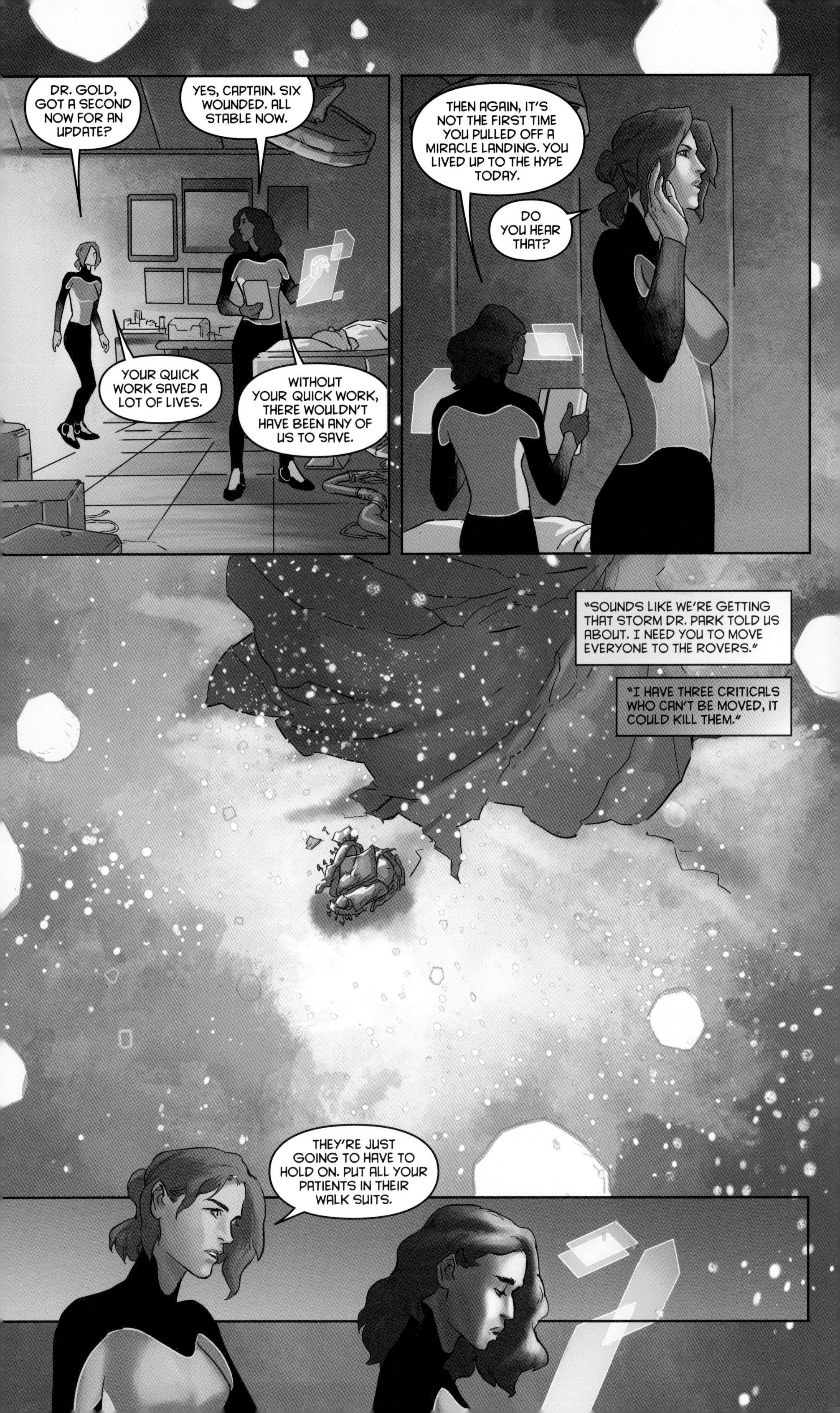
DR. GOLD, GOT A SECOND NOW FOR AN UPDATE?
YES, CAPTAIN. SIX WOUNDED. ALL STABLE NOW.
YOUR QUICK WORK SAVED A LOT OF LIVES.
WITHOUT YOUR QUICK WORK, THERE WOULDN'T HAVE BEEN ANY OF US TO SAVE.
THEN AGAIN, IT'S NOT THE FIRST TIME YOU PULLED OFF A MIRACLE LANDING. YOU LIVED UP TO THE HYPE TODAY.
DO YOU HEAR THAT?
"SOUNDS LIKE WE'RE GETTING THAT STORM DR. PARK TOLD US ABOUT. I NEED YOU TO MOVE EVERYONE TO THE ROVERS."
"I HAVE THREE CRITICALS WHO CAN'T BE MOVED, IT COULD KILL THEM."
THEY'RE JUST GOING TO HAVE TO HOLD ON. PUT ALL YOUR PATIENTS IN THEIR WALK SUITS.

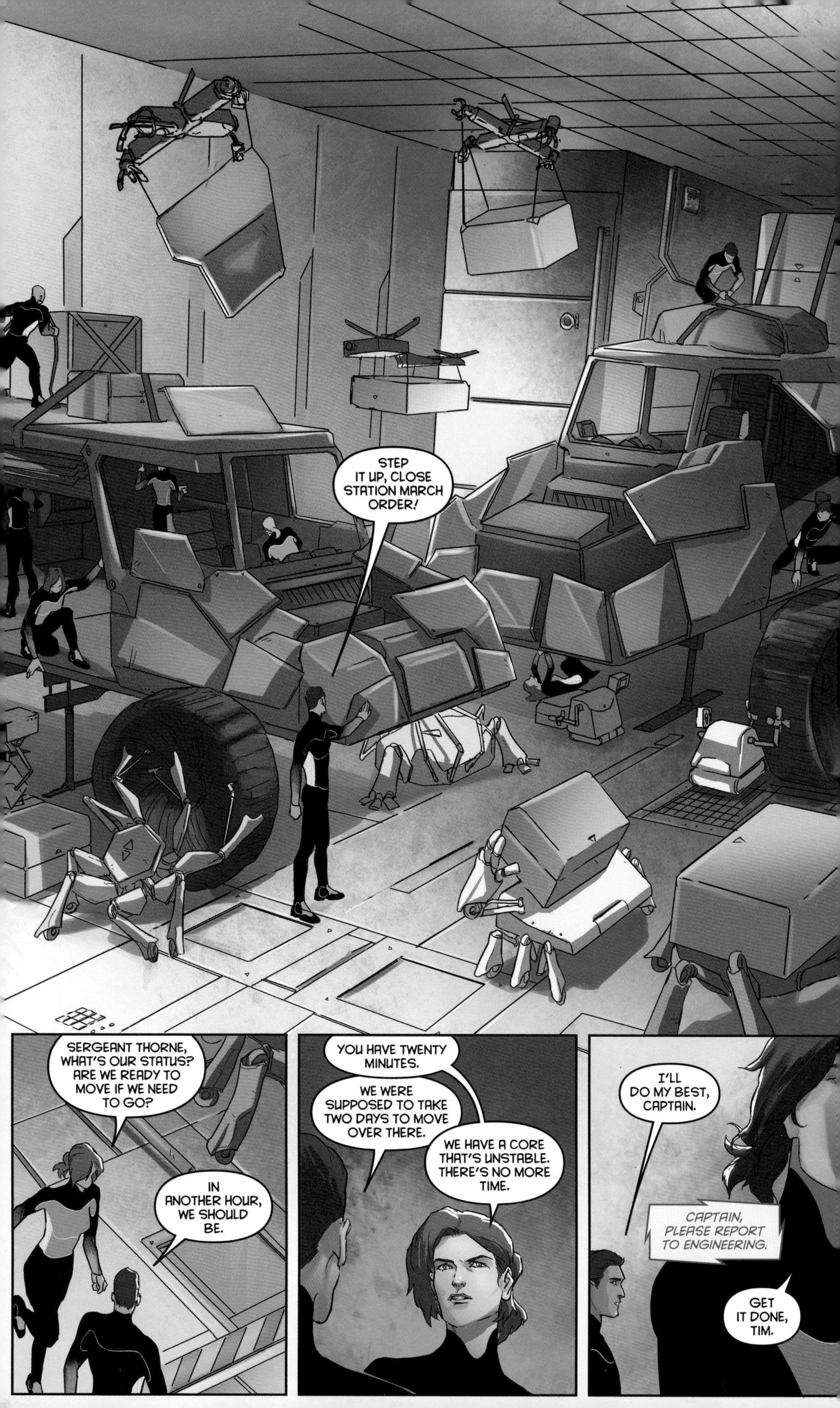
STEP IT UP, CLOSE STATION MARCH ORDER!
SERGEANT THORNE, WHAT'S OUR STATUS? ARE WE READY TO MOVE IF WE NEED TO GO?
IN ANOTHER HOUR, WE SHOULD BE.
YOU HAVE TWENTY MINUTES.
WE WERE SUPPOSED TO TAKE TWO DAYS TO MOVE OVER THERE.
WE HAVE A CORE THAT'S UNSTABLE. THERE'S NO MORE TIME.
I'LL DO MY BEST, CAPTAIN.
CAPTAIN, PLEASE REPORT TO ENGINEERING.
GET IT DONE, TIM.

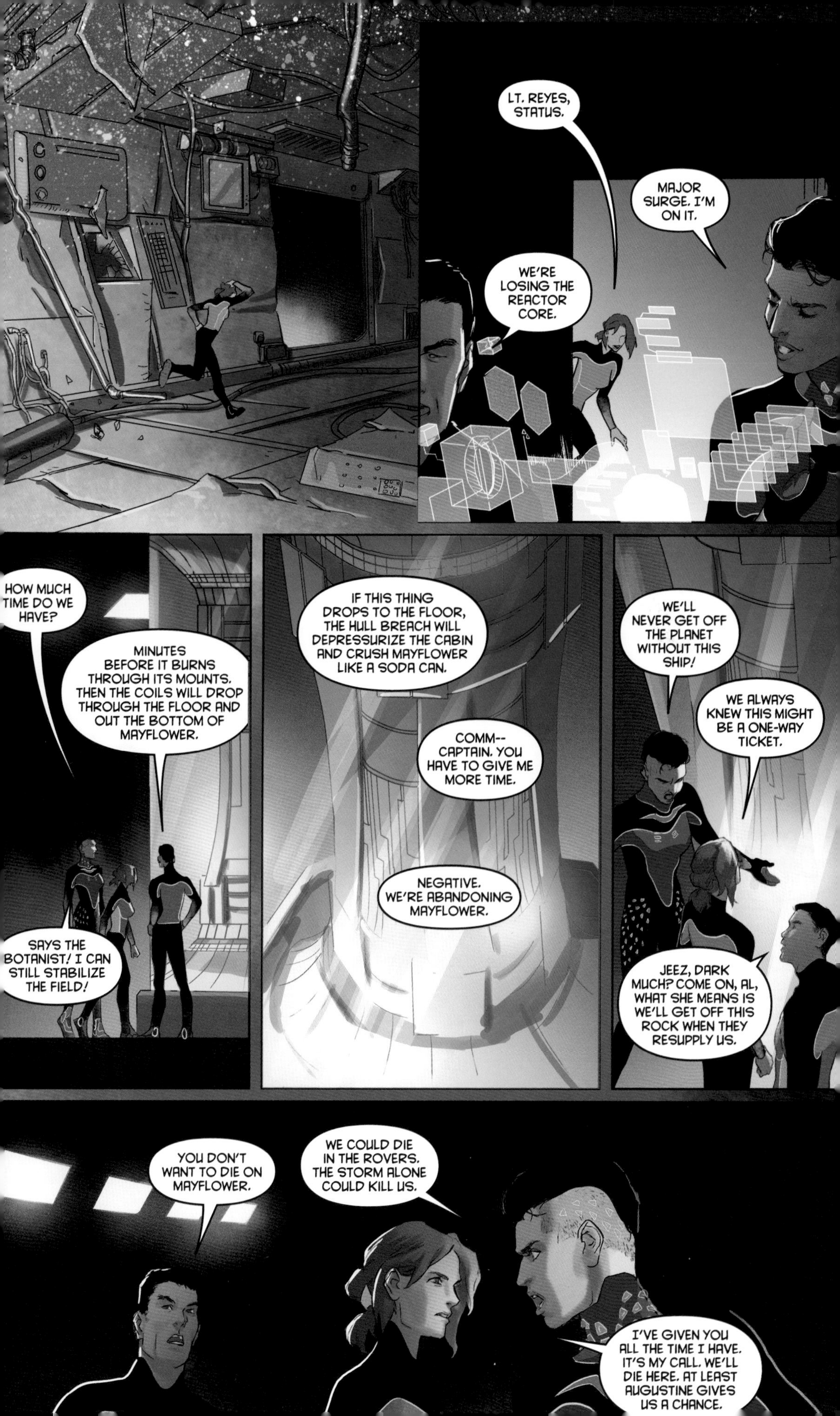
LT. REYES, STATUS.
MAJOR SURGE. I'M ON IT.
WE'RE LOSING THE REACTOR CORE.
HOW MUCH TIME DO WE HAVE?
MINUTES BEFORE IT BURNS THROUGH ITS MOUNTS. THEN THE COILS WILL DROP THROUGH THE FLOOR AND OUT THE BOTTOM OF MAYFLOWER.
SAYS THE BOTANIST! I CAN STILL STABILIZE THE FIELD!
IF THIS THING DROPS TO THE FLOOR, THE HULL BREACH WILL DEPRESSURIZE THE CABIN AND CRUSH MAYFLOWER LIKE A SODA CAN.
COMM-- CAPTAIN. YOU HAVE TO GIVE ME MORE TIME.
NEGATIVE. WE'RE ABANDONING MAYFLOWER.
WE'LL NEVER GET OFF THE PLANET WITHOUT THIS SHIP!
WE ALWAYS KNEW THIS MIGHT BE A ONE-WAY TICKET.
JEEZ, DARK MUCH? COME ON, AL, WHAT SHE MEANS IS WE'LL GET OFF THIS ROCK WHEN THEY RESUPPLY US.
YOU DON'T WANT TO DIE ON MAYFLOWER.
WE COULD DIE IN THE ROVERS. THE STORM ALONE COULD KILL US.
I'VE GIVEN YOU ALL THE TIME I HAVE. IT'S MY CALL. WE'LL DIE HERE. AT LEAST AUGUSTINE GIVES US A CHANCE.

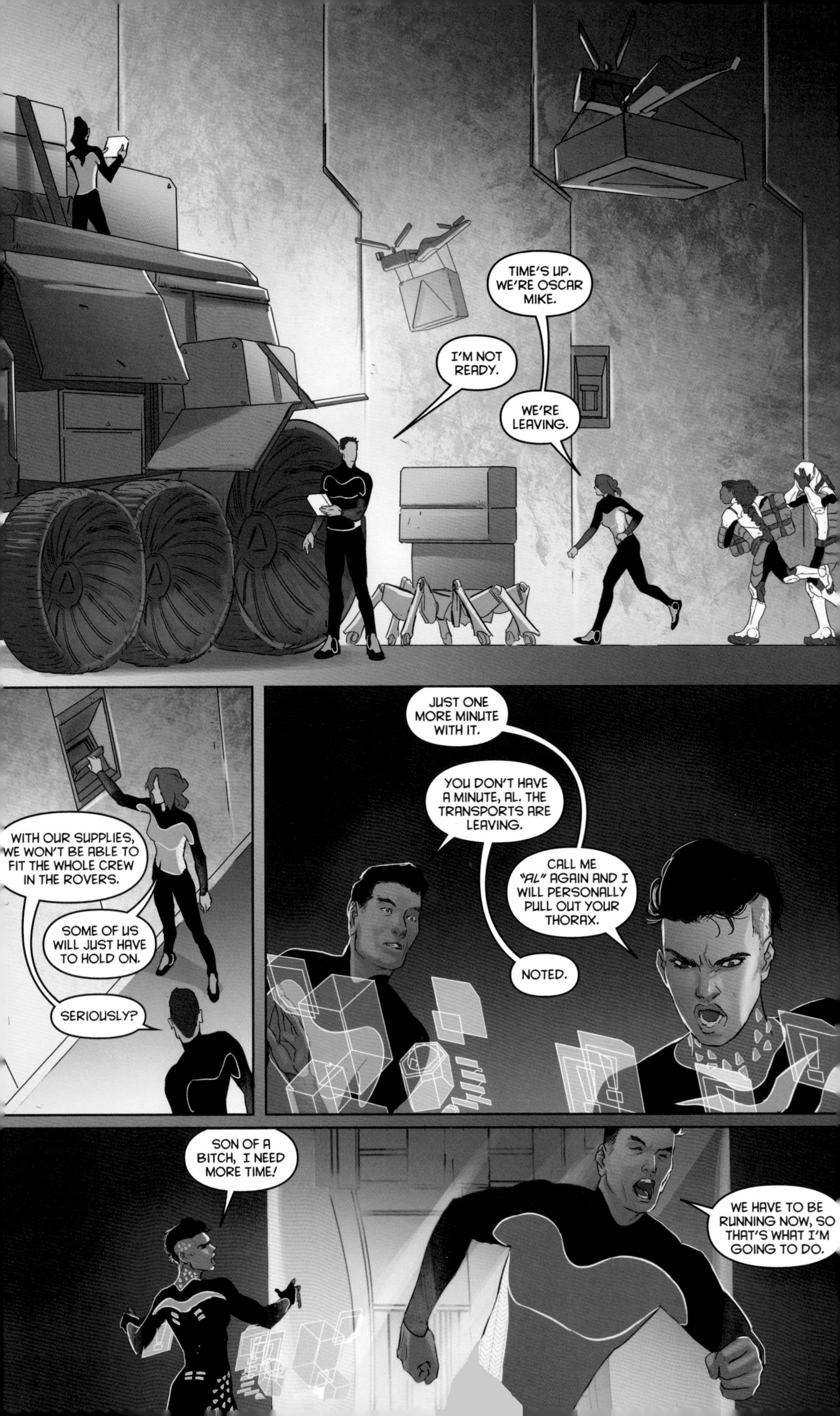
TIME'S UP. WE'RE OSCAR MIKE.
I'M NOT READY.
WE'RE LEAVING.
WITH OUR SUPPLIES, WE WON'T BE ABLE TO FIT THE WHOLE CREW IN THE ROVERS.
SOME OF US WILL JUST HAVE TO HOLD ON.
SERIOUSLY?
JUST ONE MORE MINUTE WITH IT.
YOU DON'T HAVE A MINUTE, AL. THE TRANSPORTS ARE LEAVING.
CALL ME "AL" AGAIN AND I WILL PERSONALLY PULL OUT YOUR THORAX.
NOTED.
SON OF A BITCH, I NEED MORE TIME!
WE HAVE TO BE RUNNING NOW, SO THAT'S WHAT I'M GOING TO DO.

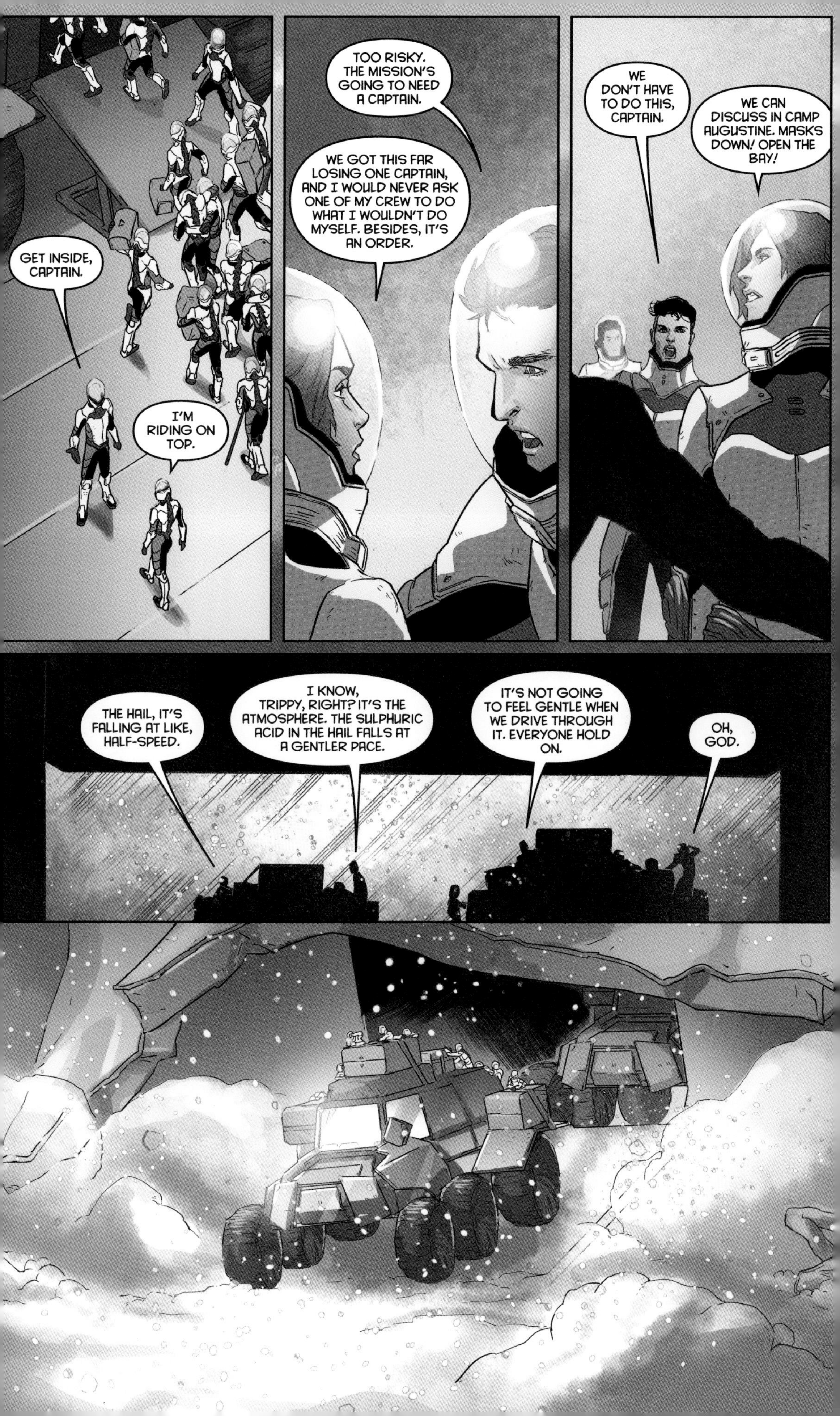
GET INSIDE, CAPTAIN.
I'M RIDING ON TOP.
TOO RISKY. THE MISSION'S GOING TO NEED A CAPTAIN.
WE GOT THIS FAR LOSING ONE CAPTAIN, AND I WOULD NEVER ASK ONE OF MY CREW TO DO WHAT I WOULDN'T DO MYSELF. BESIDES, IT'S AN ORDER.
WE DON'T HAVE TO DO THIS, CAPTAIN.
WE CAN DISCUSS IN CAMP AUGUSTINE. MASKS DOWN! OPEN THE BAY!
THE HAIL, IT'S FALLING AT LIKE, HALF-SPEED.
I KNOW, TRIPPY, RIGHT? IT'S THE ATMOSPHERE. THE SULPHURIC ACID IN THE HAIL FALLS AT A GENTLER PACE.
IT'S NOT GOING TO FEEL GENTLE WHEN WE DRIVE THROUGH IT. EVERYONE HOLD ON.
OH, GOD.

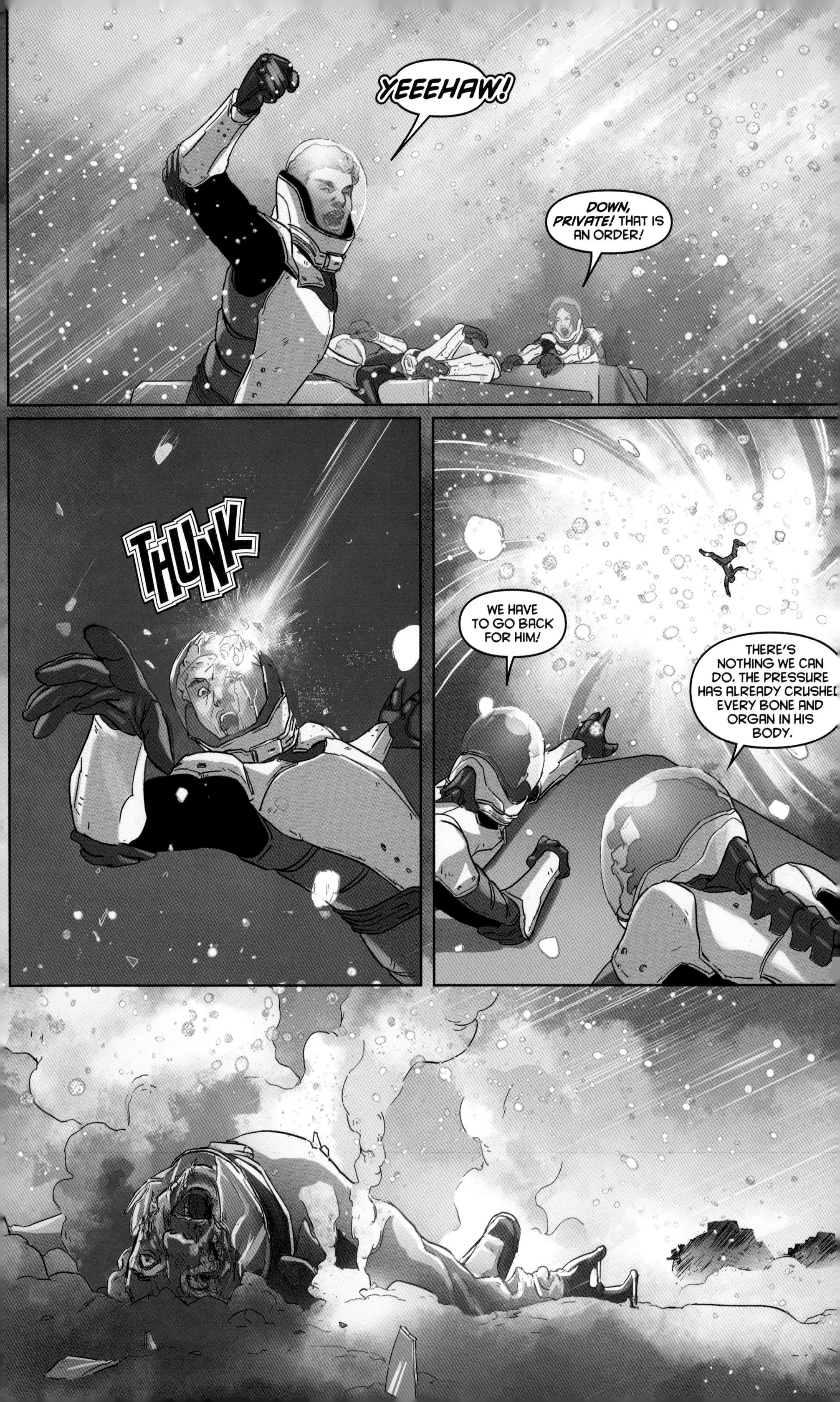
YEEEHAW!
DOWN, PRIVATE! THAT IS AN ORDER!
THUNK
WE HAVE TO GO BACK FOR HIM!
THERE'S NOTHING WE CAN DO. THE PRESSURE HAS ALREADY CRUSHED EVERY BONE AND ORGAN IN HIS BODY.

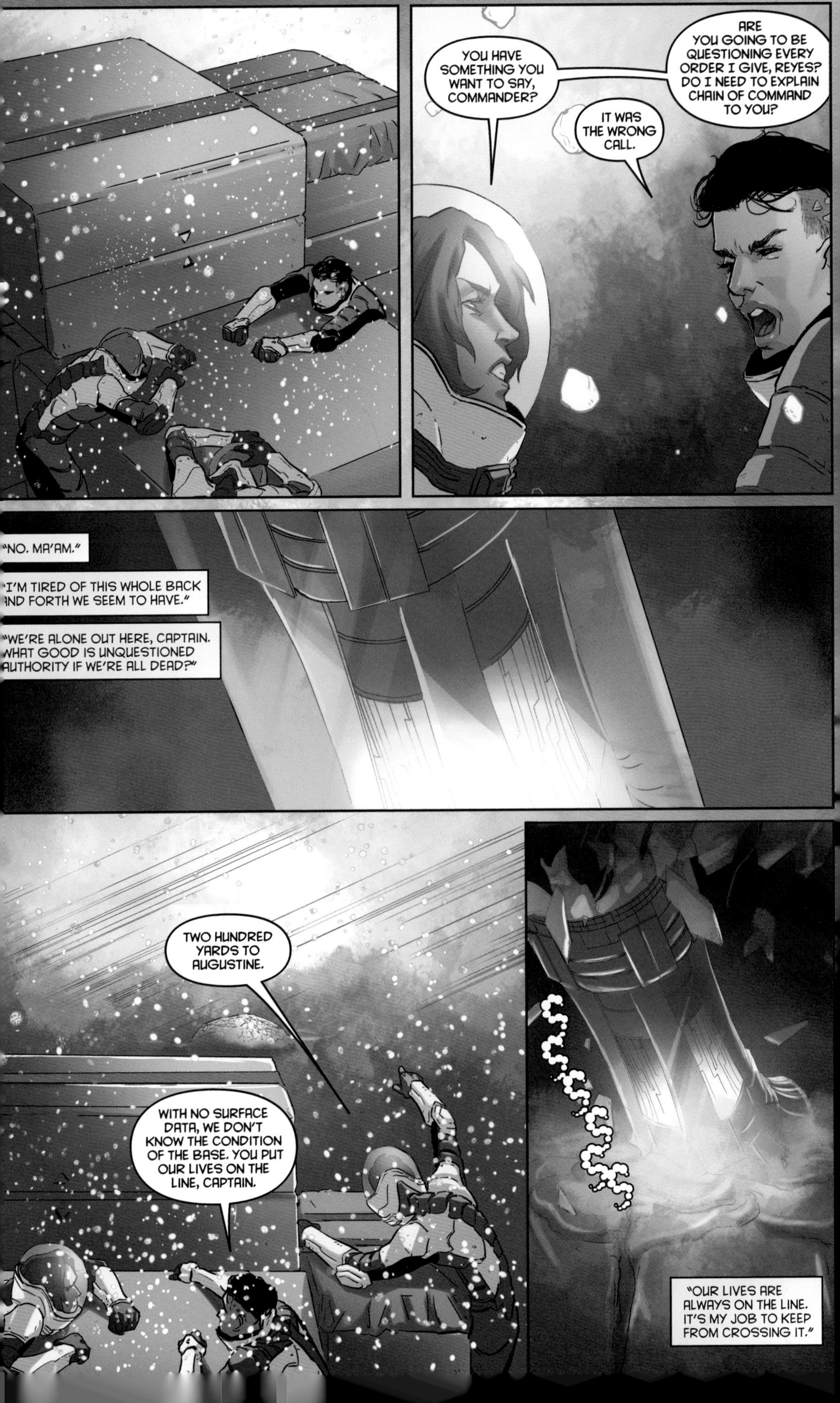

YOU HAVE SOMETHING YOU WANT TO SAY, COMMANDER?
ARE YOU GOING TO BE QUESTIONING EVERY ORDER I GIVE, REYES? DO I NEED TO EXPLAIN CHAIN OF COMMAND TO YOU?
IT WAS THE WRONG CALL.
"NO, MA'AM."
"I'M TIRED OF THIS WHOLE BACK ND FORTH WE SEEM TO HAVE."
"WE'RE ALONE OUT HERE, CAPTAIN. WHAT GOOD IS UNQUESTIONED AUTHORITY IF WE'RE ALL DEAD?"
TWO HUNDRED YARDS TO AUGUSTINE.
WITH NO SURFACE DATA, WE DON'T KNOW THE CONDITION OF THE BASE. YOU PUT OUR LIVES ON THE LINE, CAPTAIN.
SSSSSSS
"OUR LIVES ARE ALWAYS ON THE LINE. IT'S MY JOB TO KEEP FROM CROSSING IT."

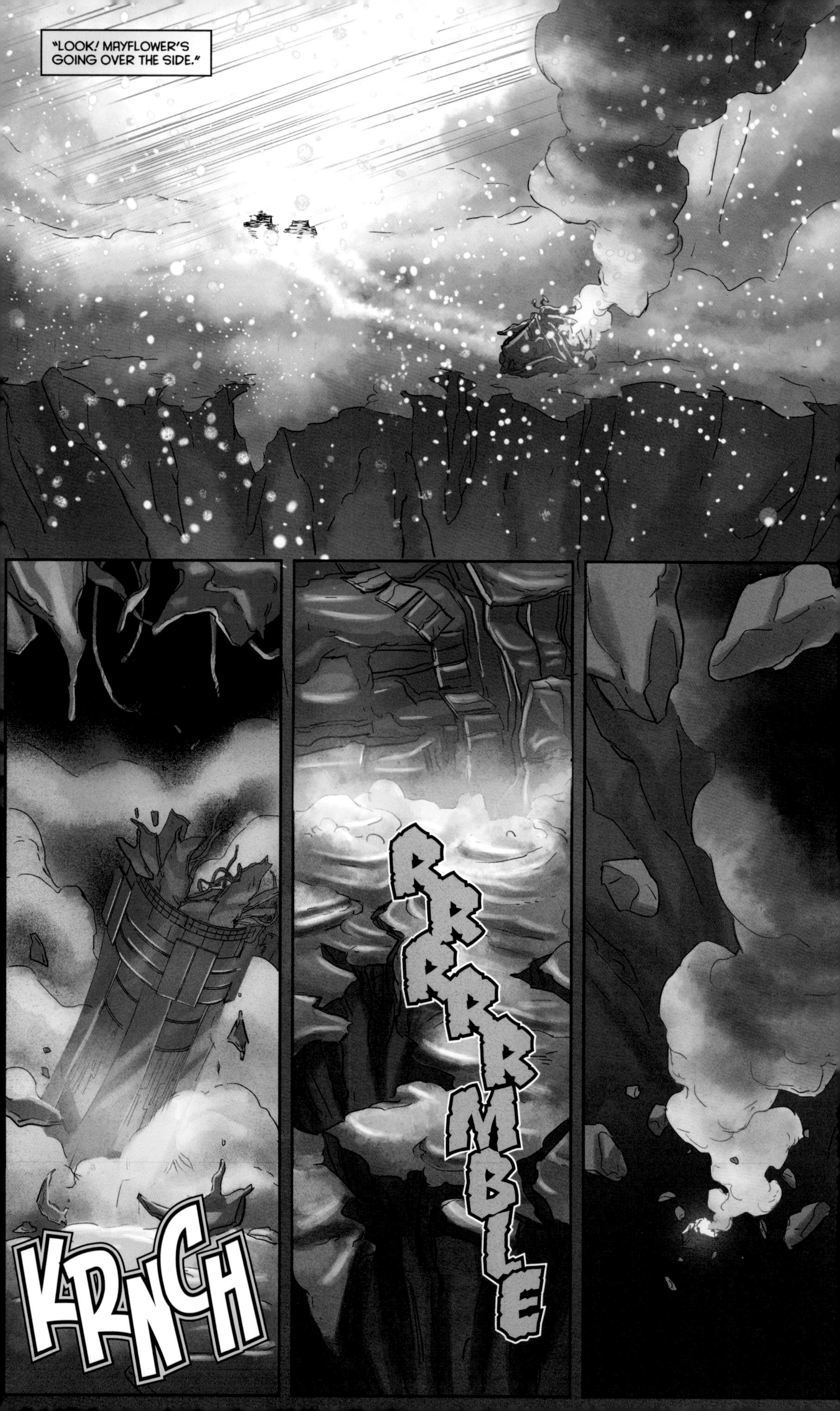
"LOOK! MAYFLOWER'S GOING OVER THE SIDE."
KRNCH
RRRRRMBLE

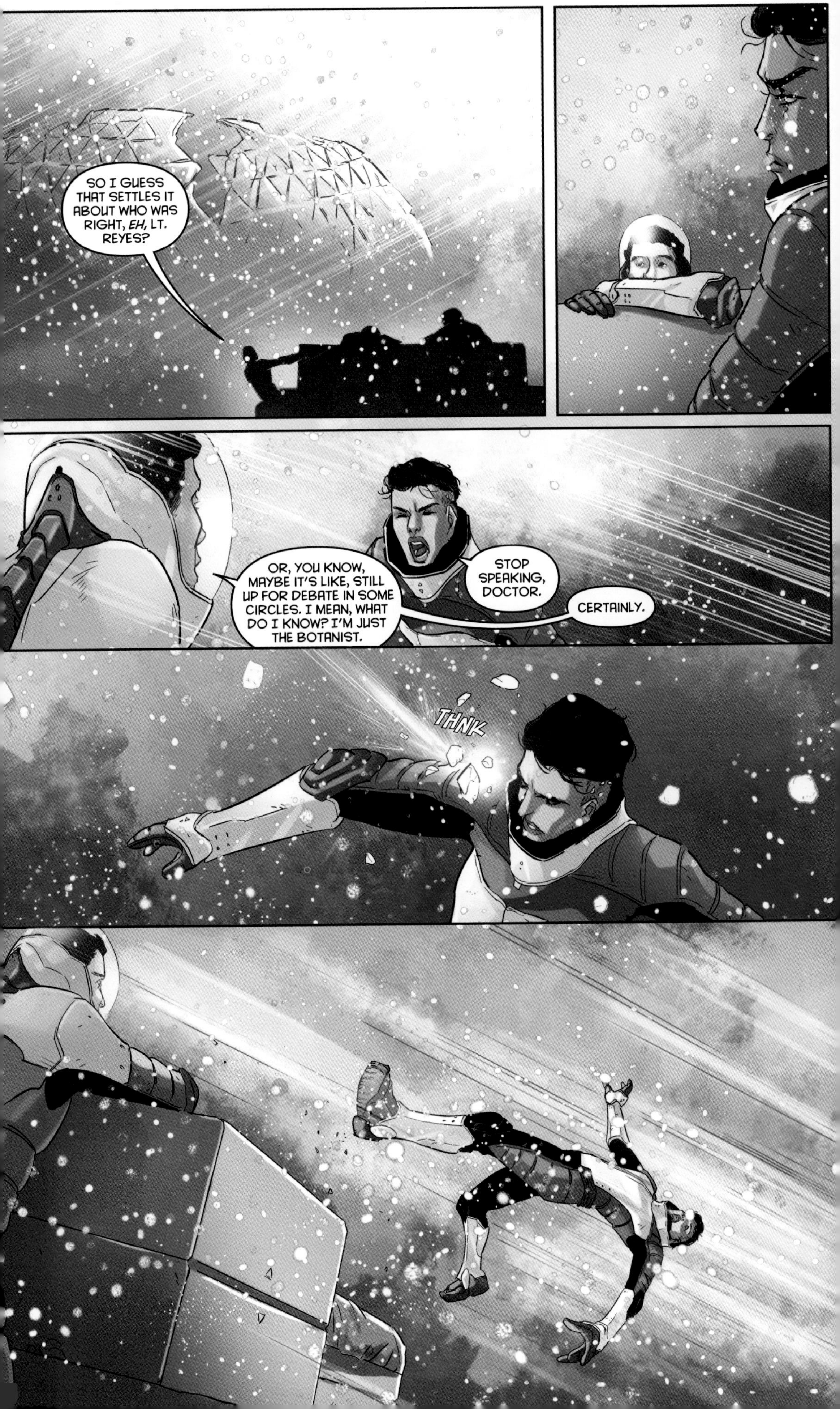
SO I GUESS THAT SETTLES IT ABOUT WHO WAS RIGHT, *EH*, LT. REYES?
OR, YOU KNOW, MAYBE IT'S LIKE, STILL UP FOR DEBATE IN SOME CIRCLES. I MEAN, WHAT DO I KNOW? I'M JUST THE BOTANIST.
STOP SPEAKING, DOCTOR.
CERTAINLY.
THNK

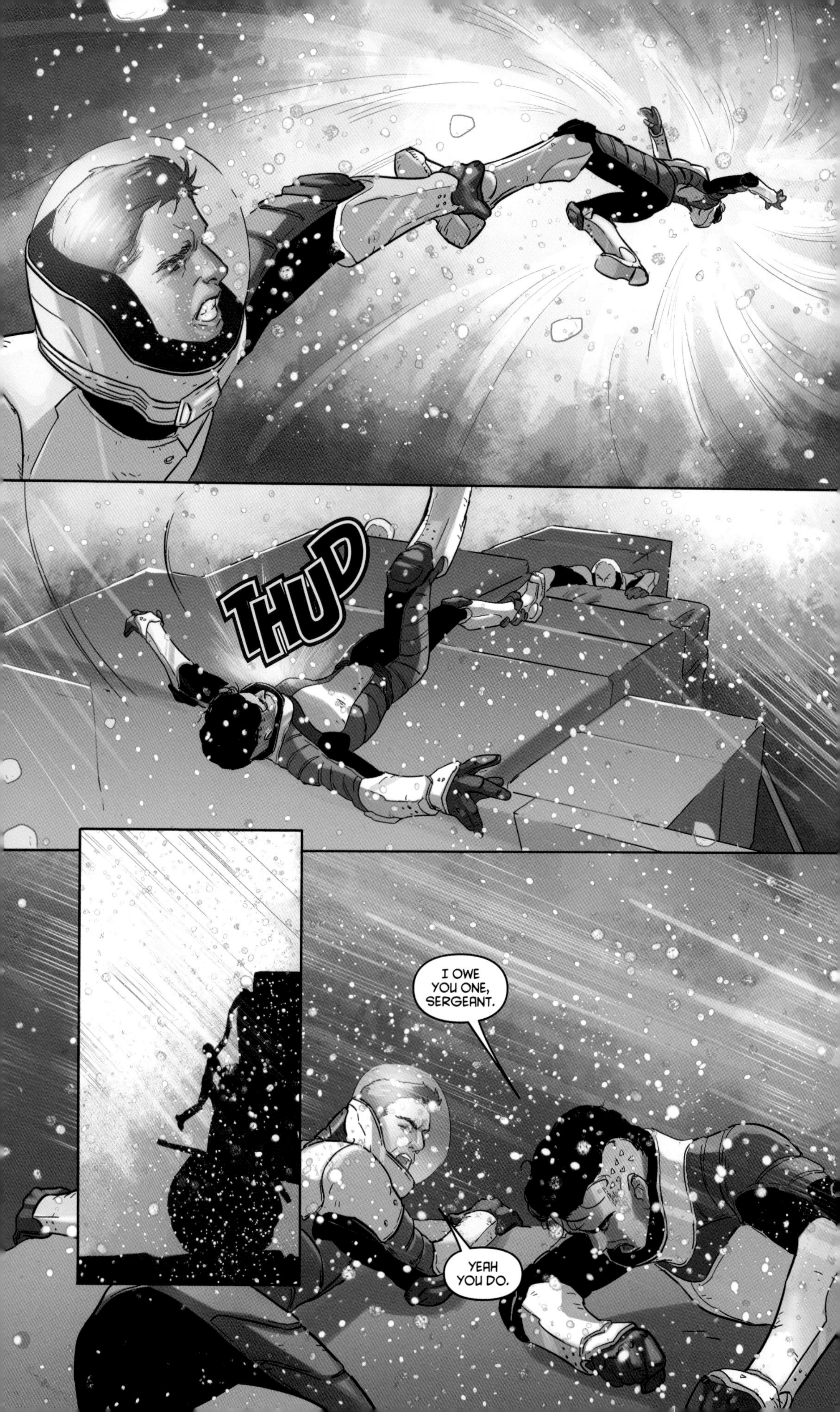
THUD
I OWE YOU ONE, SERGEANT.
YEAH YOU DO.

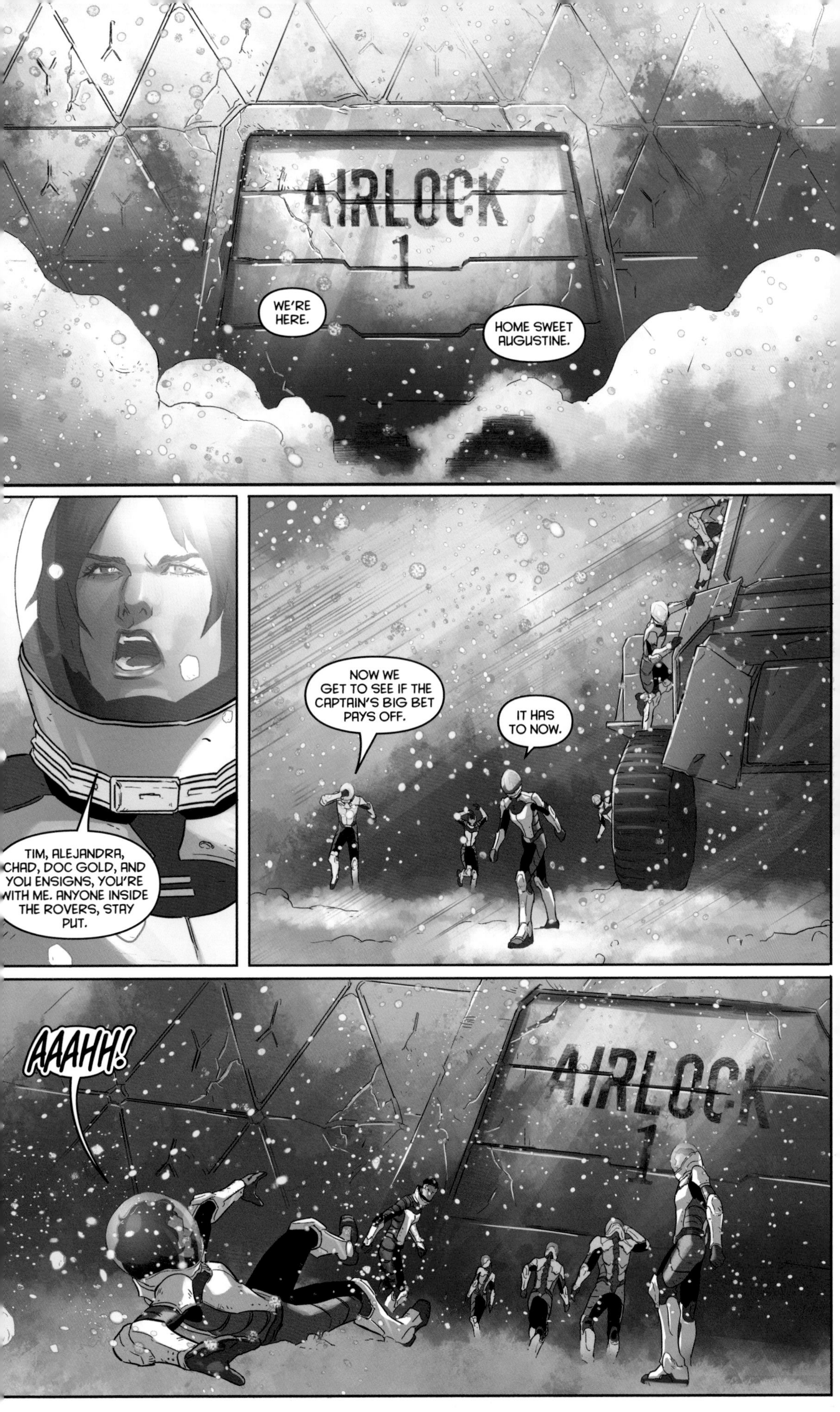
AIRLOCK 1
WE'RE HERE.
HOME SWEET AUGUSTINE.
TIM, ALEJANDRA, CHAD, DOC GOLD, AND YOU ENSIGNS, YOU'RE WITH ME. ANYONE INSIDE THE ROVERS, STAY PUT.
NOW WE GET TO SEE IF THE CAPTAIN'S BIG BET PAYS OFF.
IT HAS TO NOW.
AAAHH!
AIRLOCK 1

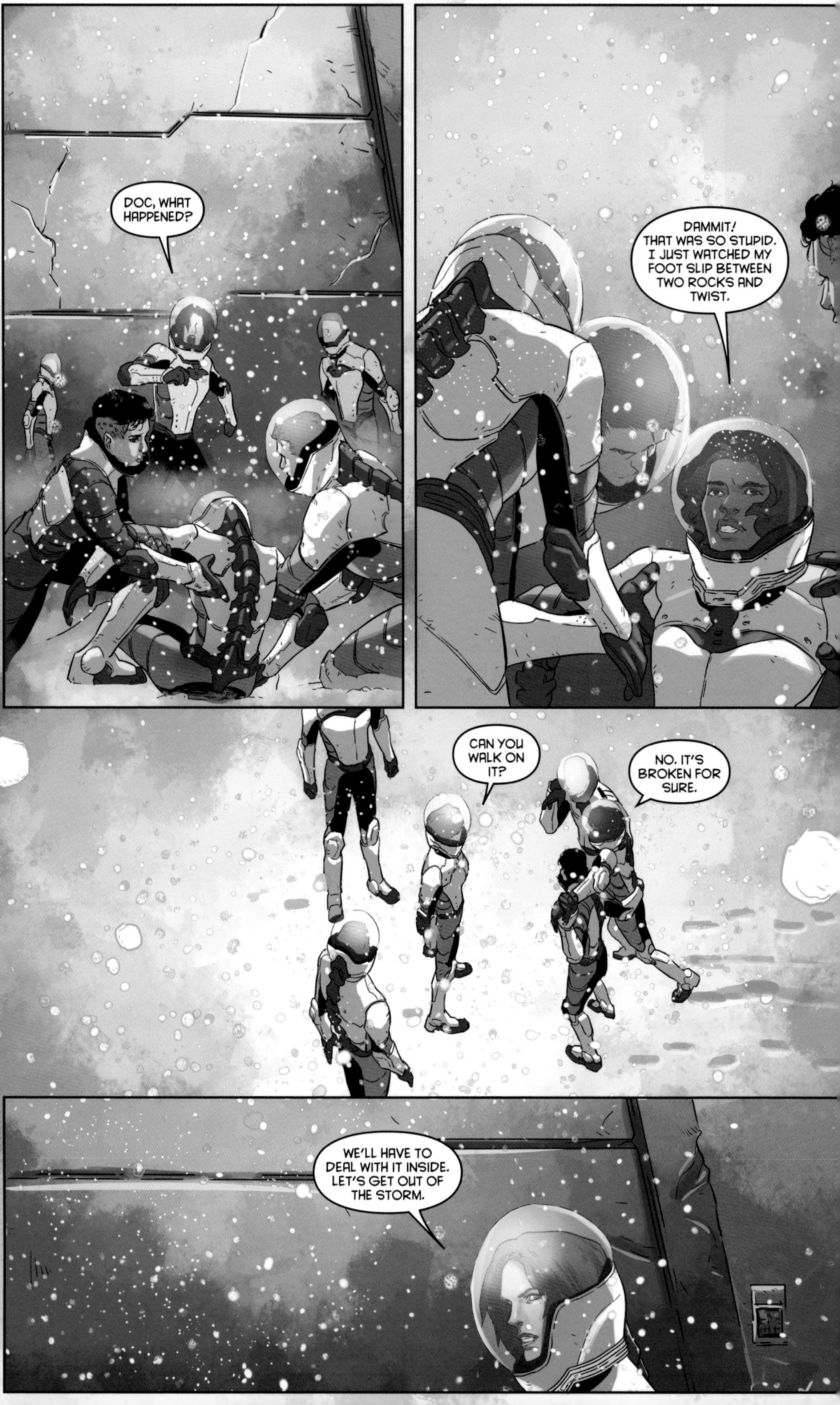
DOC, WHAT HAPPENED?
DAMMIT! THAT WAS SO STUPID. I JUST WATCHED MY FOOT SLIP BETWEEN TWO ROCKS AND TWIST.
CAN YOU WALK ON IT?
NO. IT'S BROKEN FOR SURE.
WE'LL HAVE TO DEAL WITH IT INSIDE. LET'S GET OUT OF THE STORM.

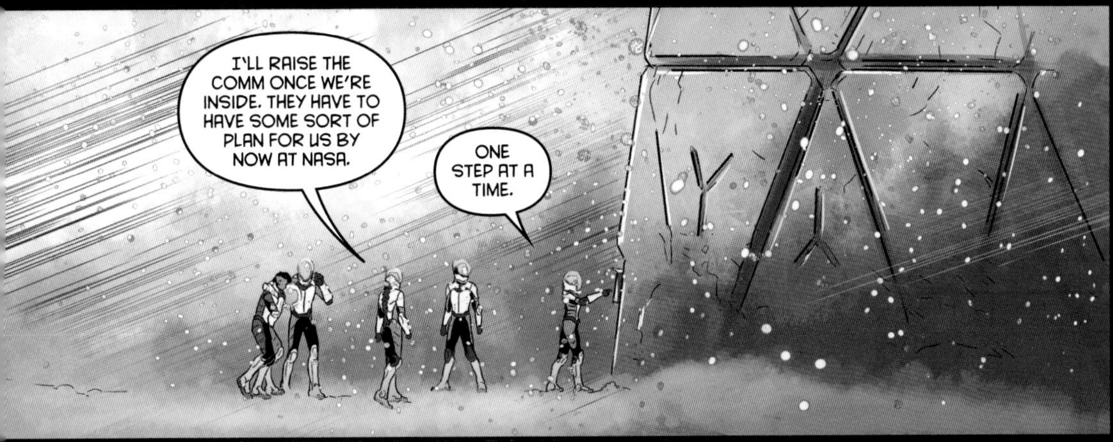
I'LL RAISE THE COMM ONCE WE'RE INSIDE. THEY HAVE TO HAVE SOME SORT OF PLAN FOR US BY NOW AT NASA.
ONE STEP AT A TIME.

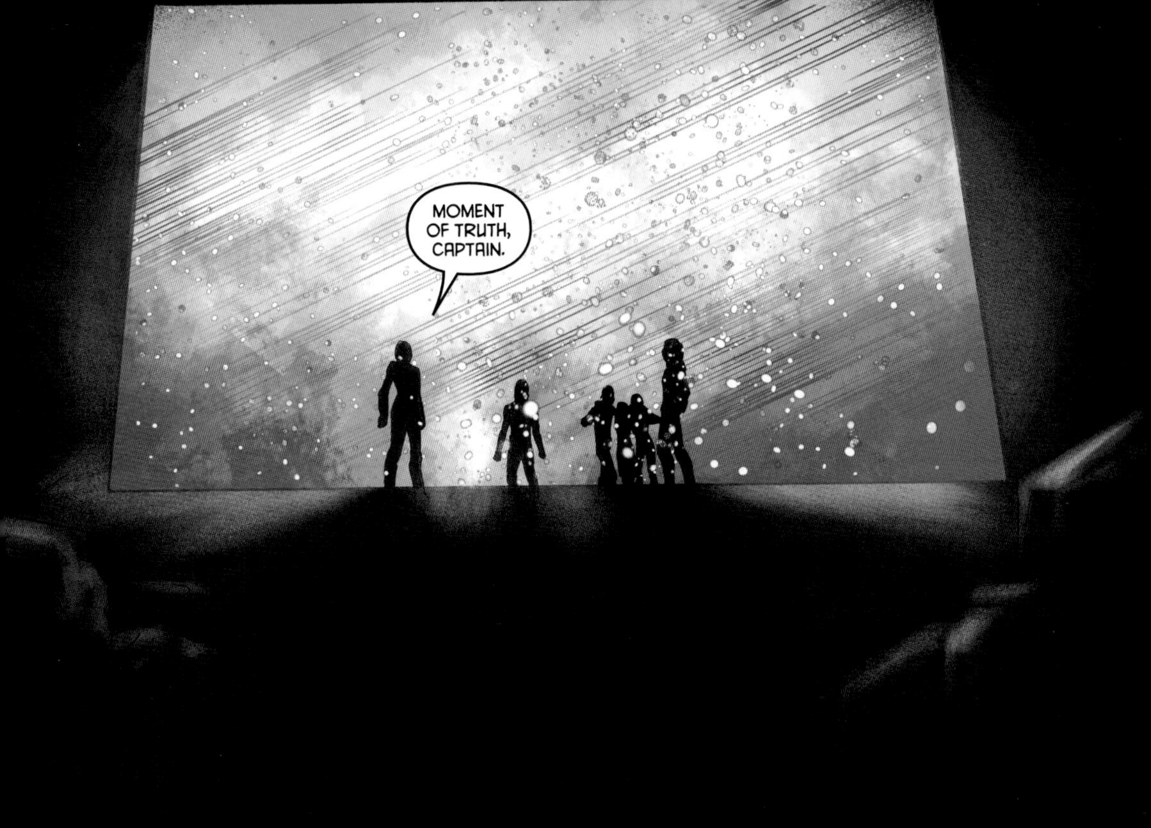
MOMENT OF TRUTH, CAPTAIN.

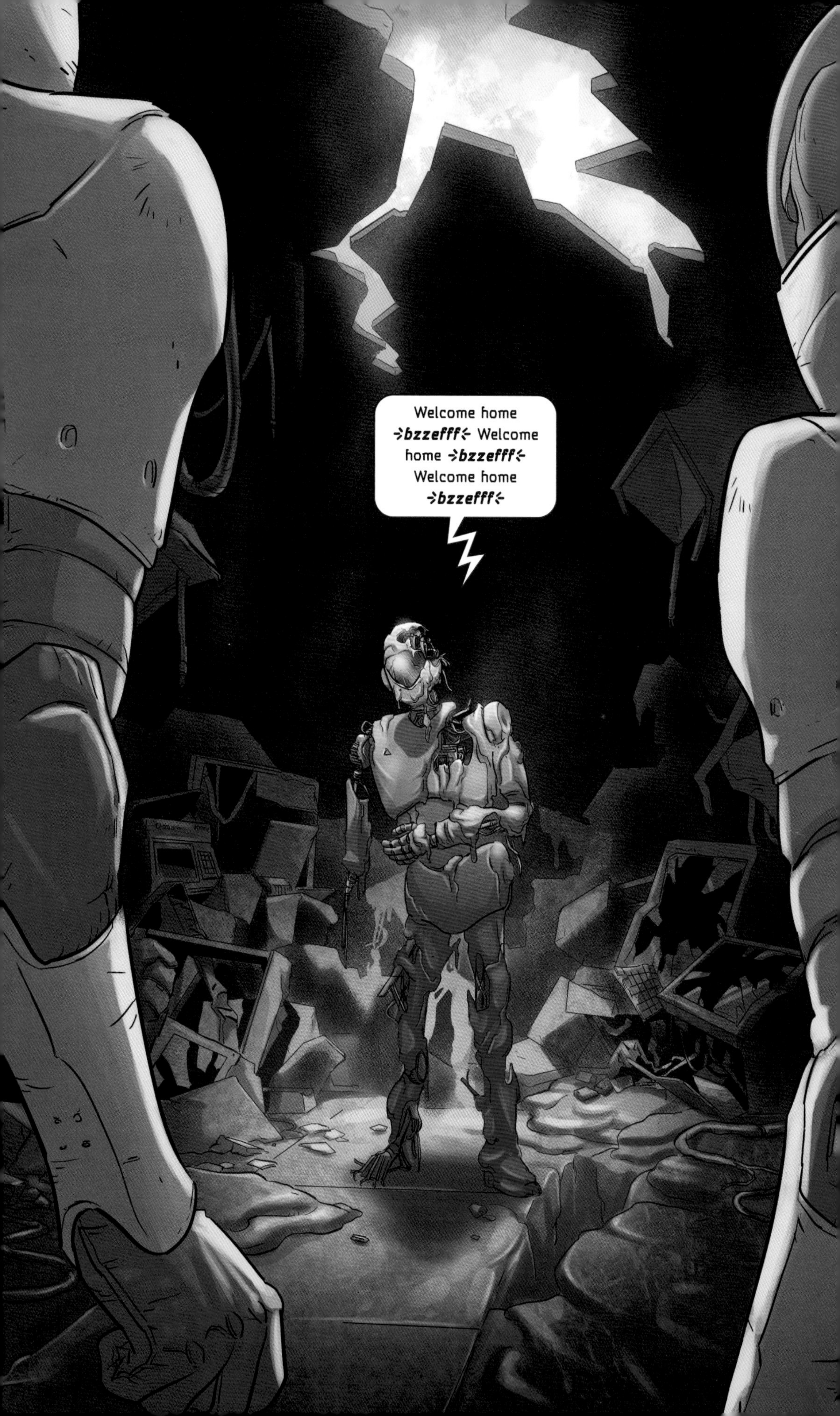
Welcome home ->bzzefff<- Welcome home ->bzzefff<- Welcome home ->bzzefff<-

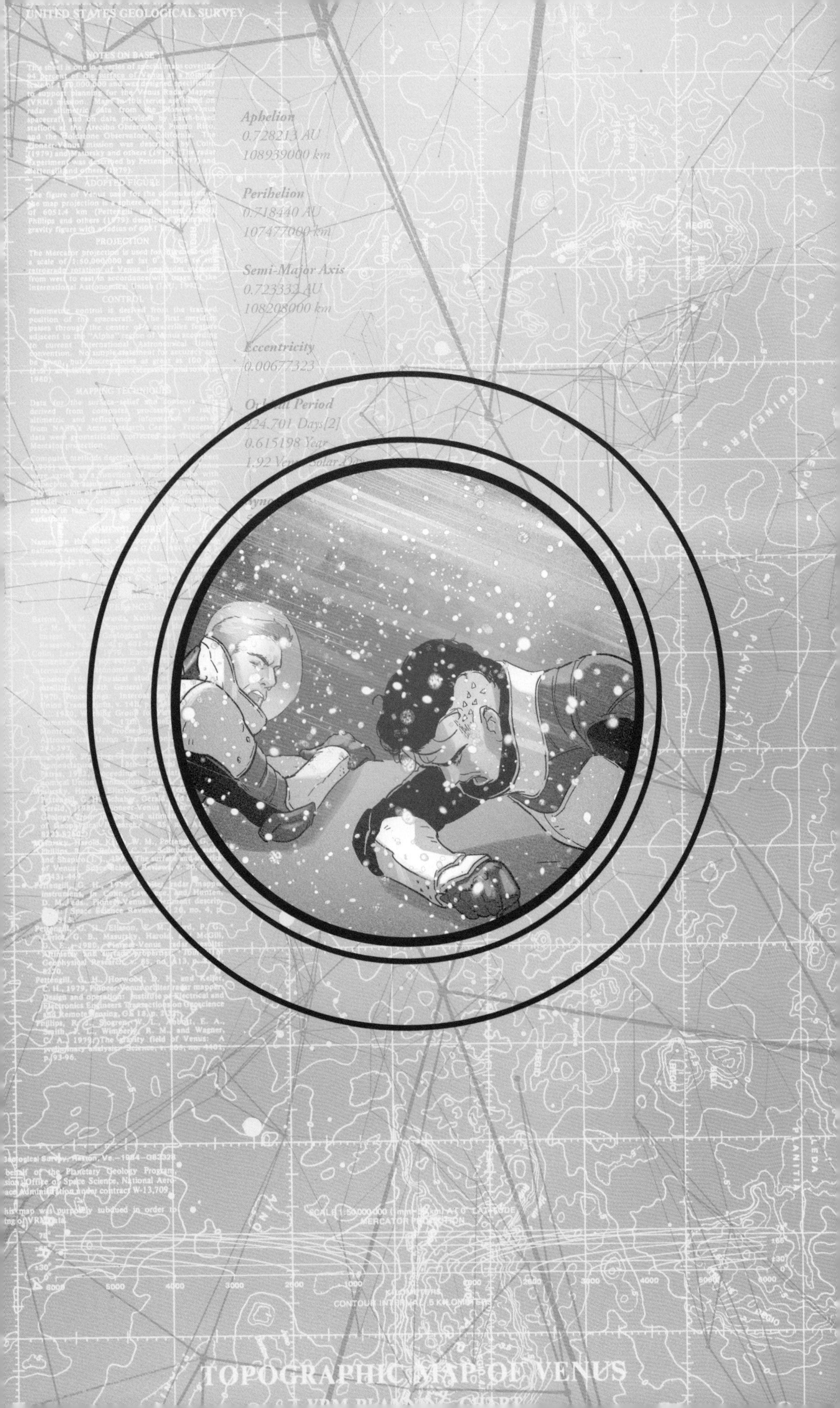

UNITED STATES GEOLOGICAL SURVEY
Aphelion
0.728213 AU
108939000 km
Perihelion
0.718440 AU
107477000 km
Semi-Major Axis
0.723332 AU
108208000 km
Eccentricity
0.00677323
Orbital Period
224.701 Days[2]
0.615198 Year
CONTOUR INTERVAL 5 KILOMETERS
TOPOGRAPHIC MAP OF VENUS

CHAPTER **TWO**

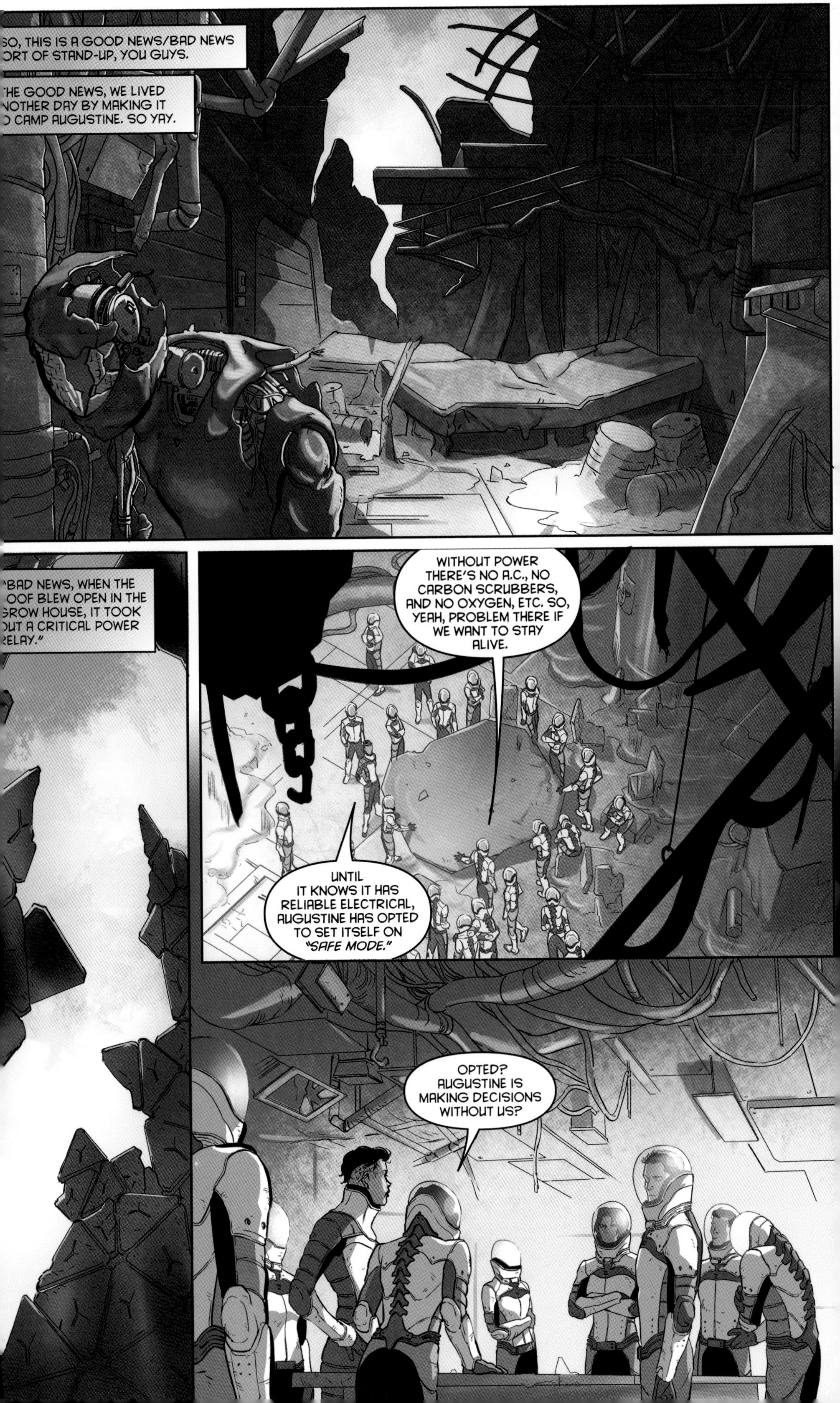

SO, THIS IS A GOOD NEWS/BAD NEWS ORT OF STAND-UP, YOU GUYS.
HE GOOD NEWS, WE LIVED NOTHER DAY BY MAKING IT CAMP AUGUSTINE. SO YAY.
"BAD NEWS, WHEN THE OOF BLEW OPEN IN THE GROW HOUSE, IT TOOK UT A CRITICAL POWER RELAY."
WITHOUT POWER THERE'S NO A.C., NO CARBON SCRUBBERS, AND NO OXYGEN, ETC. SO, YEAH, PROBLEM THERE IF WE WANT TO STAY ALIVE.
UNTIL IT KNOWS IT HAS RELIABLE ELECTRICAL, AUGUSTINE HAS OPTED TO SET ITSELF ON "SAFE MODE."
OPTED? AUGUSTINE IS MAKING DECISIONS WITHOUT US?

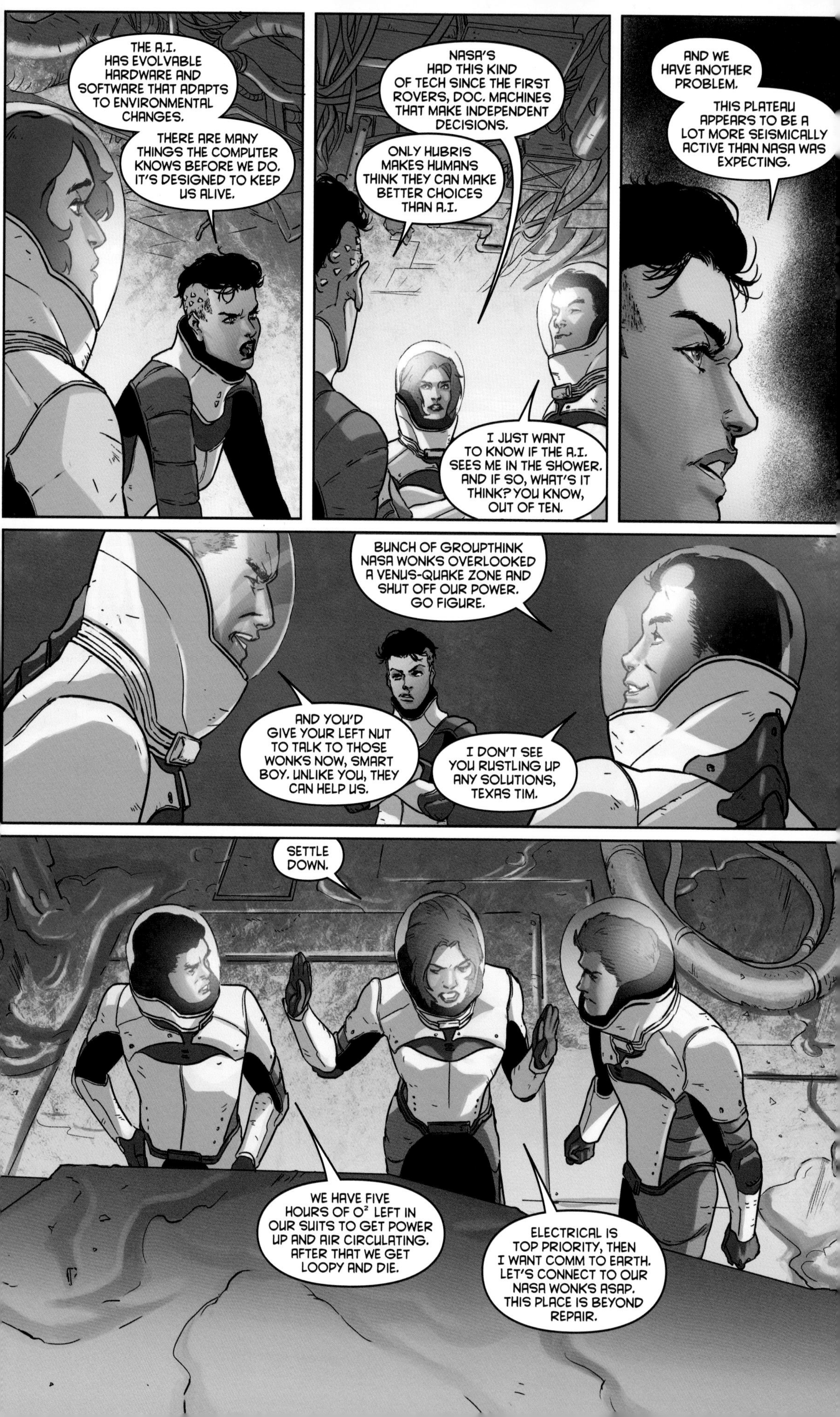
THE A.I. HAS EVOLVABLE HARDWARE AND SOFTWARE THAT ADAPTS TO ENVIRONMENTAL CHANGES.
THERE ARE MANY THINGS THE COMPUTER KNOWS BEFORE WE DO. IT'S DESIGNED TO KEEP US ALIVE.
NASA'S HAD THIS KIND OF TECH SINCE THE FIRST ROVERS, DOC. MACHINES THAT MAKE INDEPENDENT DECISIONS.
ONLY HUBRIS MAKES HUMANS THINK THEY CAN MAKE BETTER CHOICES THAN A.I.
I JUST WANT TO KNOW IF THE A.I. SEES ME IN THE SHOWER. AND IF SO, WHAT'S IT THINK? YOU KNOW, OUT OF TEN.
AND WE HAVE ANOTHER PROBLEM.
THIS PLATEAU APPEARS TO BE A LOT MORE SEISMICALLY ACTIVE THAN NASA WAS EXPECTING.
BUNCH OF GROUPTHINK NASA WONKS OVERLOOKED A VENUS-QUAKE ZONE AND SHUT OFF OUR POWER. GO FIGURE.
AND YOU'D GIVE YOUR LEFT NUT TO TALK TO THOSE WONKS NOW, SMART BOY. UNLIKE YOU, THEY CAN HELP US.
I DON'T SEE YOU RUSTLING UP ANY SOLUTIONS, TEXAS TIM.
SETTLE DOWN.
WE HAVE FIVE HOURS OF O² LEFT IN OUR SUITS TO GET POWER UP AND AIR CIRCULATING. AFTER THAT WE GET LOOPY AND DIE.
ELECTRICAL IS TOP PRIORITY, THEN I WANT COMM TO EARTH. LET'S CONNECT TO OUR NASA WONKS ASAP. THIS PLACE IS BEYOND REPAIR.

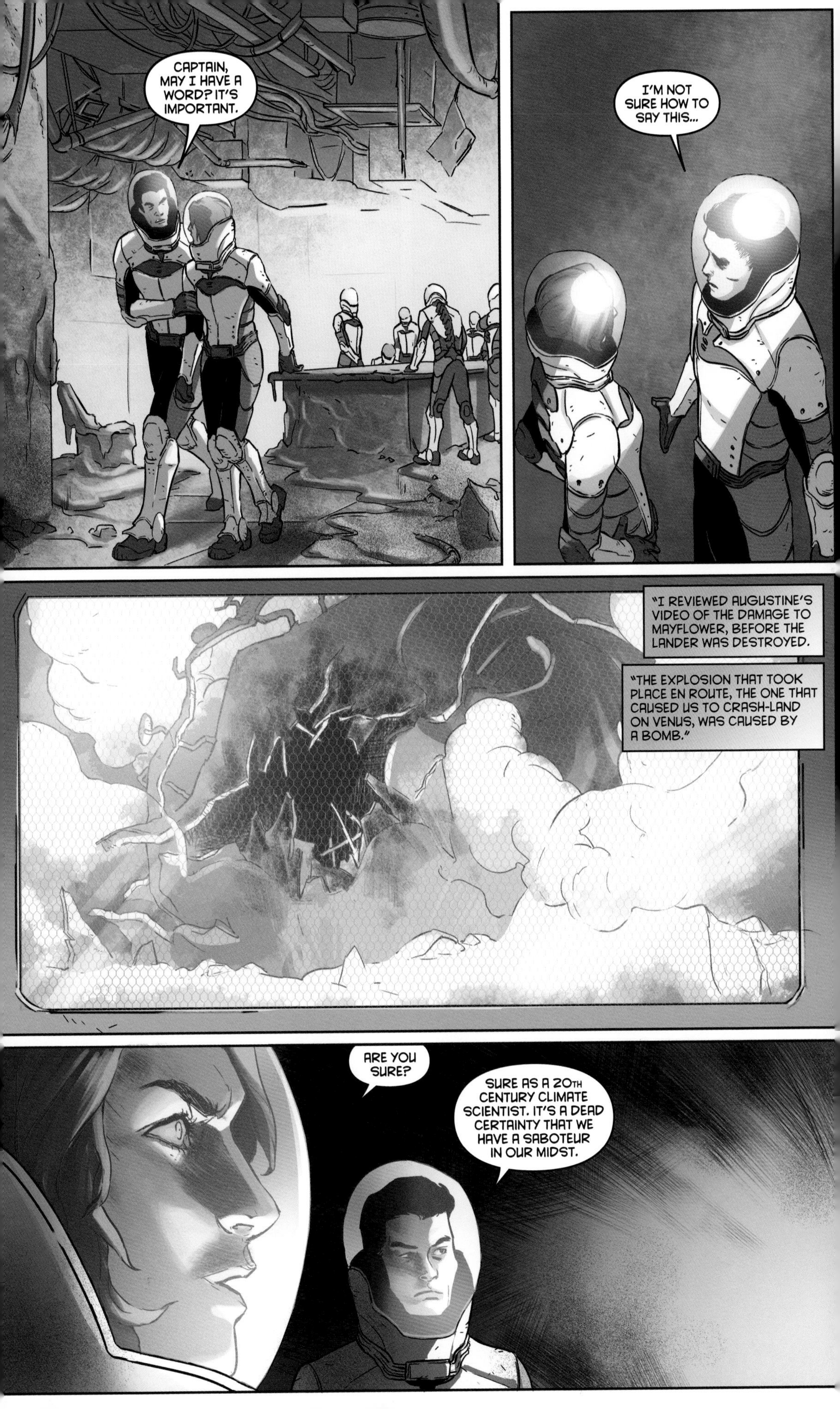
CAPTAIN, MAY I HAVE A WORD? IT'S IMPORTANT.
I'M NOT SURE HOW TO SAY THIS...
"I REVIEWED AUGUSTINE'S VIDEO OF THE DAMAGE TO MAYFLOWER, BEFORE THE LANDER WAS DESTROYED.
"THE EXPLOSION THAT TOOK PLACE EN ROUTE, THE ONE THAT CAUSED US TO CRASH-LAND ON VENUS, WAS CAUSED BY A BOMB."
ARE YOU SURE?
SURE AS A 20TH CENTURY CLIMATE SCIENTIST. IT'S A DEAD CERTAINTY THAT WE HAVE A SABOTEUR IN OUR MIDST.

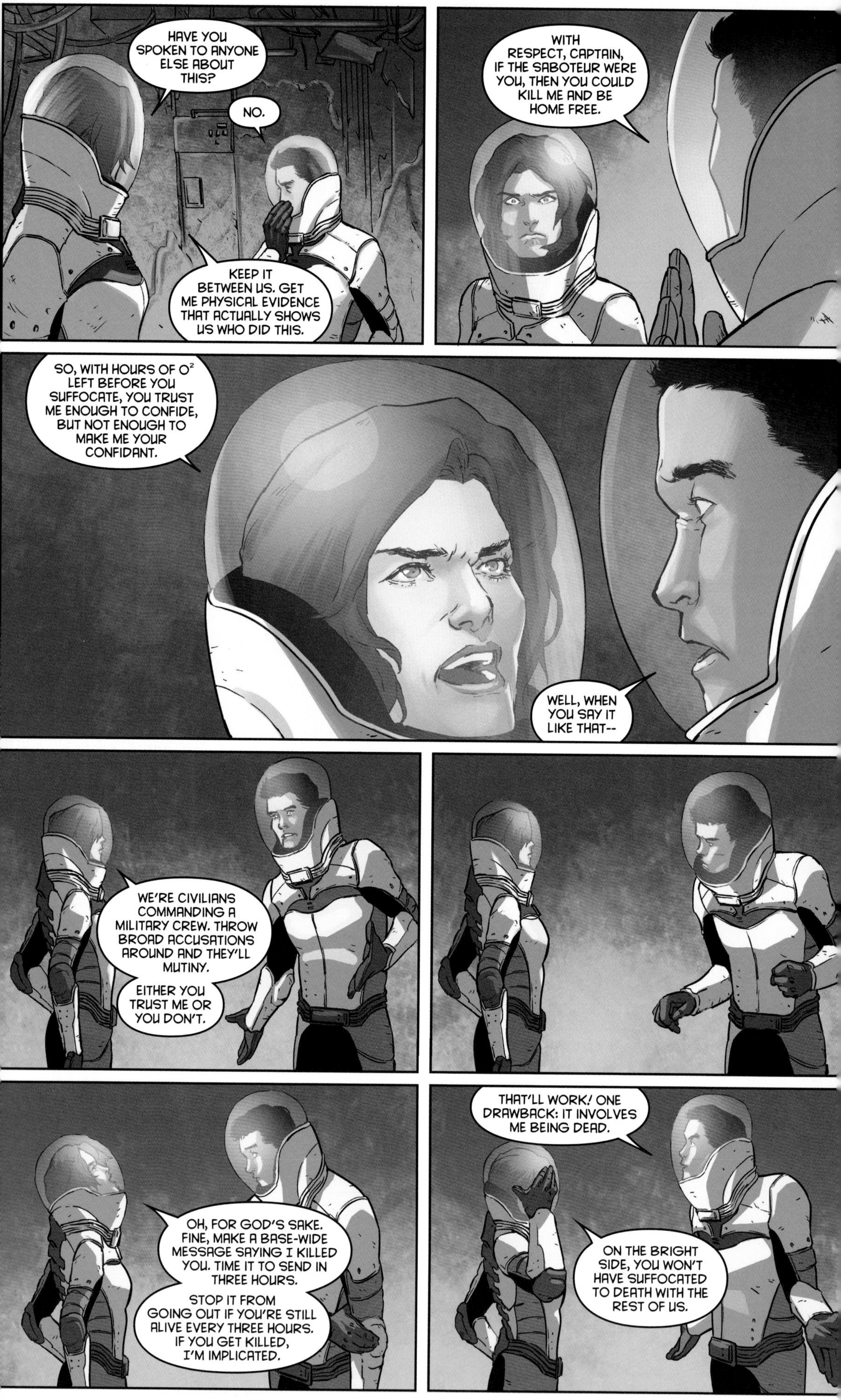
HAVE YOU SPOKEN TO ANYONE ELSE ABOUT THIS?
NO.
KEEP IT BETWEEN US. GET ME PHYSICAL EVIDENCE THAT ACTUALLY SHOWS US WHO DID THIS.
WITH RESPECT, CAPTAIN, IF THE SABOTEUR WERE YOU, THEN YOU COULD KILL ME AND BE HOME FREE.
SO, WITH HOURS OF O² LEFT BEFORE YOU SUFFOCATE, YOU TRUST ME ENOUGH TO CONFIDE, BUT NOT ENOUGH TO MAKE ME YOUR CONFIDANT.
WELL, WHEN YOU SAY IT LIKE THAT--
WE'RE CIVILIANS COMMANDING A MILITARY CREW. THROW BROAD ACCUSATIONS AROUND AND THEY'LL MUTINY.
EITHER YOU TRUST ME OR YOU DON'T.
OH, FOR GOD'S SAKE. FINE, MAKE A BASE-WIDE MESSAGE SAYING I KILLED YOU. TIME IT TO SEND IN THREE HOURS.
STOP IT FROM GOING OUT IF YOU'RE STILL ALIVE EVERY THREE HOURS. IF YOU GET KILLED, I'M IMPLICATED.
THAT'LL WORK! ONE DRAWBACK: IT INVOLVES ME BEING DEAD.
ON THE BRIGHT SIDE, YOU WON'T HAVE SUFFOCATED TO DEATH WITH THE REST OF US.

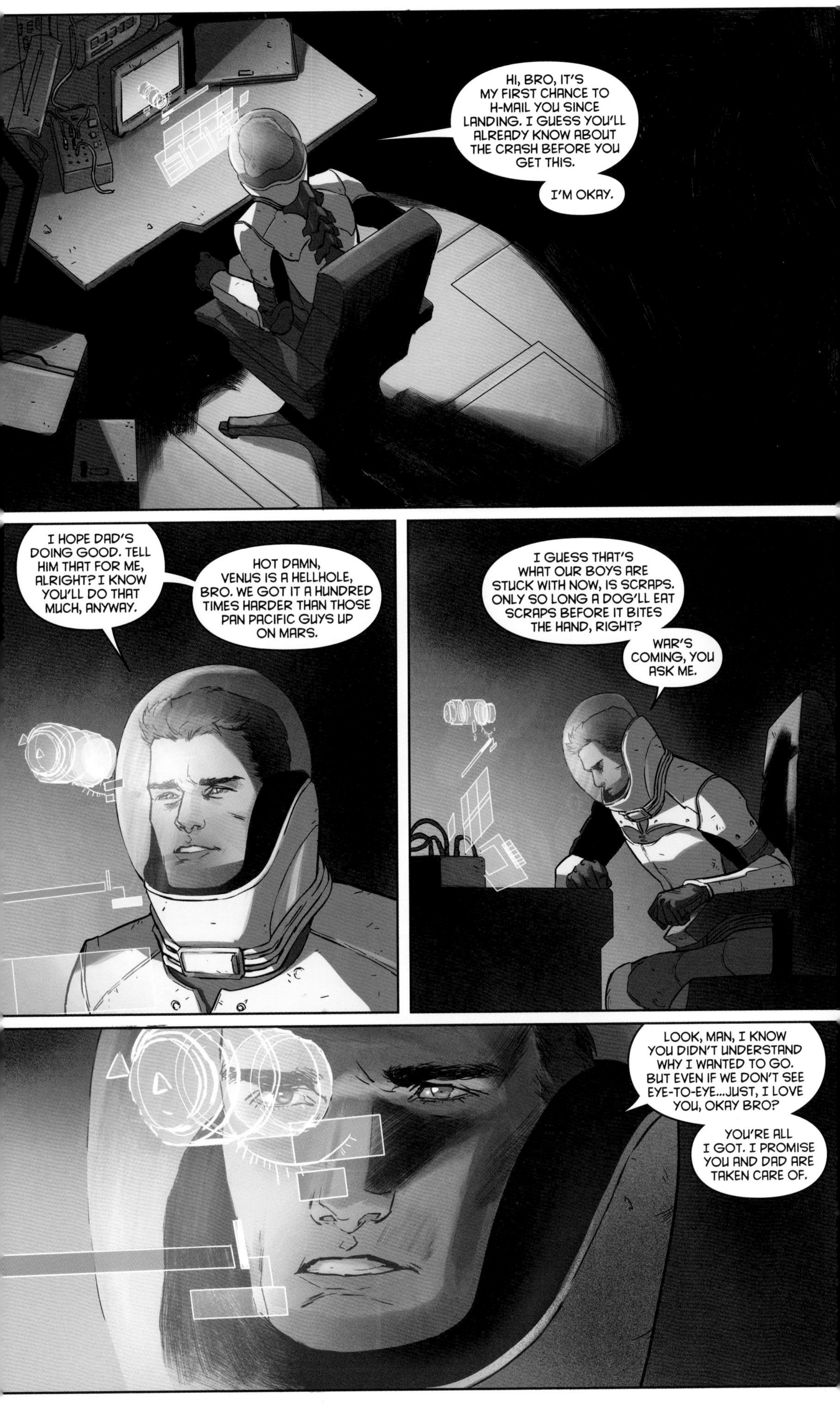
HI, BRO, IT'S MY FIRST CHANCE TO H-MAIL YOU SINCE LANDING. I GUESS YOU'LL ALREADY KNOW ABOUT THE CRASH BEFORE YOU GET THIS.
I'M OKAY.
I HOPE DAD'S DOING GOOD. TELL HIM THAT FOR ME, ALRIGHT? I KNOW YOU'LL DO THAT MUCH, ANYWAY.
HOT DAMN, VENUS IS A HELLHOLE, BRO. WE GOT IT A HUNDRED TIMES HARDER THAN THOSE PAN PACIFIC GUYS UP ON MARS.
I GUESS THAT'S WHAT OUR BOYS ARE STUCK WITH NOW, IS SCRAPS. ONLY SO LONG A DOG'LL EAT SCRAPS BEFORE IT BITES THE HAND, RIGHT?
WAR'S COMING, YOU ASK ME.
LOOK, MAN, I KNOW YOU DIDN'T UNDERSTAND WHY I WANTED TO GO. BUT EVEN IF WE DON'T SEE EYE-TO-EYE...JUST, I LOVE YOU, OKAY BRO?
YOU'RE ALL I GOT. I PROMISE YOU AND DAD ARE TAKEN CARE OF.

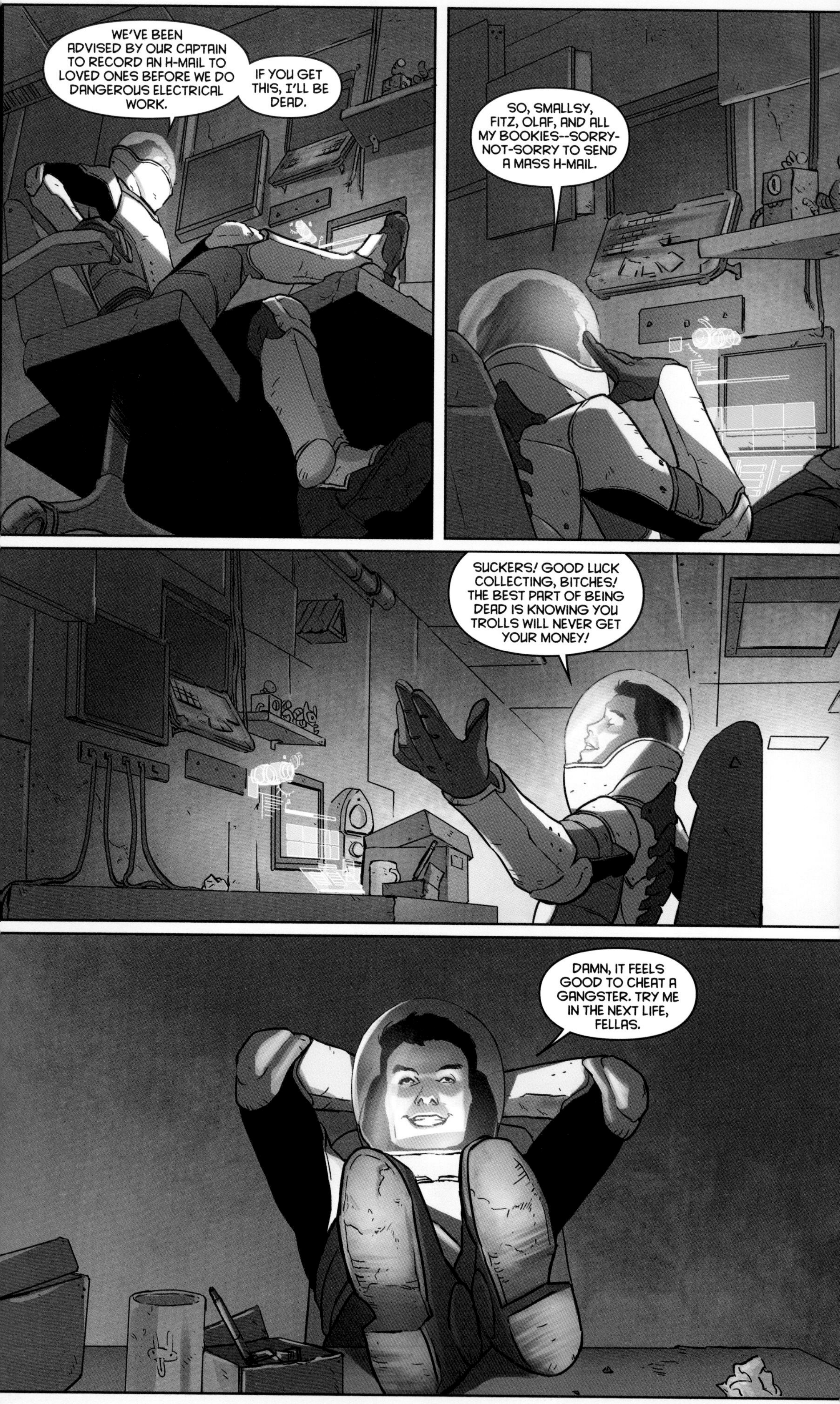
WE'VE BEEN ADVISED BY OUR CAPTAIN TO RECORD AN H-MAIL TO LOVED ONES BEFORE WE DO DANGEROUS ELECTRICAL WORK.
IF YOU GET THIS, I'LL BE DEAD.
SO, SMALLSY, FITZ, OLAF, AND ALL MY BOOKIES--SORRY-NOT-SORRY TO SEND A MASS H-MAIL.
SUCKERS! GOOD LUCK COLLECTING, BITCHES! THE BEST PART OF BEING DEAD IS KNOWING YOU TROLLS WILL NEVER GET YOUR MONEY!
DAMN, IT FEELS GOOD TO CHEAT A GANGSTER. TRY ME IN THE NEXT LIFE, FELLAS.

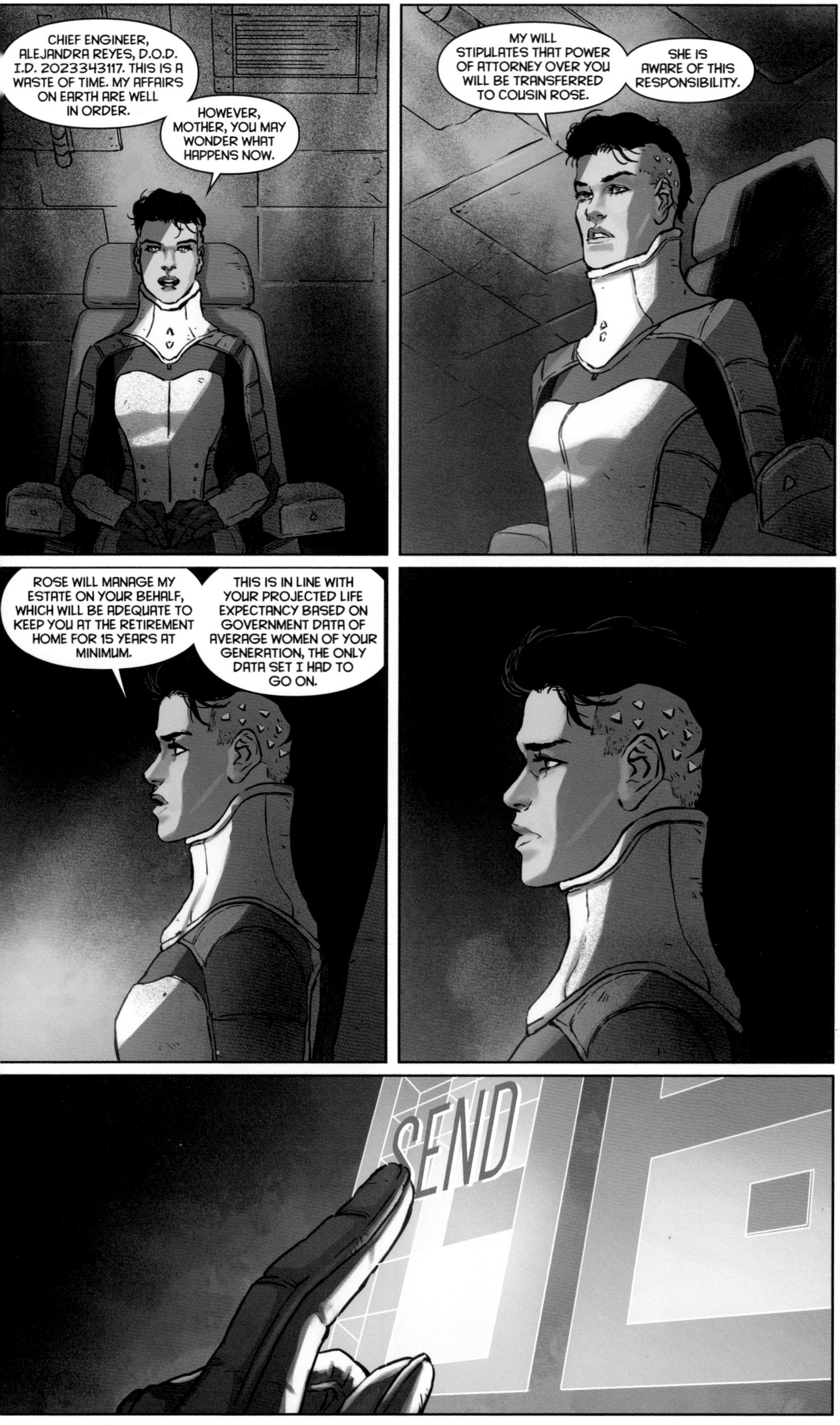

CHIEF ENGINEER, ALEJANDRA REYES, D.O.D. I.D. 2023343117. THIS IS A WASTE OF TIME. MY AFFAIRS ON EARTH ARE WELL IN ORDER.
HOWEVER, MOTHER, YOU MAY WONDER WHAT HAPPENS NOW.
MY WILL STIPULATES THAT POWER OF ATTORNEY OVER YOU WILL BE TRANSFERRED TO COUSIN ROSE.
SHE IS AWARE OF THIS RESPONSIBILITY.
ROSE WILL MANAGE MY ESTATE ON YOUR BEHALF, WHICH WILL BE ADEQUATE TO KEEP YOU AT THE RETIREMENT HOME FOR 15 YEARS AT MINIMUM.
THIS IS IN LINE WITH YOUR PROJECTED LIFE EXPECTANCY BASED ON GOVERNMENT DATA OF AVERAGE WOMEN OF YOUR GENERATION, THE ONLY DATA SET I HAD TO GO ON.
SEND

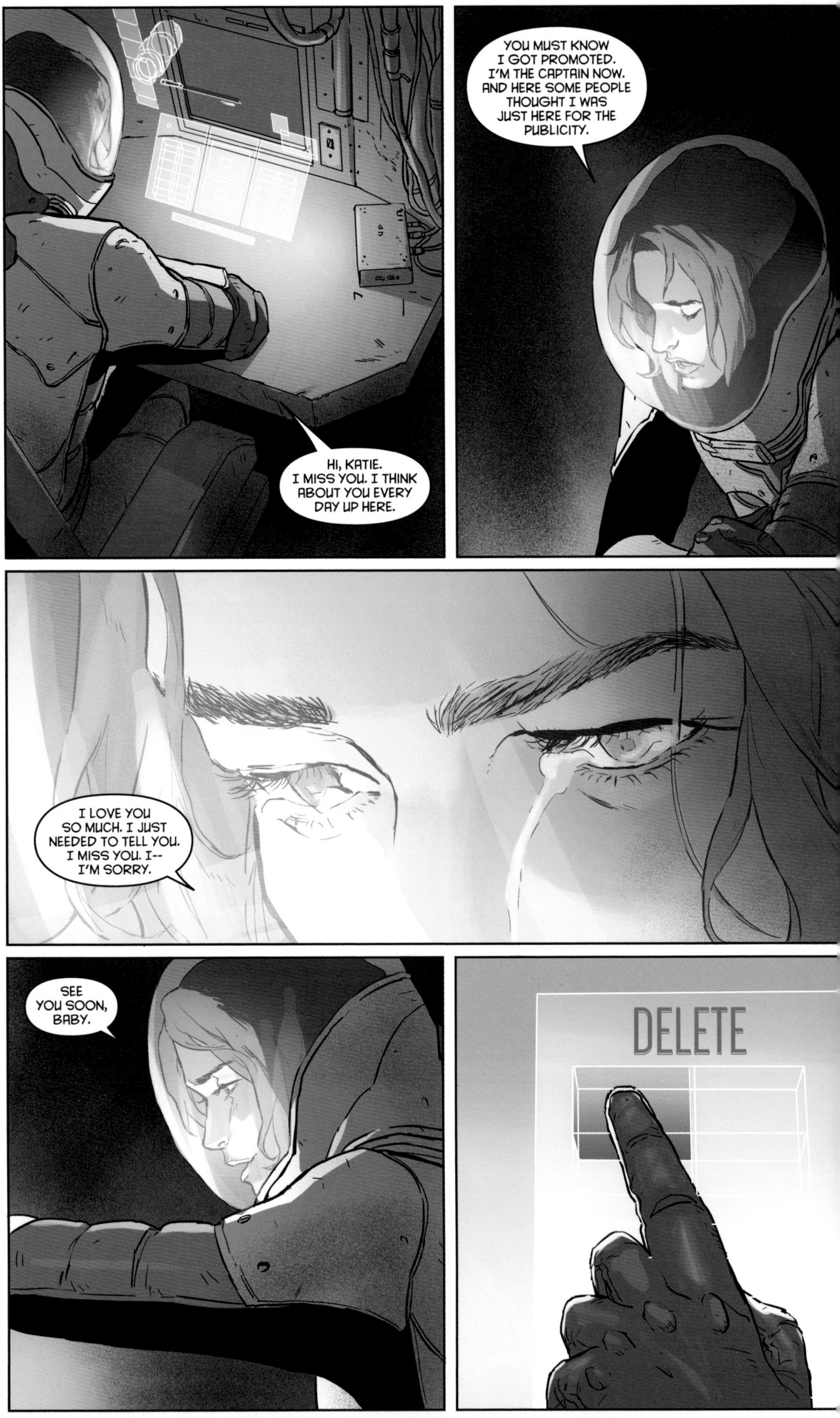
HI, KATIE. I MISS YOU. I THINK ABOUT YOU EVERY DAY UP HERE.
YOU MUST KNOW I GOT PROMOTED. I'M THE CAPTAIN NOW. AND HERE SOME PEOPLE THOUGHT I WAS JUST HERE FOR THE PUBLICITY.
I LOVE YOU SO MUCH. I JUST NEEDED TO TELL YOU. I MISS YOU. I-- I'M SORRY.
SEE YOU SOON, BABY.
DELETE

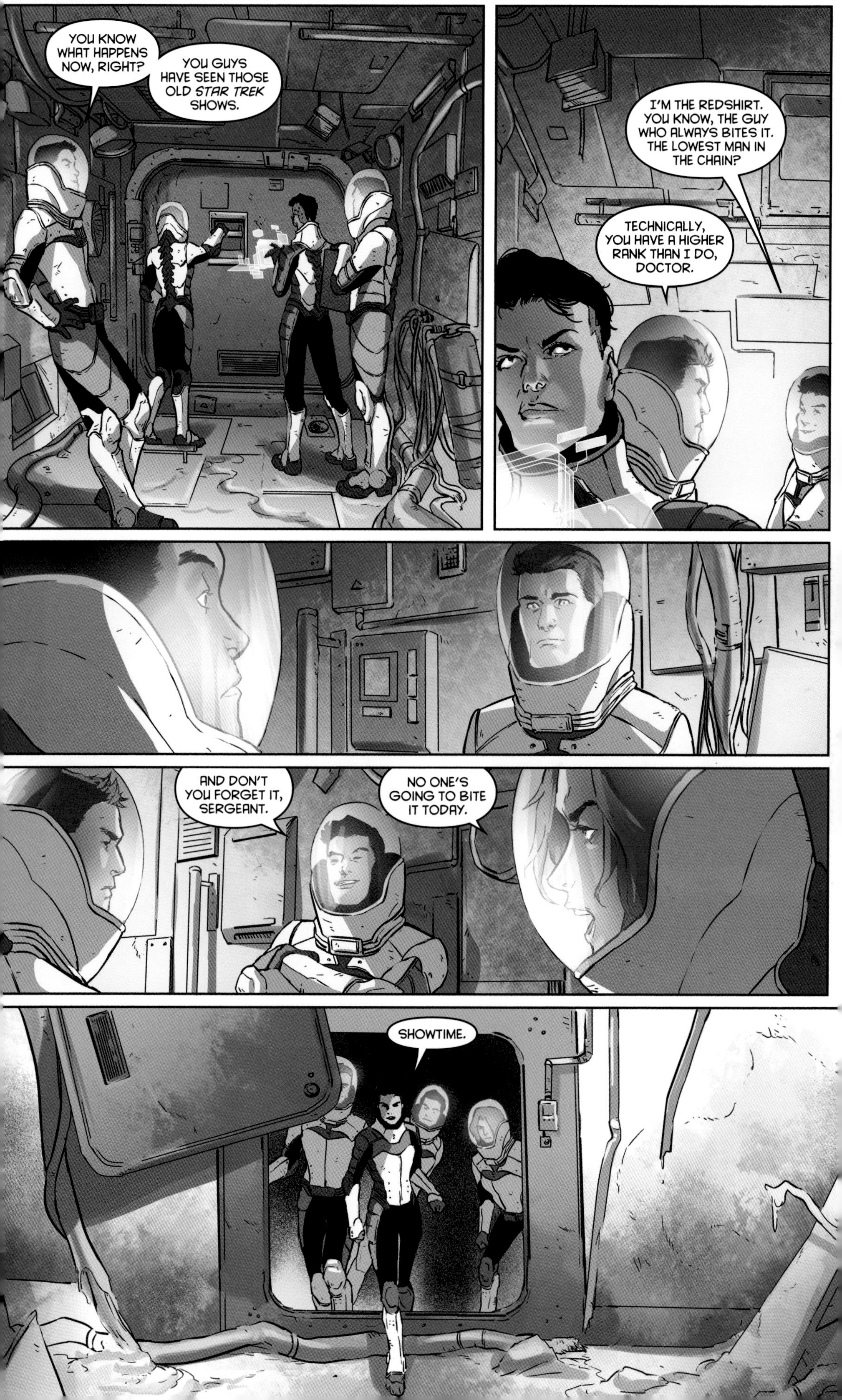
YOU KNOW WHAT HAPPENS NOW, RIGHT?
YOU GUYS HAVE SEEN THOSE OLD *STAR TREK* SHOWS.
I'M THE REDSHIRT. YOU KNOW, THE GUY WHO ALWAYS BITES IT. THE LOWEST MAN IN THE CHAIN?
TECHNICALLY, YOU HAVE A HIGHER RANK THAN I DO, DOCTOR.
AND DON'T YOU FORGET IT, SERGEANT.
NO ONE'S GOING TO BITE IT TODAY.
SHOWTIME.

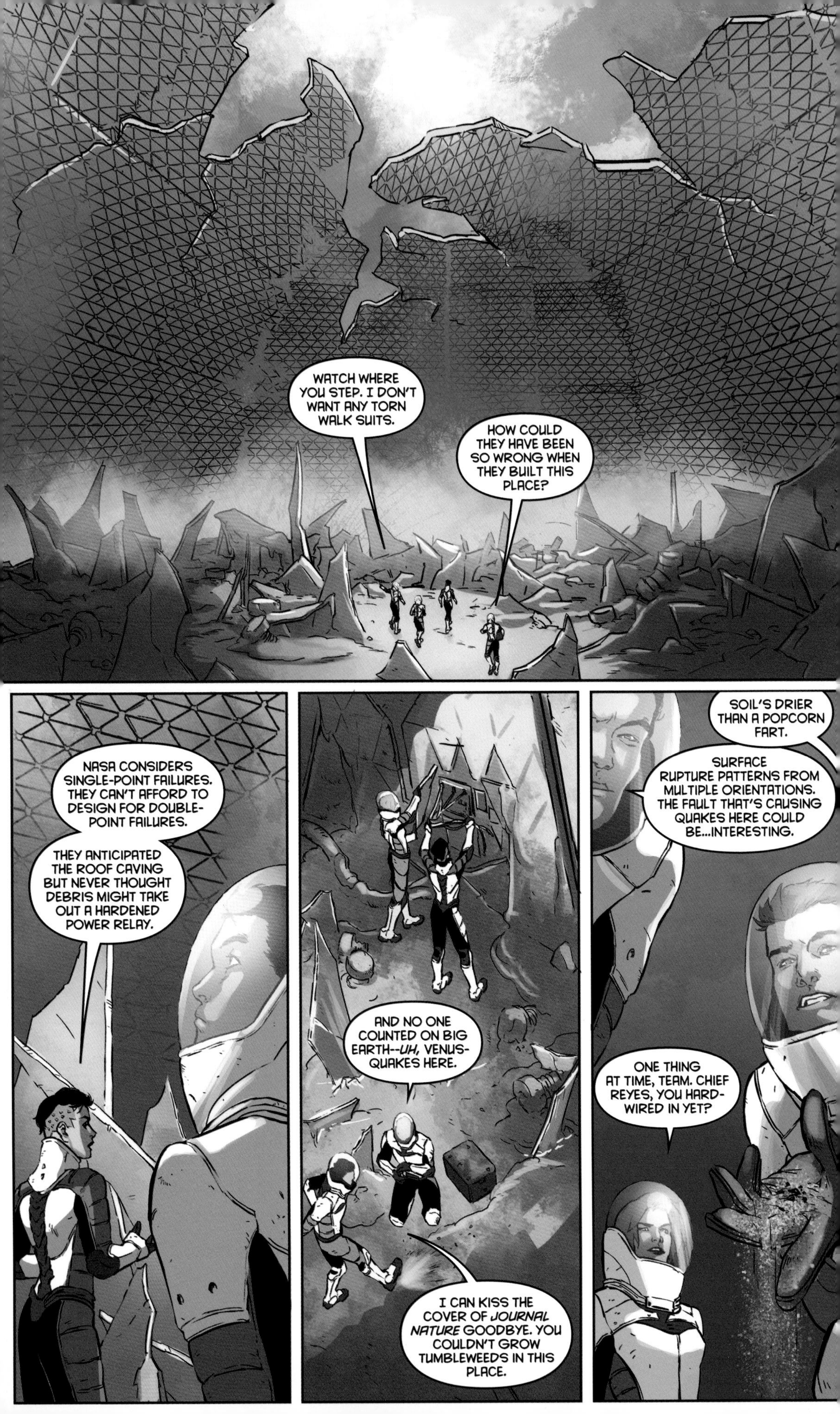
WATCH WHERE YOU STEP. I DON'T WANT ANY TORN WALK SUITS.
HOW COULD THEY HAVE BEEN SO WRONG WHEN THEY BUILT THIS PLACE?
NASA CONSIDERS SINGLE-POINT FAILURES. THEY CAN'T AFFORD TO DESIGN FOR DOUBLE-POINT FAILURES.
THEY ANTICIPATED THE ROOF CAVING BUT NEVER THOUGHT DEBRIS MIGHT TAKE OUT A HARDENED POWER RELAY.
AND NO ONE COUNTED ON BIG EARTH--*UH,* VENUS-QUAKES HERE.
I CAN KISS THE COVER OF *JOURNAL NATURE* GOODBYE. YOU COULDN'T GROW TUMBLEWEEDS IN THIS PLACE.
SOIL'S DRIER THAN A POPCORN FART.
SURFACE RUPTURE PATTERNS FROM MULTIPLE ORIENTATIONS. THE FAULT THAT'S CAUSING QUAKES HERE COULD BE...INTERESTING.
ONE THING AT TIME, TEAM. CHIEF REYES, YOU HARD-WIRED IN YET?

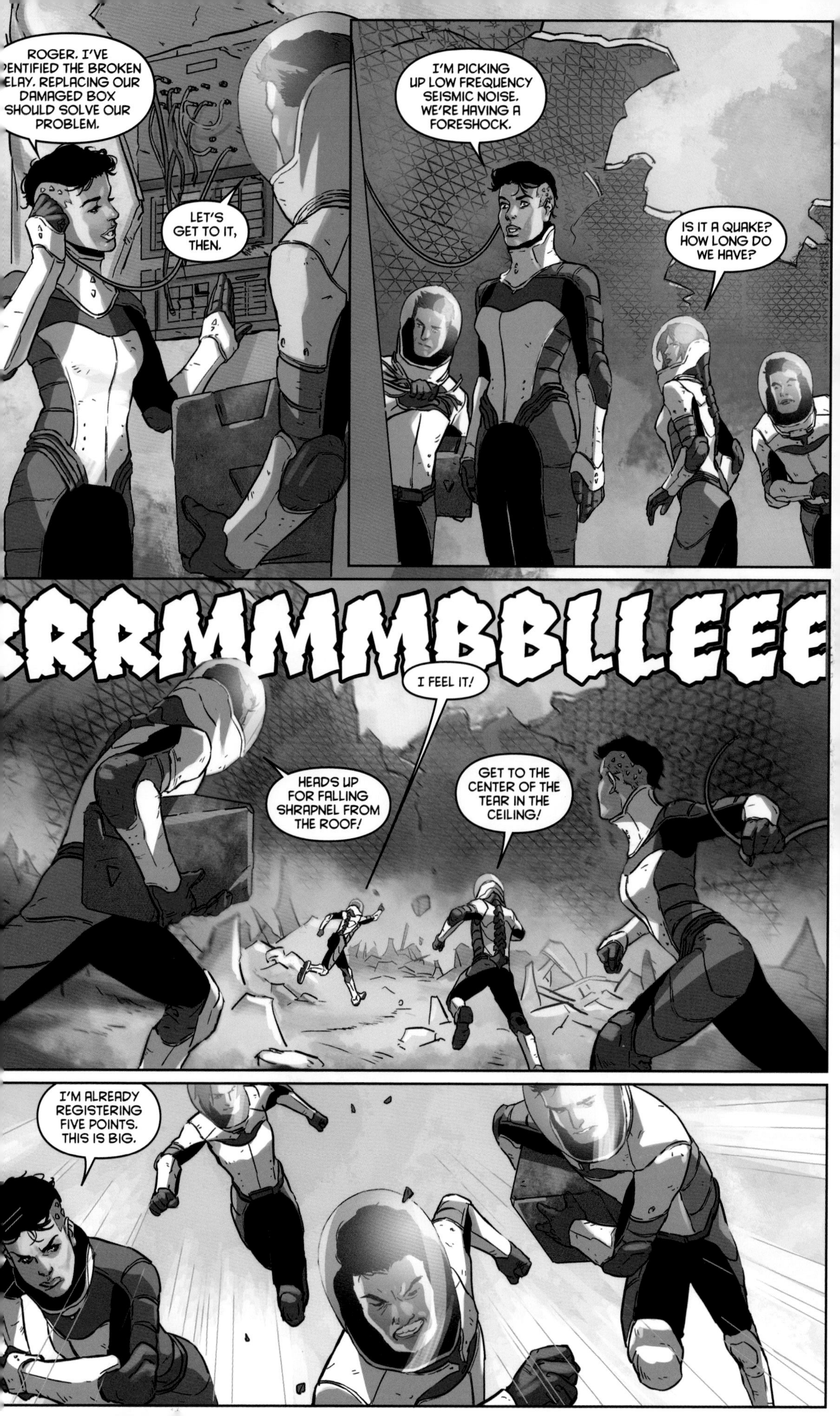

ROGER. I'VE ENTIFIED THE BROKEN ELAY. REPLACING OUR DAMAGED BOX SHOULD SOLVE OUR PROBLEM.
LET'S GET TO IT, THEN.
I'M PICKING UP LOW FREQUENCY SEISMIC NOISE. WE'RE HAVING A FORESHOCK.
IS IT A QUAKE? HOW LONG DO WE HAVE?
RRMMMBBLLEEE
I FEEL IT!
HEADS UP FOR FALLING SHRAPNEL FROM THE ROOF!
GET TO THE CENTER OF THE TEAR IN THE CEILING!
I'M ALREADY REGISTERING FIVE POINTS. THIS IS BIG.

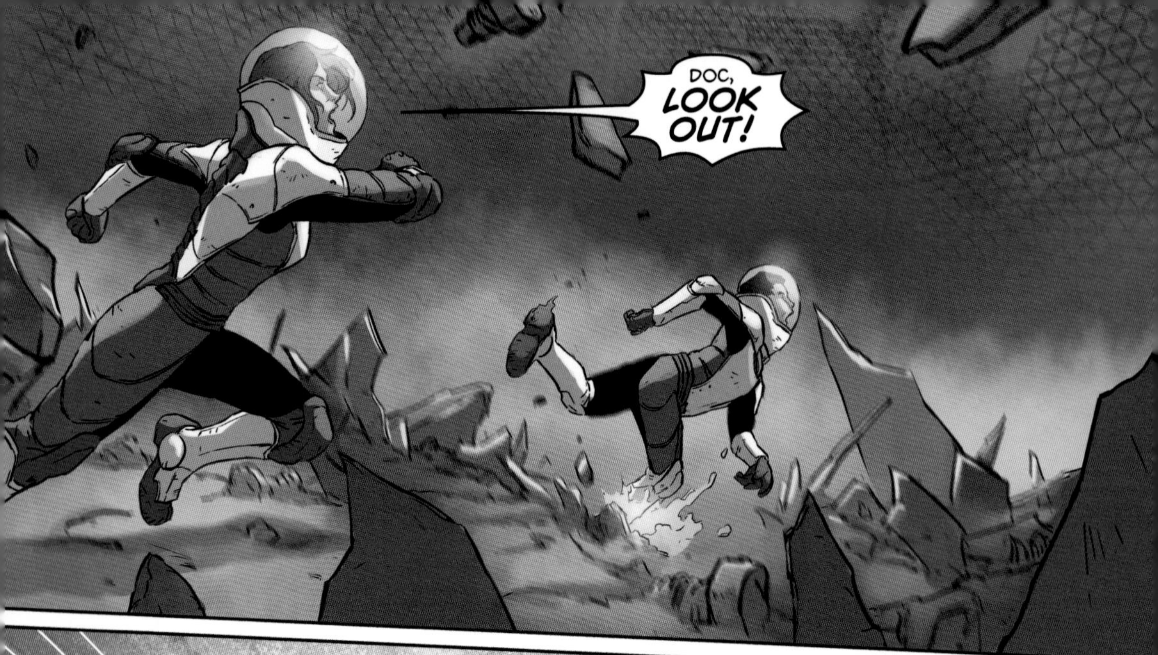
DOC, LOOK OUT!

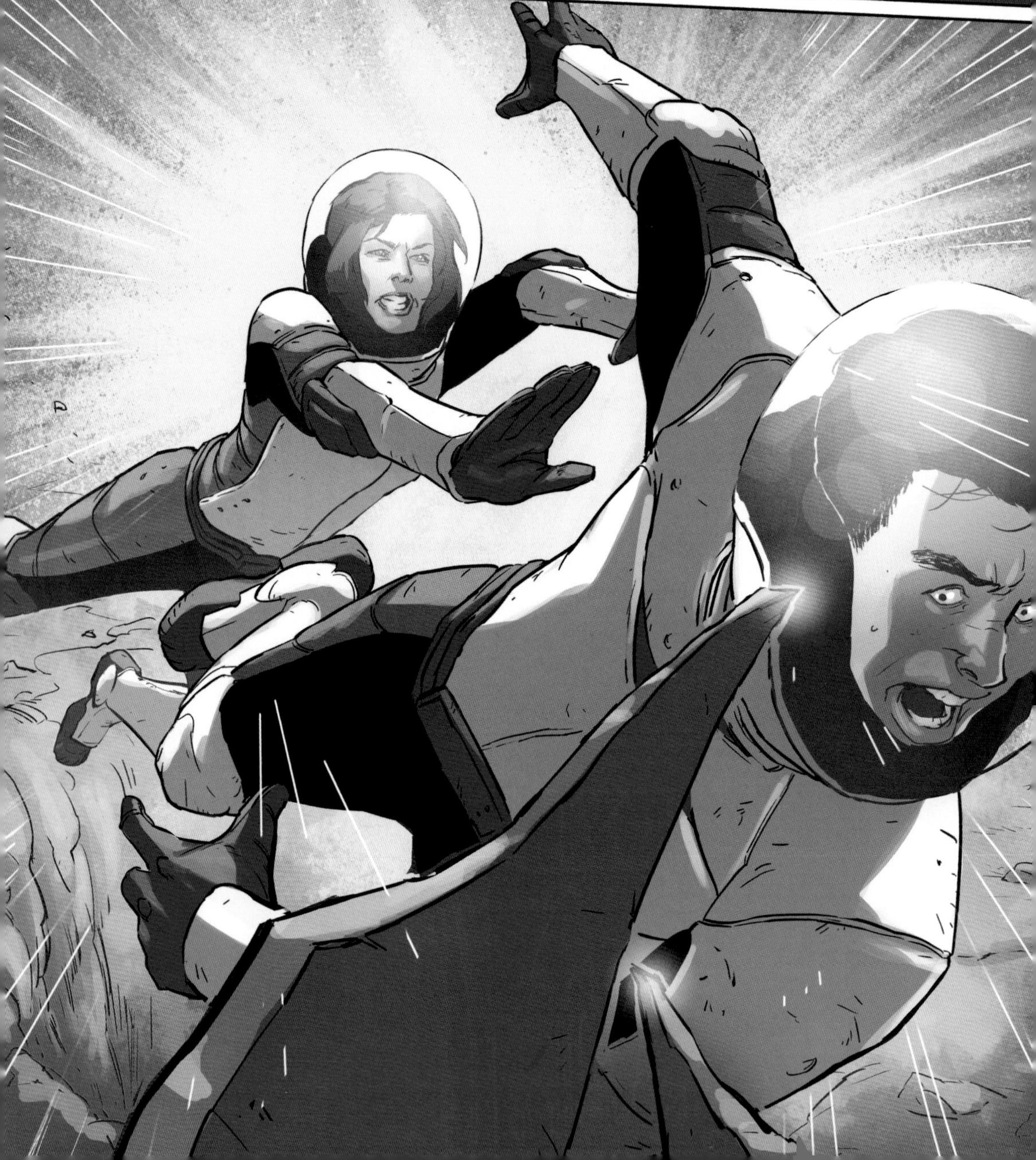

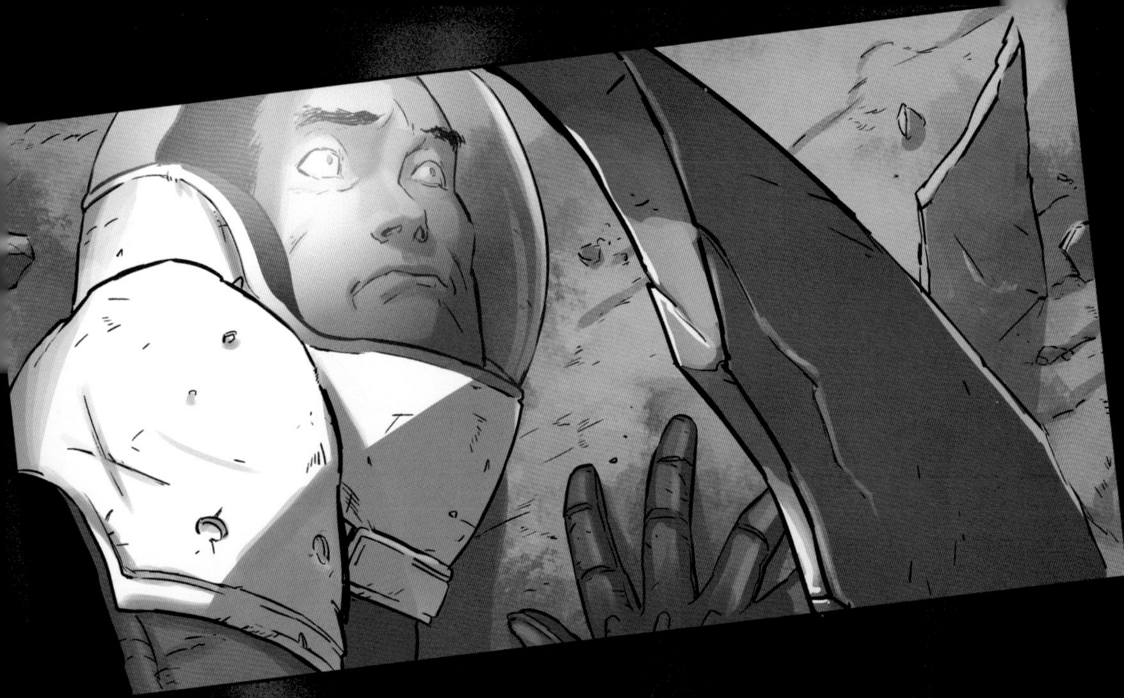

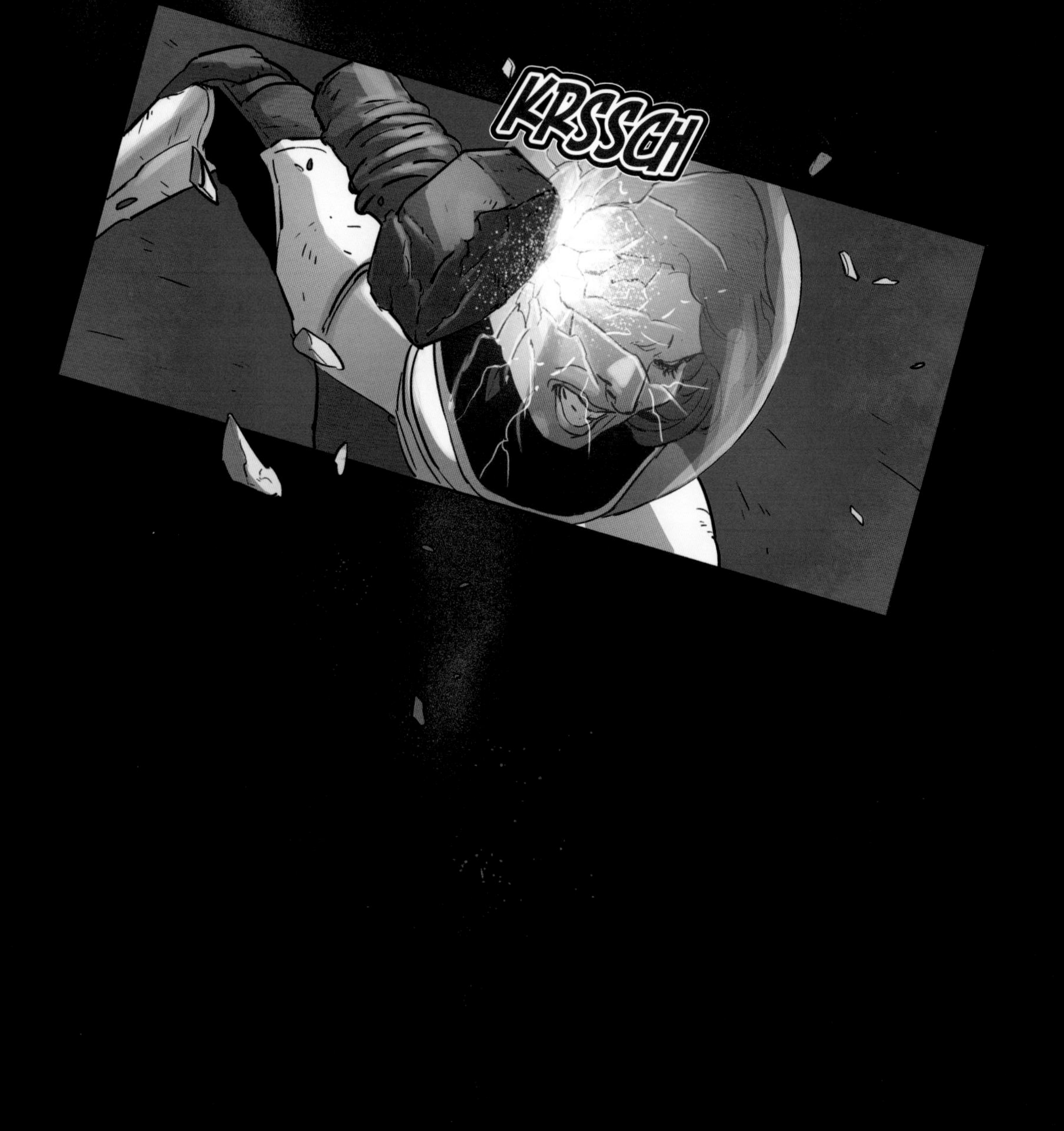

KRSSCH

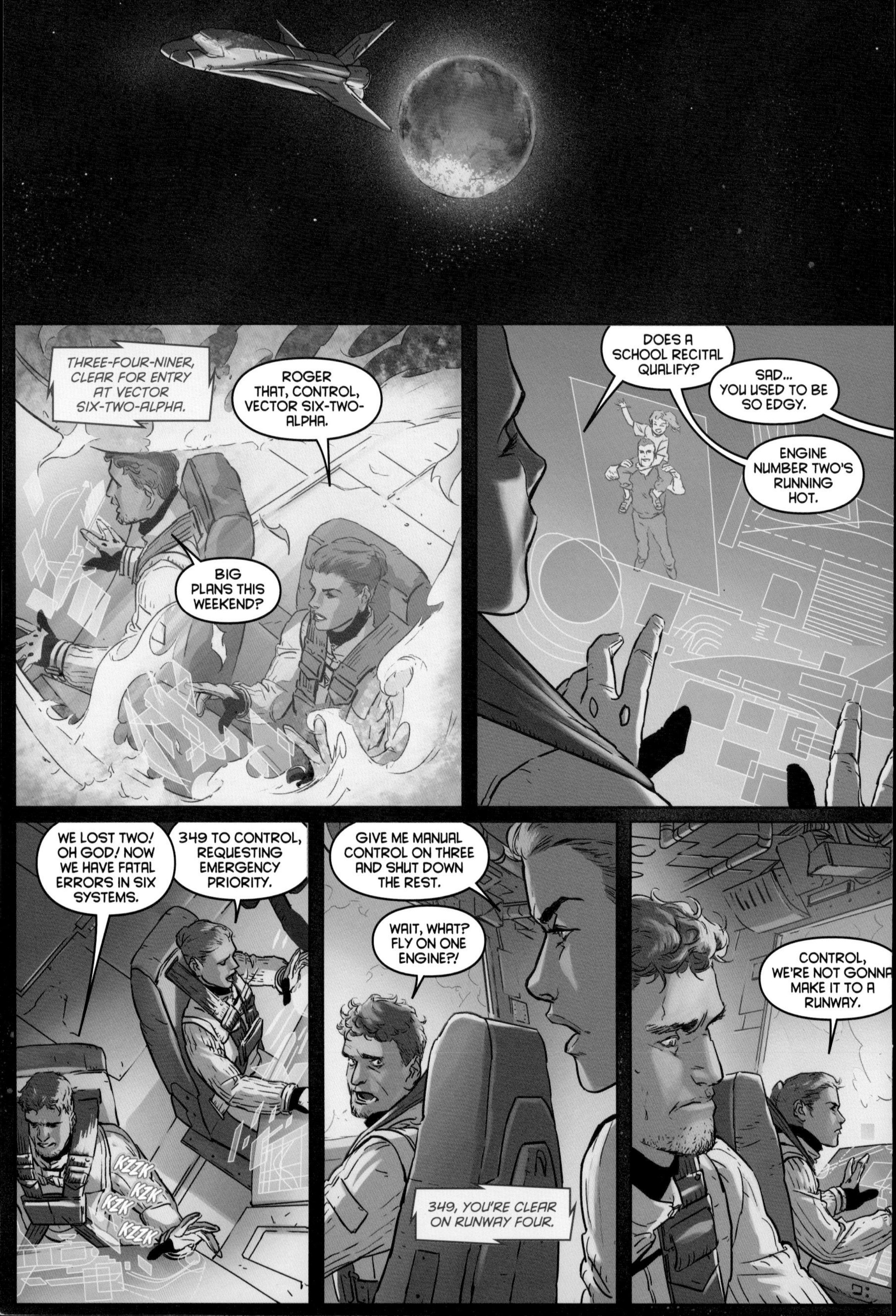
THREE-FOUR-NINER, CLEAR FOR ENTRY AT VECTOR SIX-TWO-ALPHA.
ROGER THAT, CONTROL, VECTOR SIX-TWO-ALPHA.
BIG PLANS THIS WEEKEND?
DOES A SCHOOL RECITAL QUALIFY?
SAD... YOU USED TO BE SO EDGY.
ENGINE NUMBER TWO'S RUNNING HOT.
WE LOST TWO! OH GOD! NOW WE HAVE FATAL ERRORS IN SIX SYSTEMS.
349 TO CONTROL, REQUESTING EMERGENCY PRIORITY.
KZZK
KZK
KZK
KZZK
GIVE ME MANUAL CONTROL ON THREE AND SHUT DOWN THE REST.
WAIT, WHAT? FLY ON ONE ENGINE?!
349, YOU'RE CLEAR ON RUNWAY FOUR.
CONTROL, WE'RE NOT GONNA MAKE IT TO A RUNWAY.

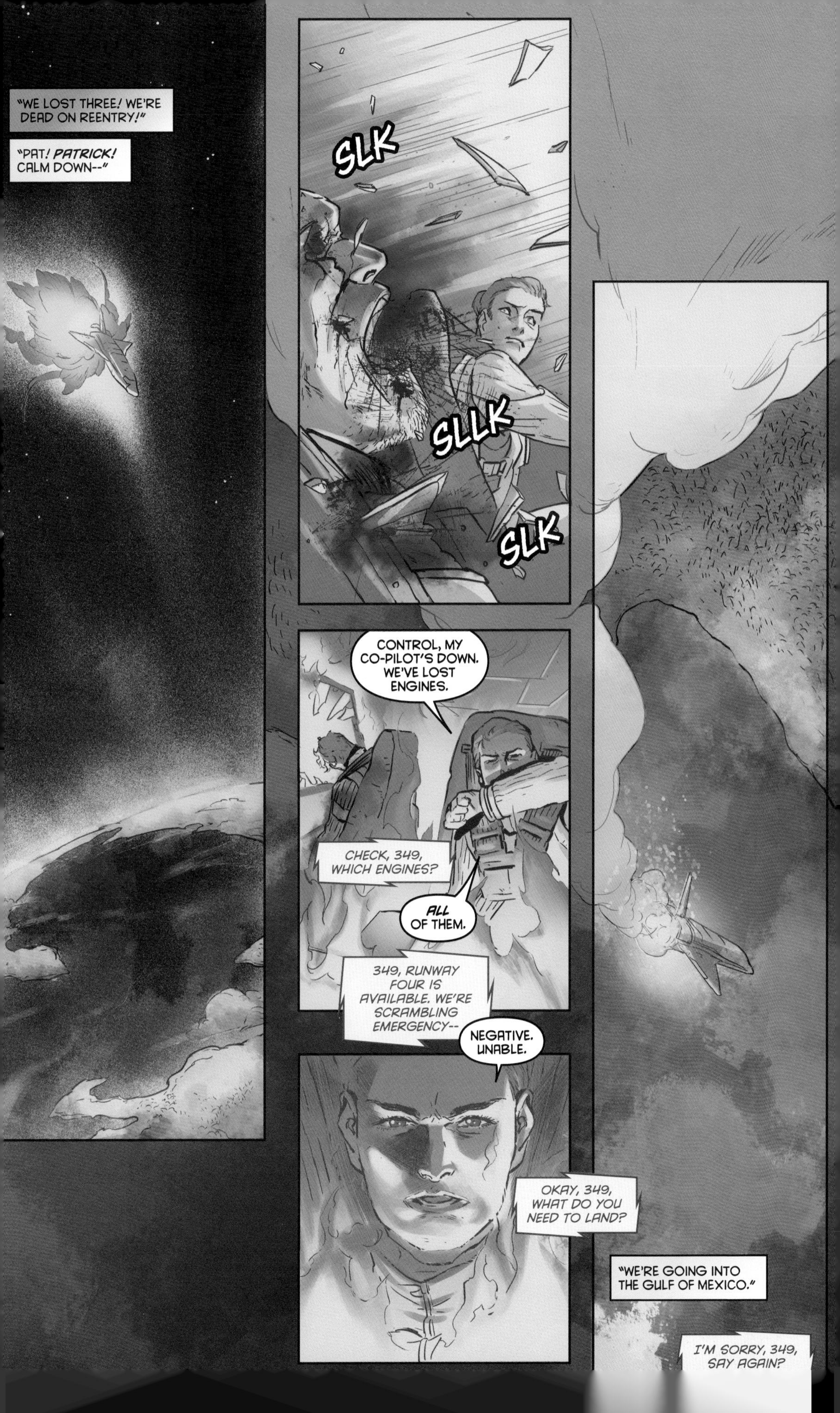
"WE LOST THREE! WE'RE DEAD ON REENTRY!"
"PAT! PATRICK! CALM DOWN--"
SLK
SLLK
SLK
CONTROL, MY CO-PILOT'S DOWN. WE'VE LOST ENGINES.
CHECK, 349, WHICH ENGINES?
ALL OF THEM.
349, RUNWAY FOUR IS AVAILABLE. WE'RE SCRAMBLING EMERGENCY--
NEGATIVE. UNABLE.
OKAY, 349, WHAT DO YOU NEED TO LAND?
"WE'RE GOING INTO THE GULF OF MEXICO."
I'M SORRY, 349, SAY AGAIN?

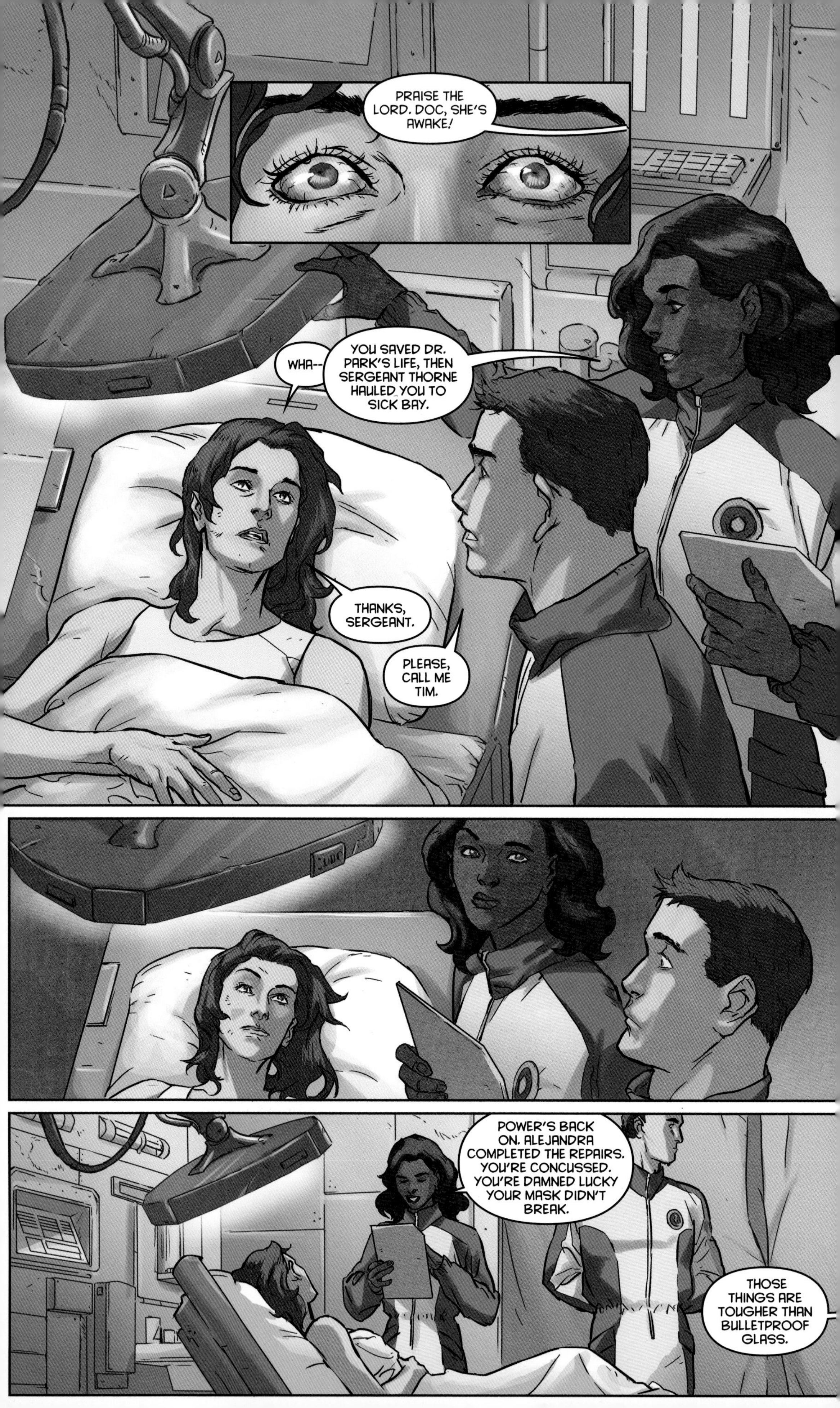
PRAISE THE LORD. DOC, SHE'S AWAKE!
WHA--
YOU SAVED DR. PARK'S LIFE, THEN SERGEANT THORNE HAULED YOU TO SICK BAY.
THANKS, SERGEANT.
PLEASE, CALL ME TIM.
POWER'S BACK ON. ALEJANDRA COMPLETED THE REPAIRS. YOU'RE CONCUSSED. YOU'RE DAMNED LUCKY YOUR MASK DIDN'T BREAK.
THOSE THINGS ARE TOUGHER THAN BULLETPROOF GLASS.

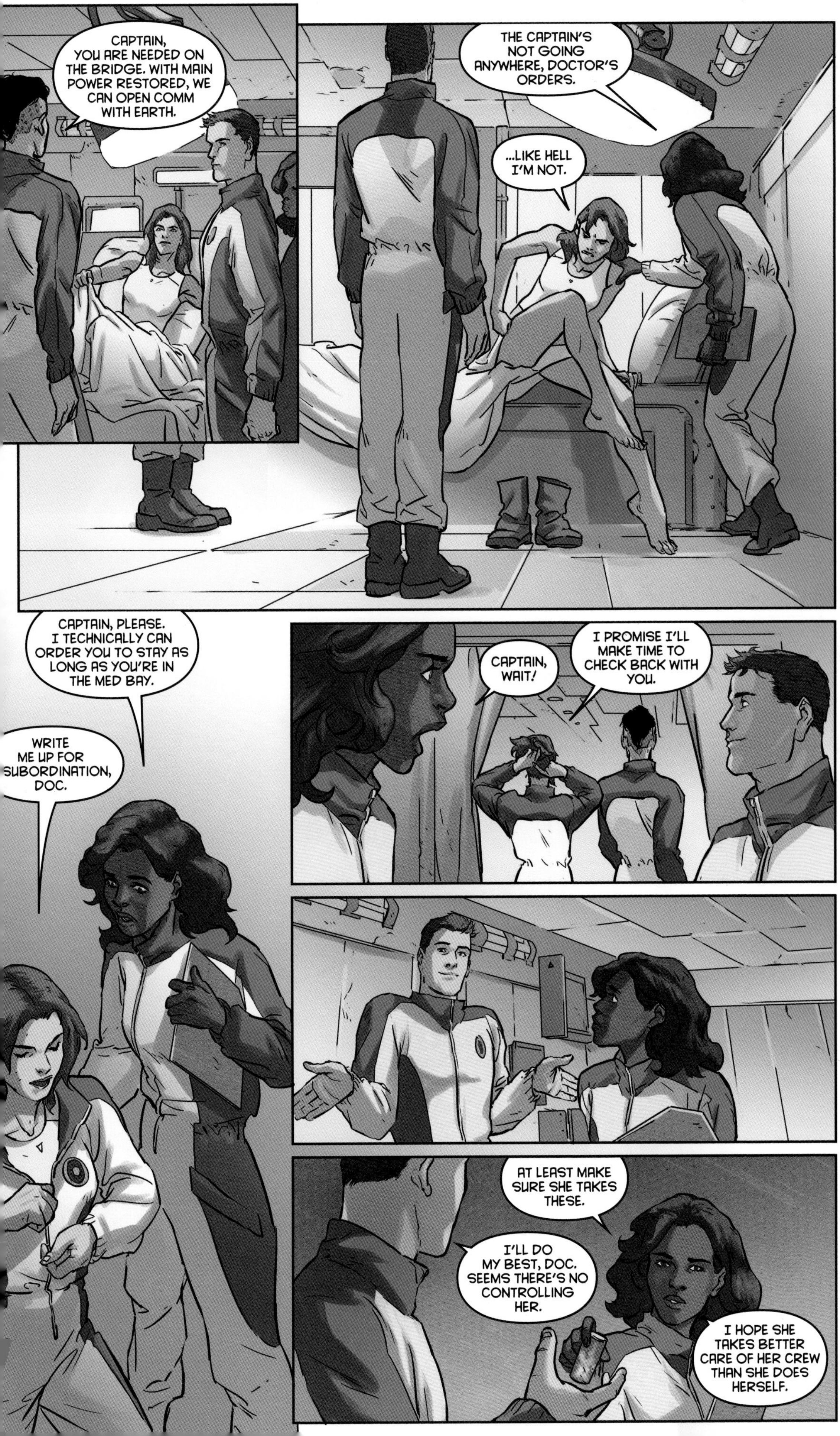
CAPTAIN, YOU ARE NEEDED ON THE BRIDGE. WITH MAIN POWER RESTORED, WE CAN OPEN COMM WITH EARTH.
THE CAPTAIN'S NOT GOING ANYWHERE, DOCTOR'S ORDERS.
...LIKE HELL I'M NOT.
CAPTAIN, PLEASE. I TECHNICALLY CAN ORDER YOU TO STAY AS LONG AS YOU'RE IN THE MED BAY.
WRITE ME UP FOR SUBORDINATION, DOC.
CAPTAIN, WAIT!
I PROMISE I'LL MAKE TIME TO CHECK BACK WITH YOU.
AT LEAST MAKE SURE SHE TAKES THESE.
I'LL DO MY BEST, DOC. SEEMS THERE'S NO CONTROLLING HER.
I HOPE SHE TAKES BETTER CARE OF HER CREW THAN SHE DOES HERSELF.

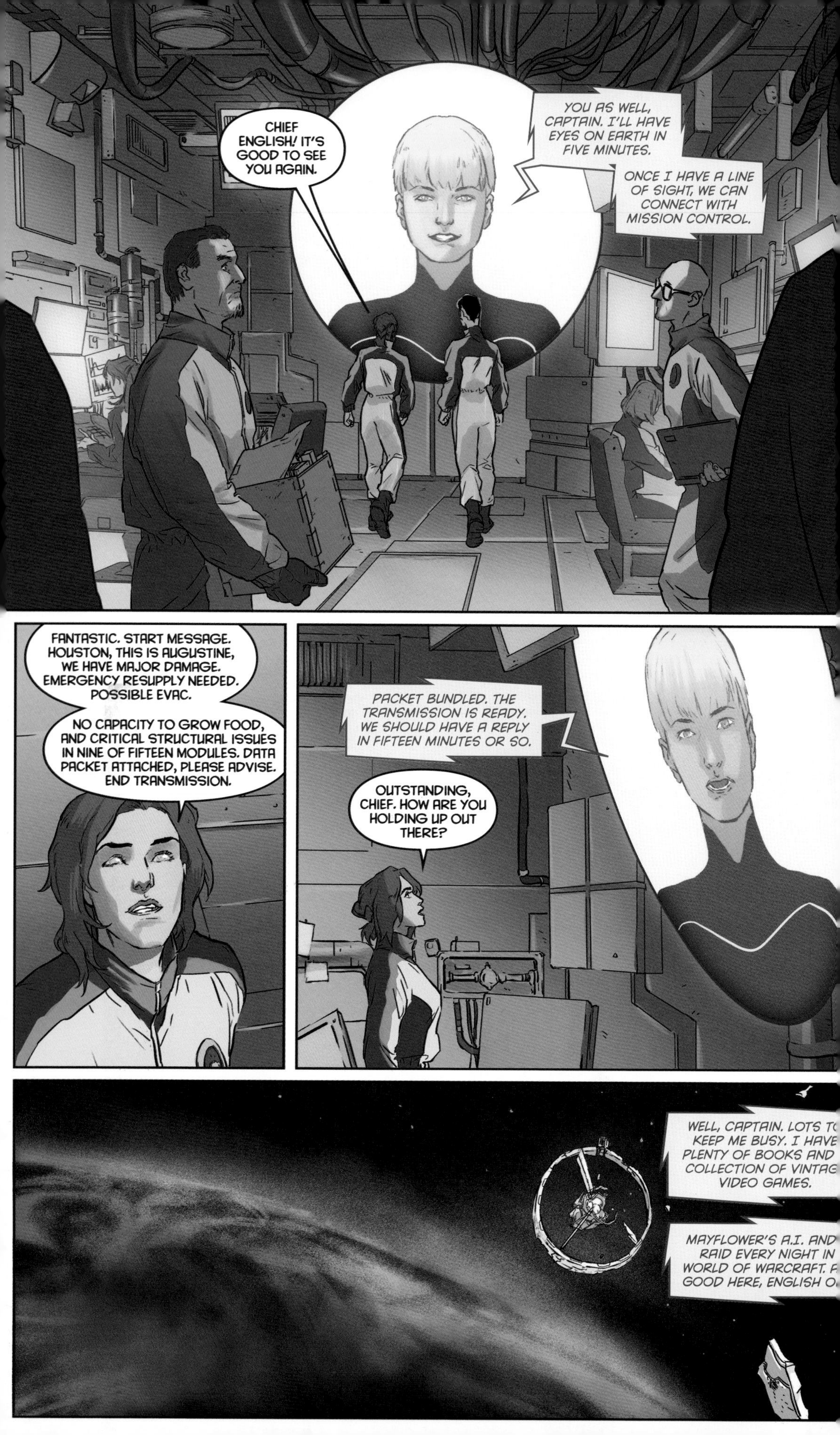
CHIEF ENGLISH! IT'S GOOD TO SEE YOU AGAIN.
YOU AS WELL, CAPTAIN. I'LL HAVE EYES ON EARTH IN FIVE MINUTES.
ONCE I HAVE A LINE OF SIGHT, WE CAN CONNECT WITH MISSION CONTROL.
FANTASTIC. START MESSAGE. HOUSTON, THIS IS AUGUSTINE, WE HAVE MAJOR DAMAGE. EMERGENCY RESUPPLY NEEDED. POSSIBLE EVAC.
NO CAPACITY TO GROW FOOD, AND CRITICAL STRUCTURAL ISSUES IN NINE OF FIFTEEN MODULES. DATA PACKET ATTACHED, PLEASE ADVISE. END TRANSMISSION.
PACKET BUNDLED. THE TRANSMISSION IS READY. WE SHOULD HAVE A REPLY IN FIFTEEN MINUTES OR SO.
OUTSTANDING, CHIEF. HOW ARE YOU HOLDING UP OUT THERE?
WELL, CAPTAIN. LOTS TO KEEP ME BUSY. I HAVE PLENTY OF BOOKS AND COLLECTION OF VINTAG VIDEO GAMES.
MAYFLOWER'S A.I. AND RAID EVERY NIGHT IN WORLD OF WARCRAFT. GOOD HERE, ENGLISH O

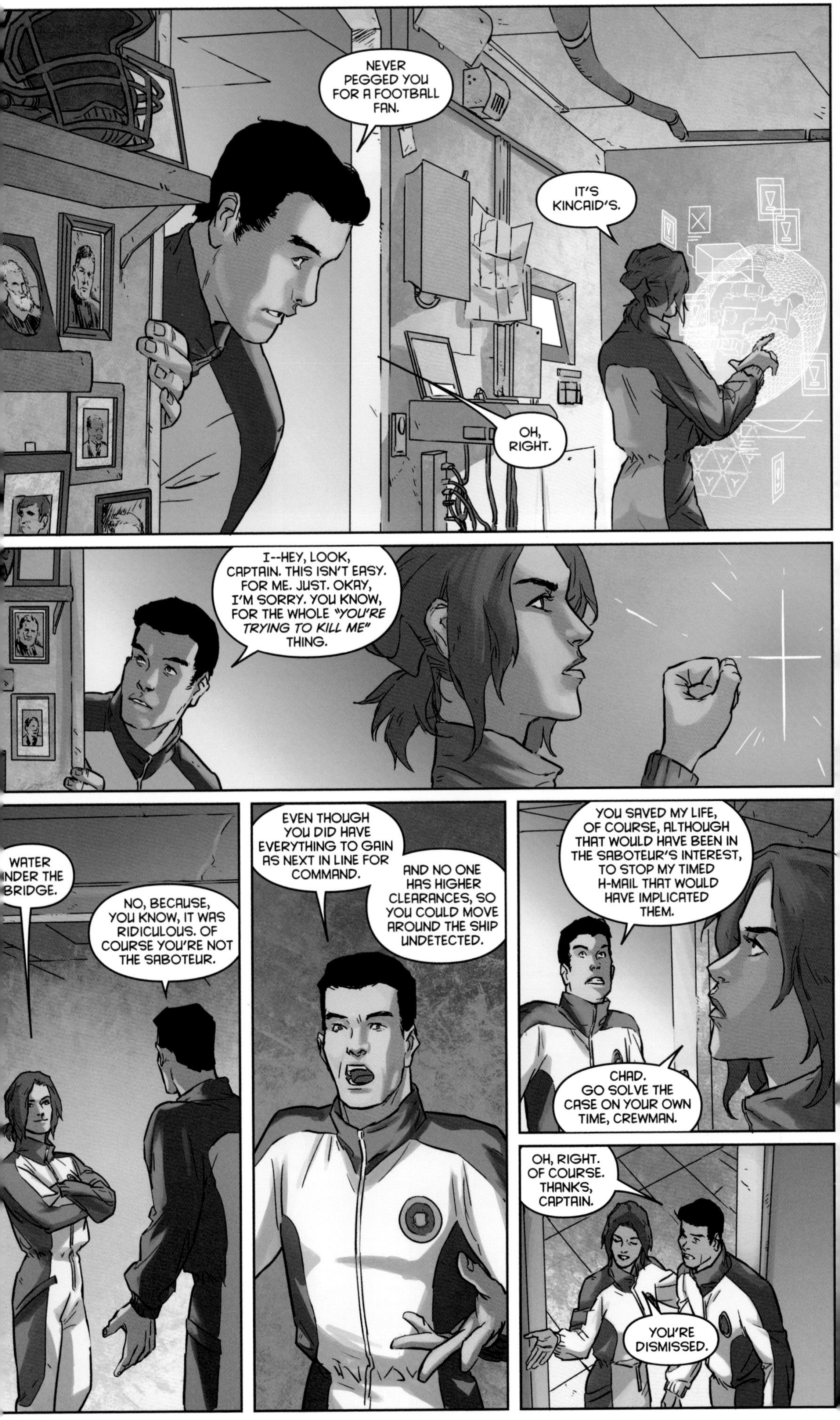
NEVER PEGGED YOU FOR A FOOTBALL FAN.
IT'S KINCAID'S.
OH, RIGHT.
I--HEY, LOOK, CAPTAIN. THIS ISN'T EASY. FOR ME. JUST. OKAY, I'M SORRY. YOU KNOW, FOR THE WHOLE *"YOU'RE TRYING TO KILL ME"* THING.
WATER UNDER THE BRIDGE.
NO, BECAUSE, YOU KNOW, IT WAS RIDICULOUS. OF COURSE YOU'RE NOT THE SABOTEUR.
EVEN THOUGH YOU DID HAVE EVERYTHING TO GAIN AS NEXT IN LINE FOR COMMAND.
AND NO ONE HAS HIGHER CLEARANCES, SO YOU COULD MOVE AROUND THE SHIP UNDETECTED.
YOU SAVED MY LIFE, OF COURSE, ALTHOUGH THAT WOULD HAVE BEEN IN THE SABOTEUR'S INTEREST, TO STOP MY TIMED H-MAIL THAT WOULD HAVE IMPLICATED THEM.
CHAD. GO SOLVE THE CASE ON YOUR OWN TIME, CREWMAN.
OH, RIGHT. OF COURSE. THANKS, CAPTAIN.
YOU'RE DISMISSED.

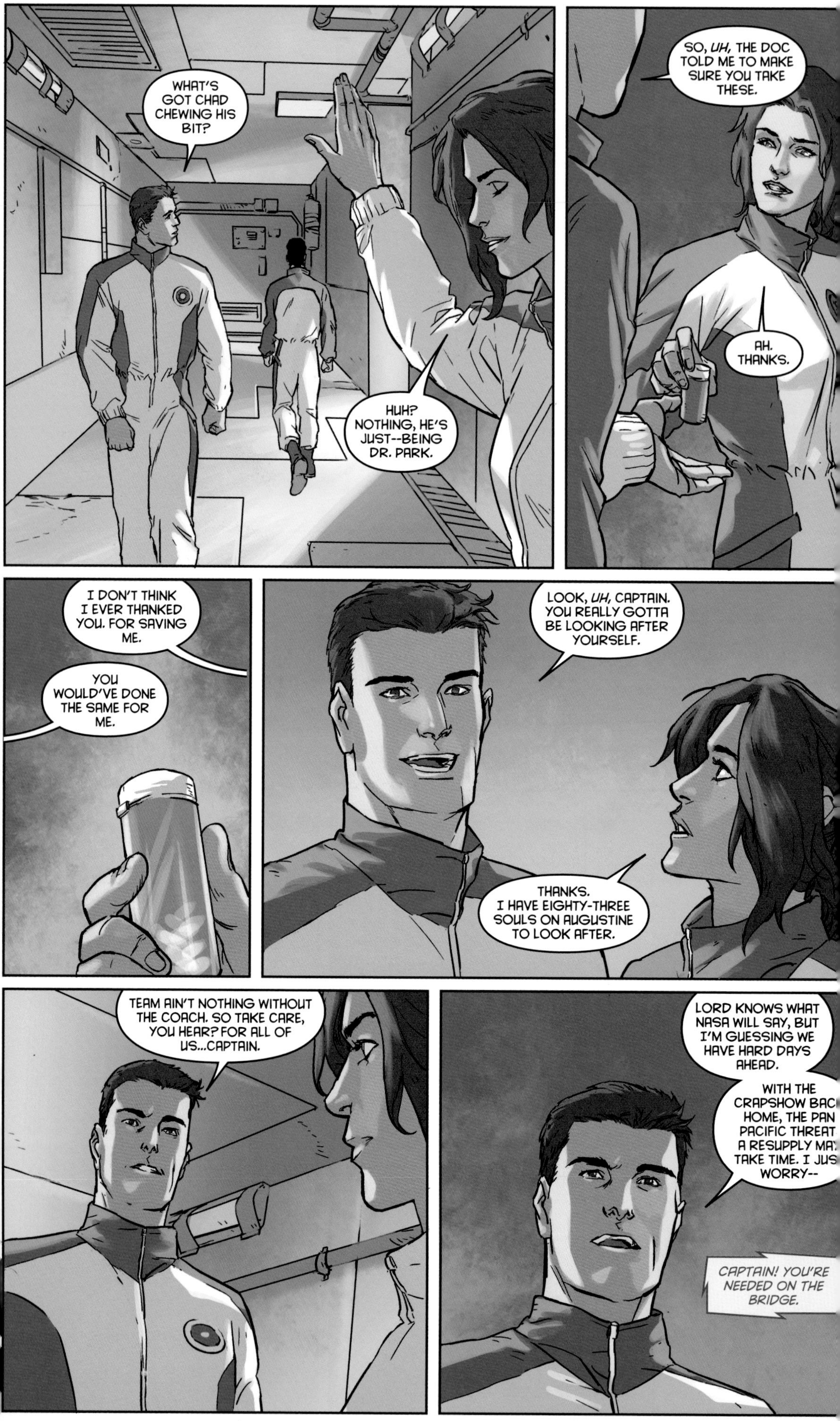

WHAT'S GOT CHAD CHEWING HIS BIT?
HUH? NOTHING, HE'S JUST--BEING DR. PARK.
SO, *UH*, THE DOC TOLD ME TO MAKE SURE YOU TAKE THESE.
AH. THANKS.
I DON'T THINK I EVER THANKED YOU. FOR SAVING ME.
YOU WOULD'VE DONE THE SAME FOR ME.
LOOK, *UH*, CAPTAIN. YOU REALLY GOTTA BE LOOKING AFTER YOURSELF.
THANKS. I HAVE EIGHTY-THREE SOULS ON AUGUSTINE TO LOOK AFTER.
TEAM AIN'T NOTHING WITHOUT THE COACH. SO TAKE CARE, YOU HEAR? FOR ALL OF US...CAPTAIN.
LORD KNOWS WHAT NASA WILL SAY, BUT I'M GUESSING WE HAVE HARD DAYS AHEAD.
WITH THE CRAPSHOW BAC HOME, THE PAN PACIFIC THREAT A RESUPPLY MA TAKE TIME. I JUS WORRY--
CAPTAIN! YOU'RE NEEDED ON THE BRIDGE.

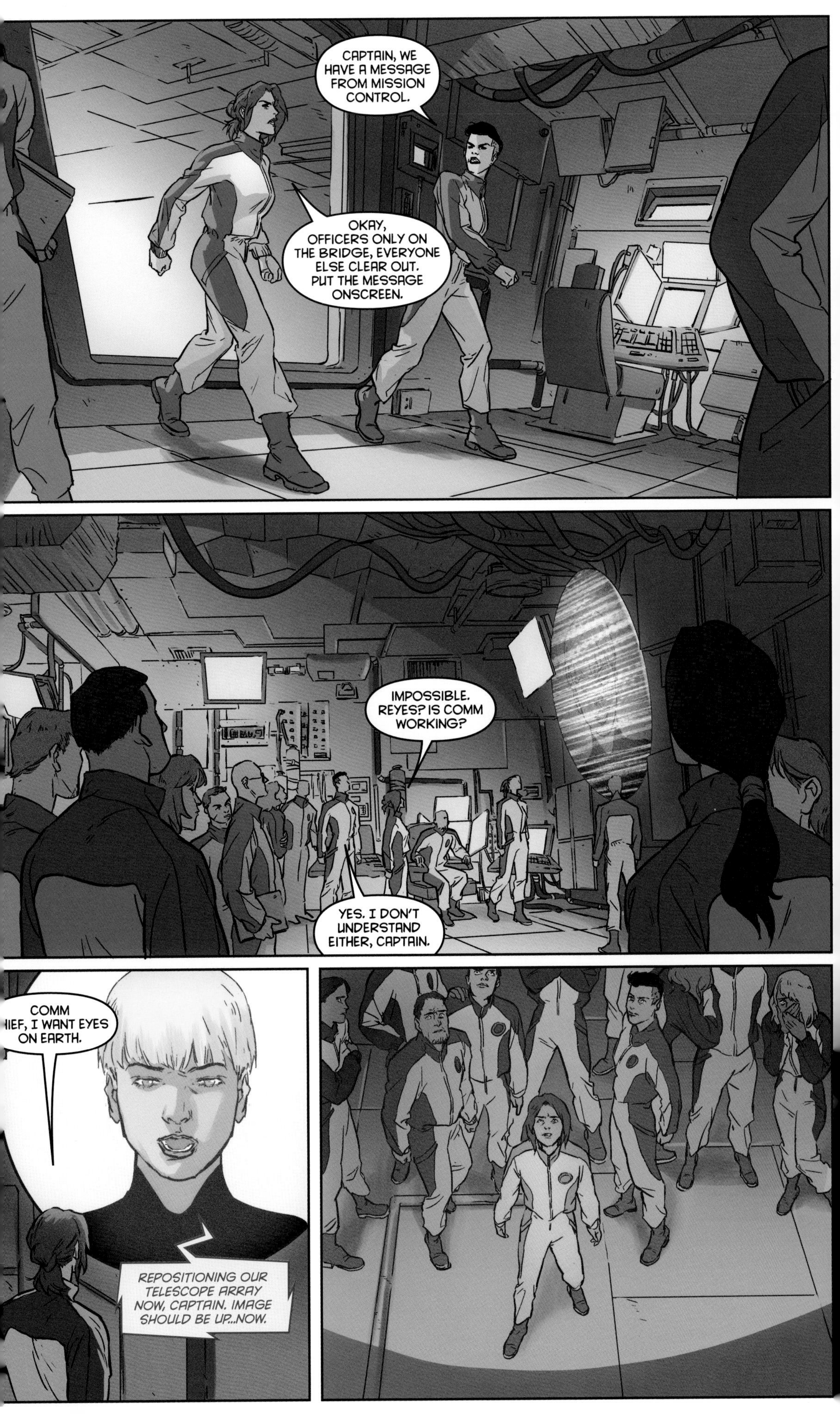
CAPTAIN, WE HAVE A MESSAGE FROM MISSION CONTROL.
OKAY, OFFICERS ONLY ON THE BRIDGE, EVERYONE ELSE CLEAR OUT. PUT THE MESSAGE ONSCREEN.
IMPOSSIBLE. REYES? IS COMM WORKING?
YES. I DON'T UNDERSTAND EITHER, CAPTAIN.
COMM HIEF, I WANT EYES ON EARTH.
REPOSITIONING OUR TELESCOPE ARRAY NOW, CAPTAIN. IMAGE SHOULD BE UP...NOW.

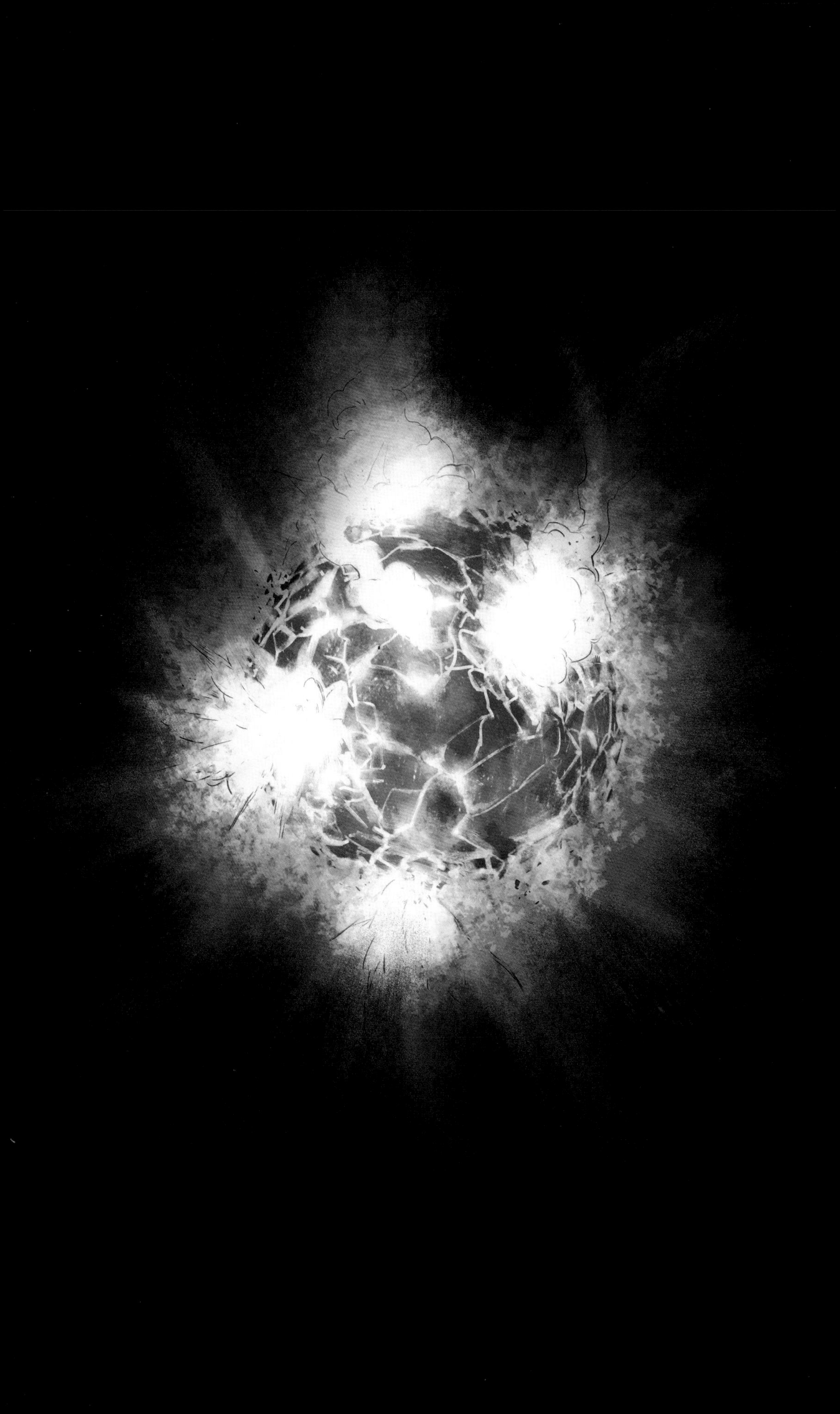

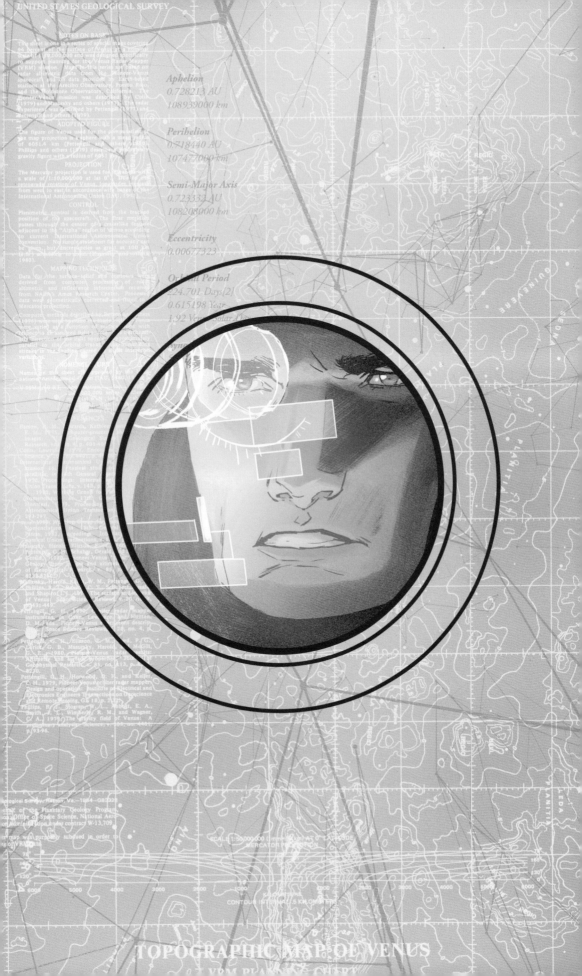

Aphelion
0.728213 AU
108939000 km

Perihelion
0.718440 AU
107477000 km

Semi-Major Axis
0.723333 AU
108208000 km

Eccentricity
0.00677323

Orbital Period
224.701 Days (2)
0.615198 Year
1.92 Venus Solar Days

CHAPTER **THREE**

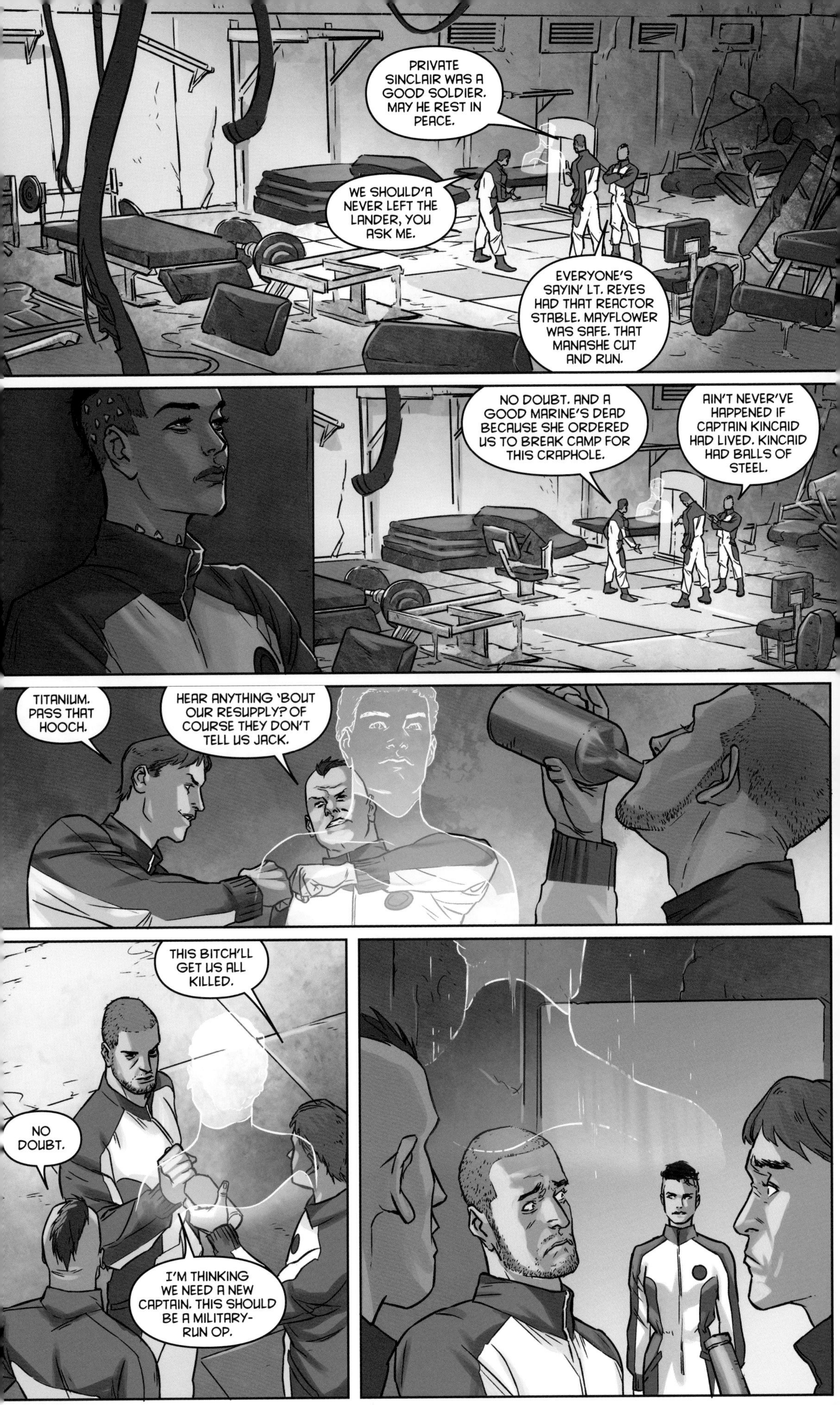
PRIVATE SINCLAIR WAS A GOOD SOLDIER. MAY HE REST IN PEACE.
WE SHOULD'A NEVER LEFT THE LANDER, YOU ASK ME.
EVERYONE'S SAYIN' LT. REYES HAD THAT REACTOR STABLE. MAYFLOWER WAS SAFE. THAT MANASHE CUT AND RUN.
NO DOUBT. AND A GOOD MARINE'S DEAD BECAUSE SHE ORDERED US TO BREAK CAMP FOR THIS CRAPHOLE.
AIN'T NEVER'VE HAPPENED IF CAPTAIN KINCAID HAD LIVED. KINCAID HAD BALLS OF STEEL.
TITANIUM. PASS THAT HOOCH.
HEAR ANYTHING 'BOUT OUR RESUPPLY? OF COURSE THEY DON'T TELL US JACK.
THIS BITCH'LL GET US ALL KILLED.
NO DOUBT.
I'M THINKING WE NEED A NEW CAPTAIN. THIS SHOULD BE A MILITARY-RUN OP.

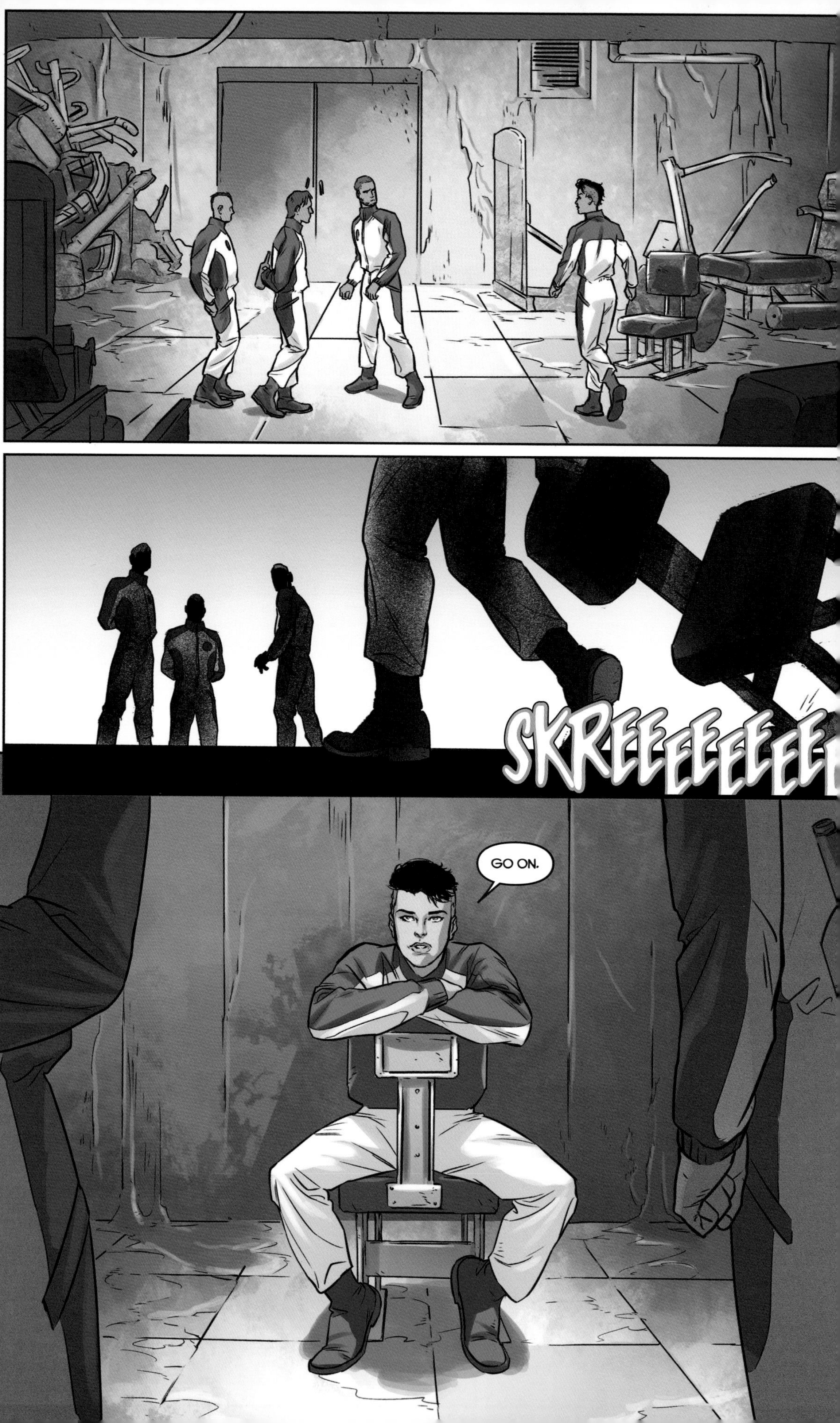
SKREEEEEEEE
GO ON.

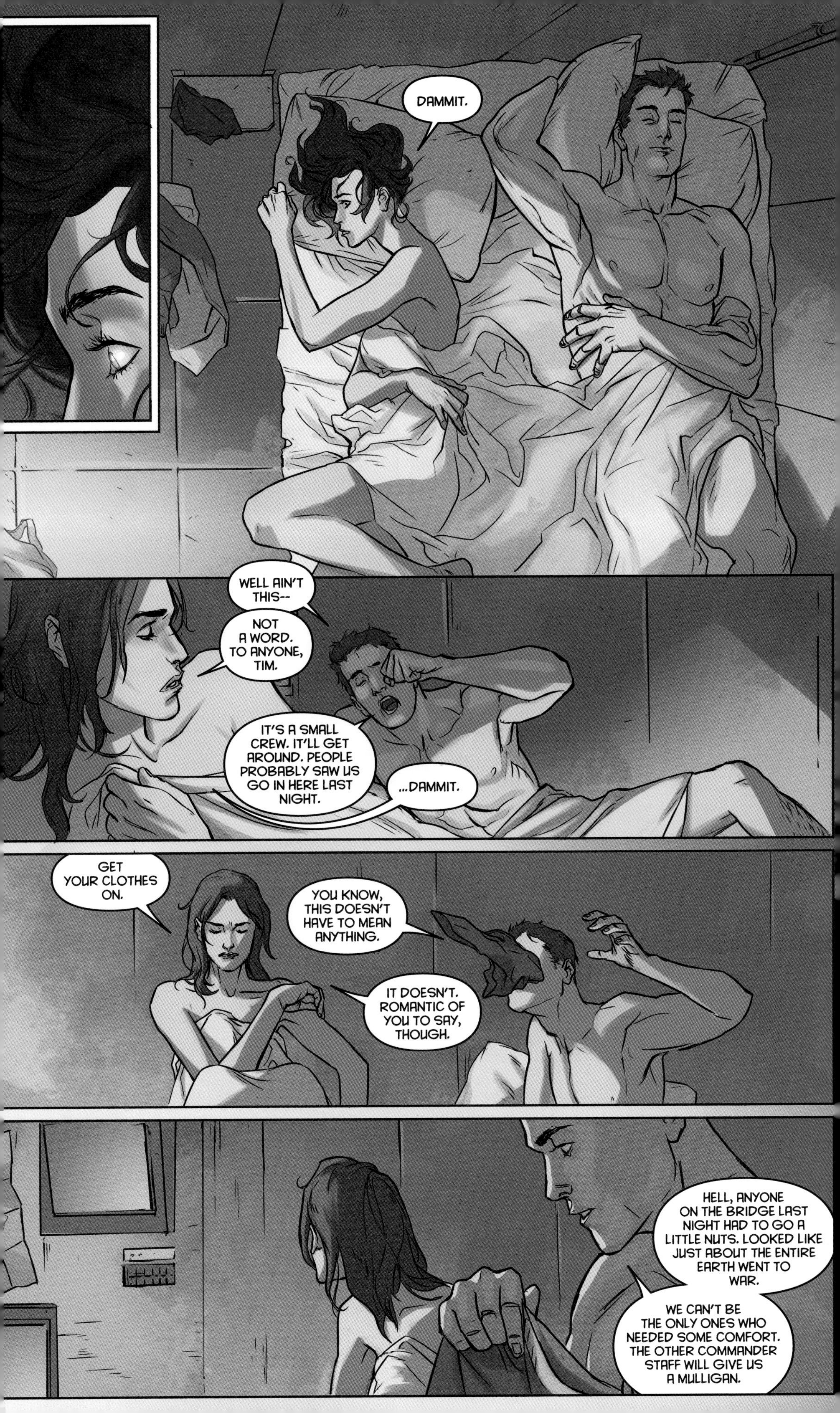
DAMMIT.
WELL AIN'T THIS--
NOT A WORD. TO ANYONE, TIM.
IT'S A SMALL CREW. IT'LL GET AROUND. PEOPLE PROBABLY SAW US GO IN HERE LAST NIGHT.
...DAMMIT.
GET YOUR CLOTHES ON.
YOU KNOW, THIS DOESN'T HAVE TO MEAN ANYTHING.
IT DOESN'T. ROMANTIC OF YOU TO SAY, THOUGH.
HELL, ANYONE ON THE BRIDGE LAST NIGHT HAD TO GO A LITTLE NUTS. LOOKED LIKE JUST ABOUT THE ENTIRE EARTH WENT TO WAR.
WE CAN'T BE THE ONLY ONES WHO NEEDED SOME COMFORT. THE OTHER COMMANDER STAFF WILL GIVE US A MULLIGAN.

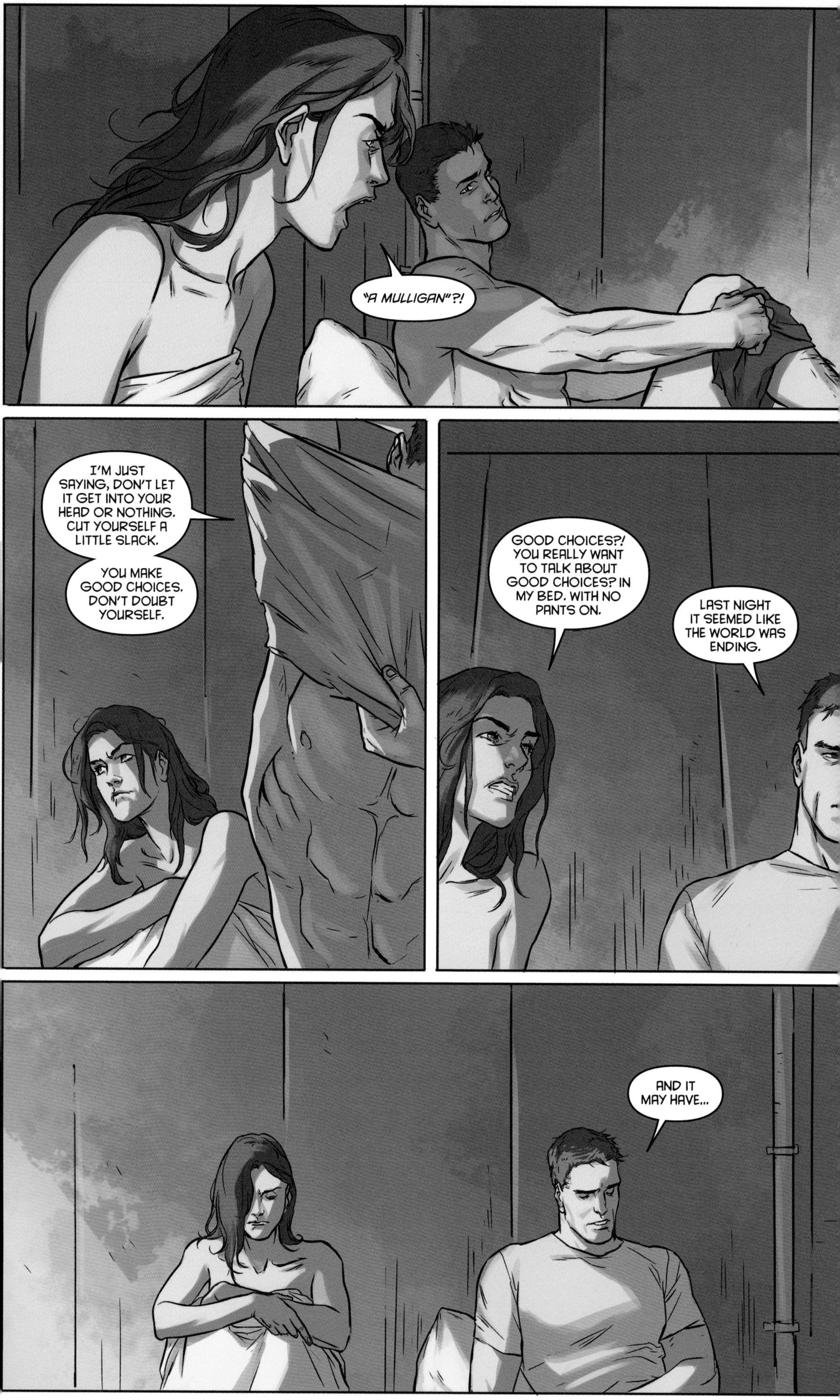
"A MULLIGAN"?!
I'M JUST SAYING, DON'T LET IT GET INTO YOUR HEAD OR NOTHING. CUT YOURSELF A LITTLE SLACK.
YOU MAKE GOOD CHOICES. DON'T DOUBT YOURSELF.
GOOD CHOICES?! YOU REALLY WANT TO TALK ABOUT GOOD CHOICES? IN MY BED. WITH NO PANTS ON.
LAST NIGHT IT SEEMED LIKE THE WORLD WAS ENDING.
AND IT MAY HAVE...

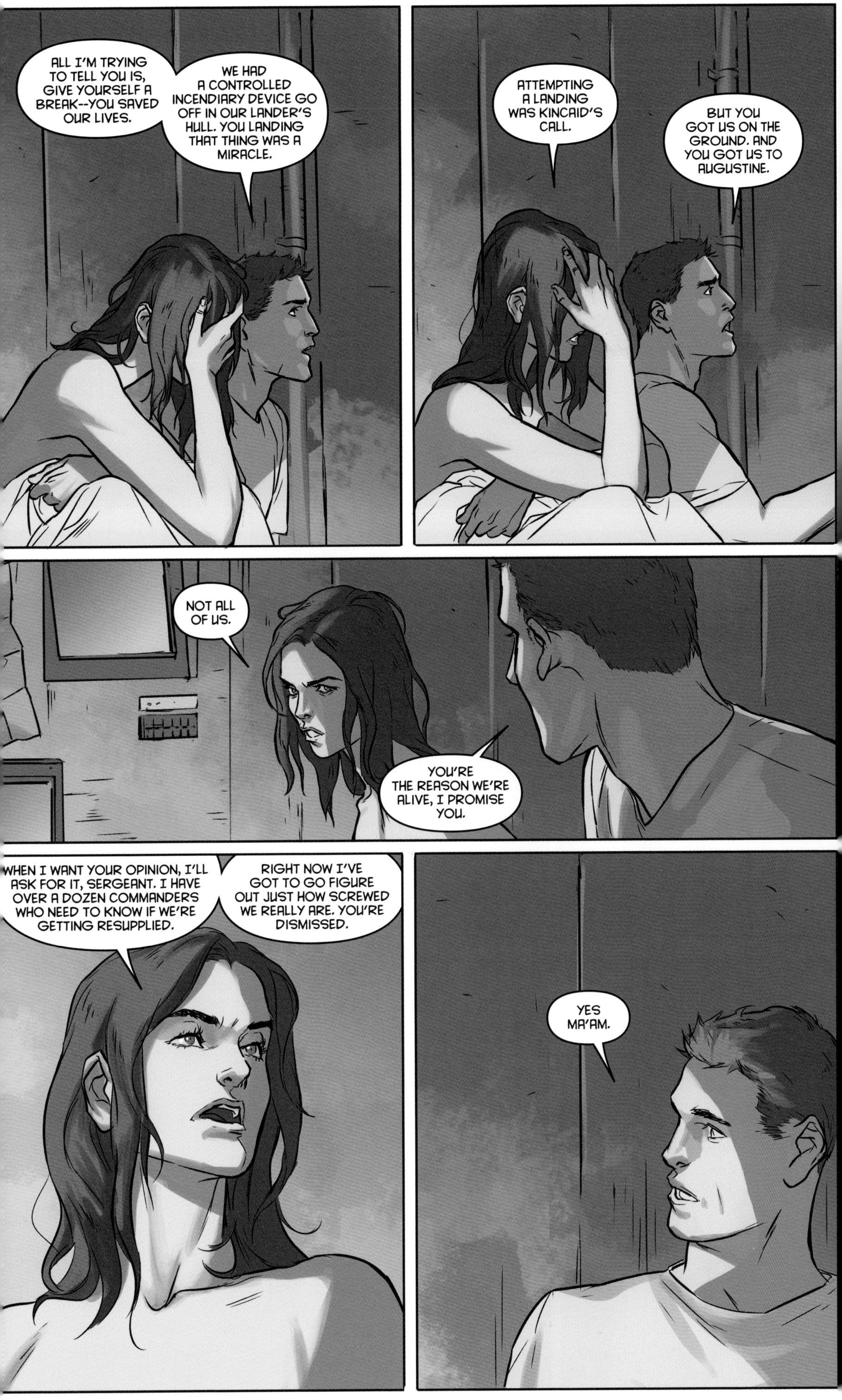
ALL I'M TRYING TO TELL YOU IS, GIVE YOURSELF A BREAK--YOU SAVED OUR LIVES.
WE HAD A CONTROLLED INCENDIARY DEVICE GO OFF IN OUR LANDER'S HULL. YOU LANDING THAT THING WAS A MIRACLE.
ATTEMPTING A LANDING WAS KINCAID'S CALL.
BUT YOU GOT US ON THE GROUND. AND YOU GOT US TO AUGUSTINE.
NOT ALL OF US.
YOU'RE THE REASON WE'RE ALIVE, I PROMISE YOU.
WHEN I WANT YOUR OPINION, I'LL ASK FOR IT, SERGEANT. I HAVE OVER A DOZEN COMMANDERS WHO NEED TO KNOW IF WE'RE GETTING RESUPPLIED.
RIGHT NOW I'VE GOT TO GO FIGURE OUT JUST HOW SCREWED WE REALLY ARE. YOU'RE DISMISSED.
YES MA'AM.

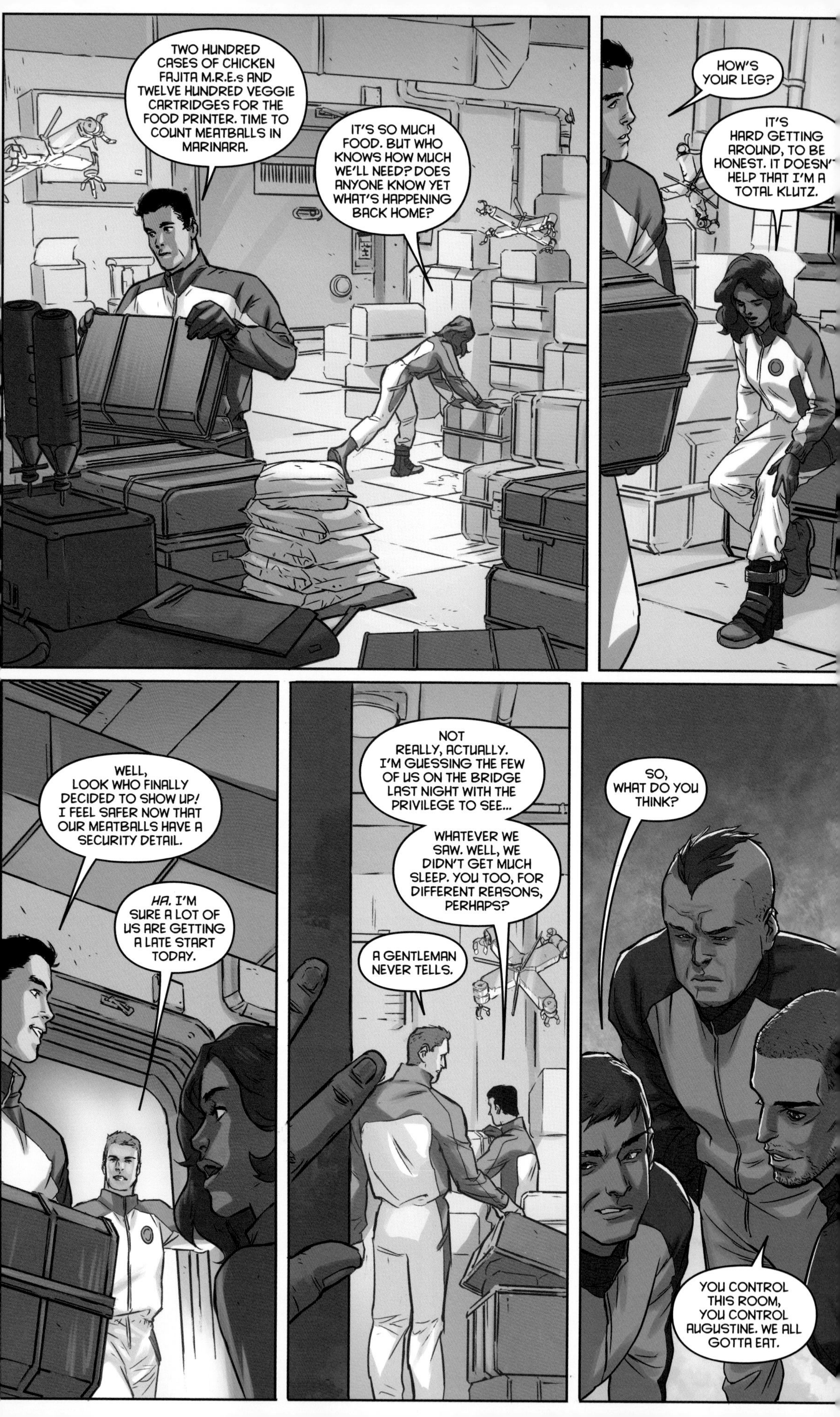
TWO HUNDRED CASES OF CHICKEN FAJITA M.R.E.s AND TWELVE HUNDRED VEGGIE CARTRIDGES FOR THE FOOD PRINTER. TIME TO COUNT MEATBALLS IN MARINARA.
IT'S SO MUCH FOOD. BUT WHO KNOWS HOW MUCH WE'LL NEED? DOES ANYONE KNOW YET WHAT'S HAPPENING BACK HOME?
HOW'S YOUR LEG?
IT'S HARD GETTING AROUND, TO BE HONEST. IT DOESN'T HELP THAT I'M A TOTAL KLUTZ.
WELL, LOOK WHO FINALLY DECIDED TO SHOW UP! I FEEL SAFER NOW THAT OUR MEATBALLS HAVE A SECURITY DETAIL.
HA. I'M SURE A LOT OF US ARE GETTING A LATE START TODAY.
NOT REALLY, ACTUALLY. I'M GUESSING THE FEW OF US ON THE BRIDGE LAST NIGHT WITH THE PRIVILEGE TO SEE...
WHATEVER WE SAW. WELL, WE DIDN'T GET MUCH SLEEP. YOU TOO, FOR DIFFERENT REASONS, PERHAPS?
A GENTLEMAN NEVER TELLS.
SO, WHAT DO YOU THINK?
YOU CONTROL THIS ROOM, YOU CONTROL AUGUSTINE. WE ALL GOTTA EAT.

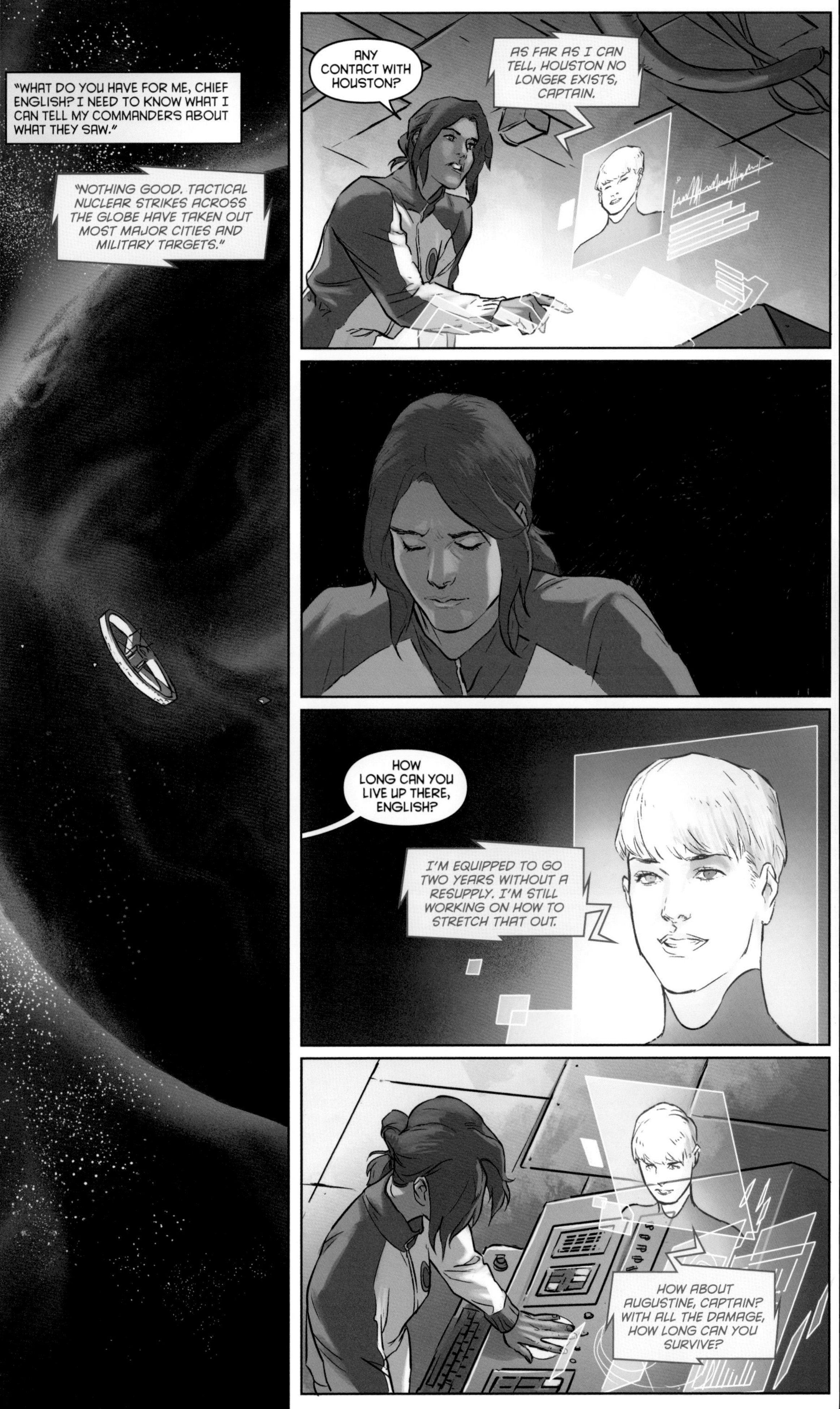
"WHAT DO YOU HAVE FOR ME, CHIEF ENGLISH? I NEED TO KNOW WHAT I CAN TELL MY COMMANDERS ABOUT WHAT THEY SAW."
"NOTHING GOOD. TACTICAL NUCLEAR STRIKES ACROSS THE GLOBE HAVE TAKEN OUT MOST MAJOR CITIES AND MILITARY TARGETS."
ANY CONTACT WITH HOUSTON?
AS FAR AS I CAN TELL, HOUSTON NO LONGER EXISTS, CAPTAIN.
HOW LONG CAN YOU LIVE UP THERE, ENGLISH?
I'M EQUIPPED TO GO TWO YEARS WITHOUT A RESUPPLY. I'M STILL WORKING ON HOW TO STRETCH THAT OUT.
HOW ABOUT AUGUSTINE, CAPTAIN? WITH ALL THE DAMAGE, HOW LONG CAN YOU SURVIVE?

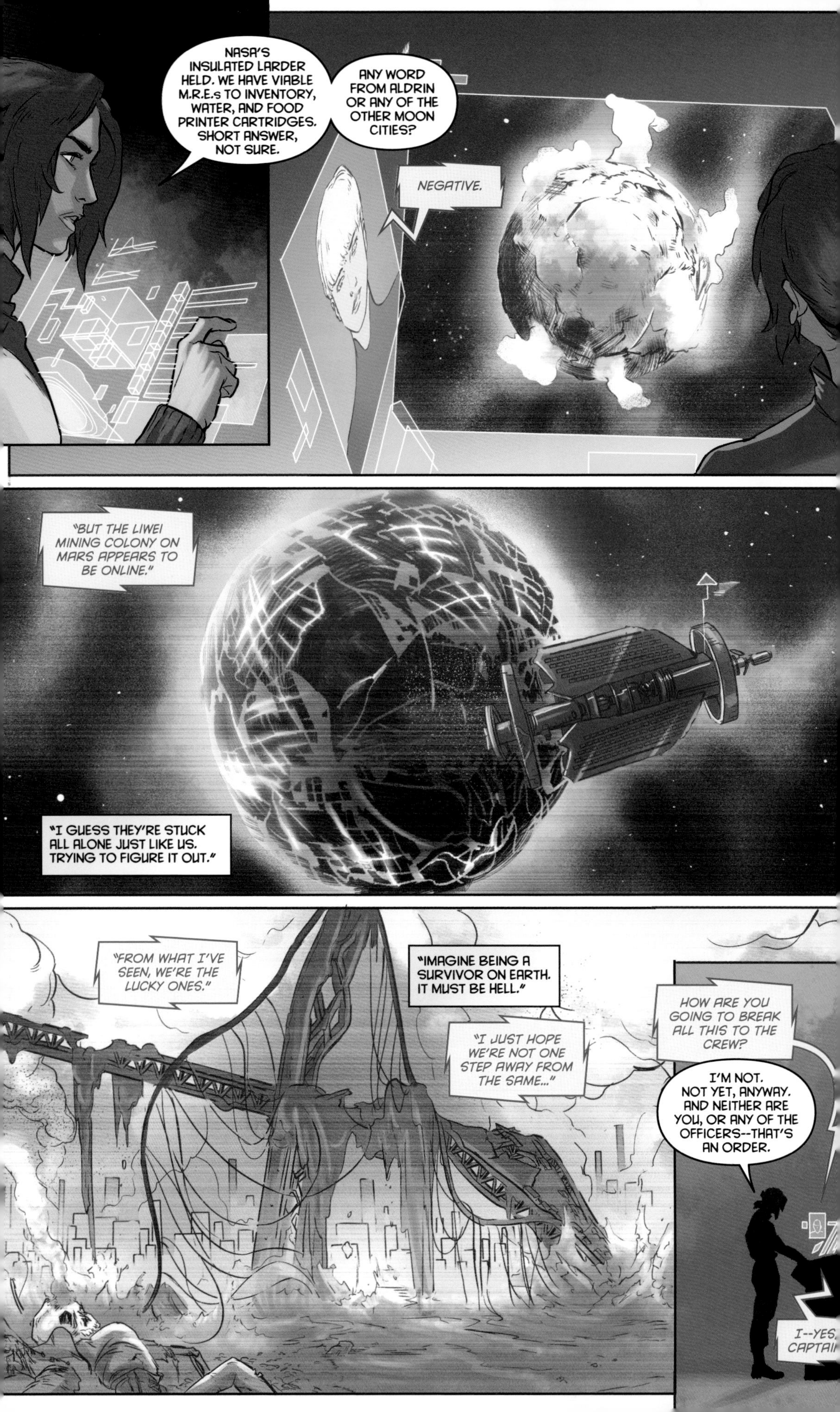
NASA'S INSULATED LARDER HELD. WE HAVE VIABLE M.R.E.s TO INVENTORY, WATER, AND FOOD PRINTER CARTRIDGES. SHORT ANSWER, NOT SURE.
ANY WORD FROM ALDRIN OR ANY OF THE OTHER MOON CITIES?
NEGATIVE.
"BUT THE LIWEI MINING COLONY ON MARS APPEARS TO BE ONLINE."
"I GUESS THEY'RE STUCK ALL ALONE JUST LIKE US. TRYING TO FIGURE IT OUT."
"FROM WHAT I'VE SEEN, WE'RE THE LUCKY ONES."
"IMAGINE BEING A SURVIVOR ON EARTH. IT MUST BE HELL."
"I JUST HOPE WE'RE NOT ONE STEP AWAY FROM THE SAME..."
HOW ARE YOU GOING TO BREAK ALL THIS TO THE CREW?
I'M NOT. NOT YET, ANYWAY. AND NEITHER ARE YOU, OR ANY OF THE OFFICERS--THAT'S AN ORDER.
I--YES, CAPTAI

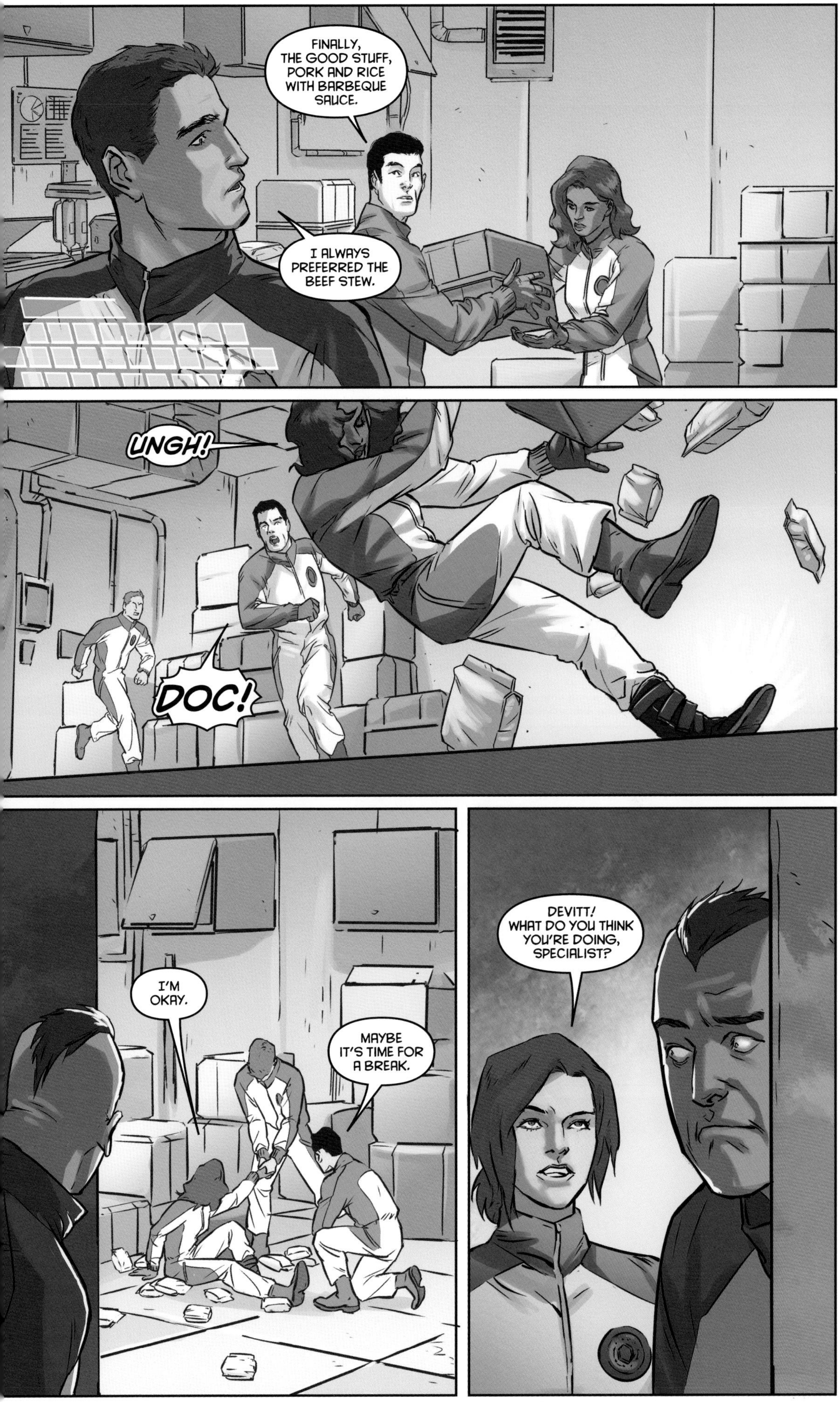
FINALLY, THE GOOD STUFF, PORK AND RICE WITH BARBEQUE SAUCE.
I ALWAYS PREFERRED THE BEEF STEW.
UNGH!
DOC!
I'M OKAY.
MAYBE IT'S TIME FOR A BREAK.
DEVITT! WHAT DO YOU THINK YOU'RE DOING, SPECIALIST?

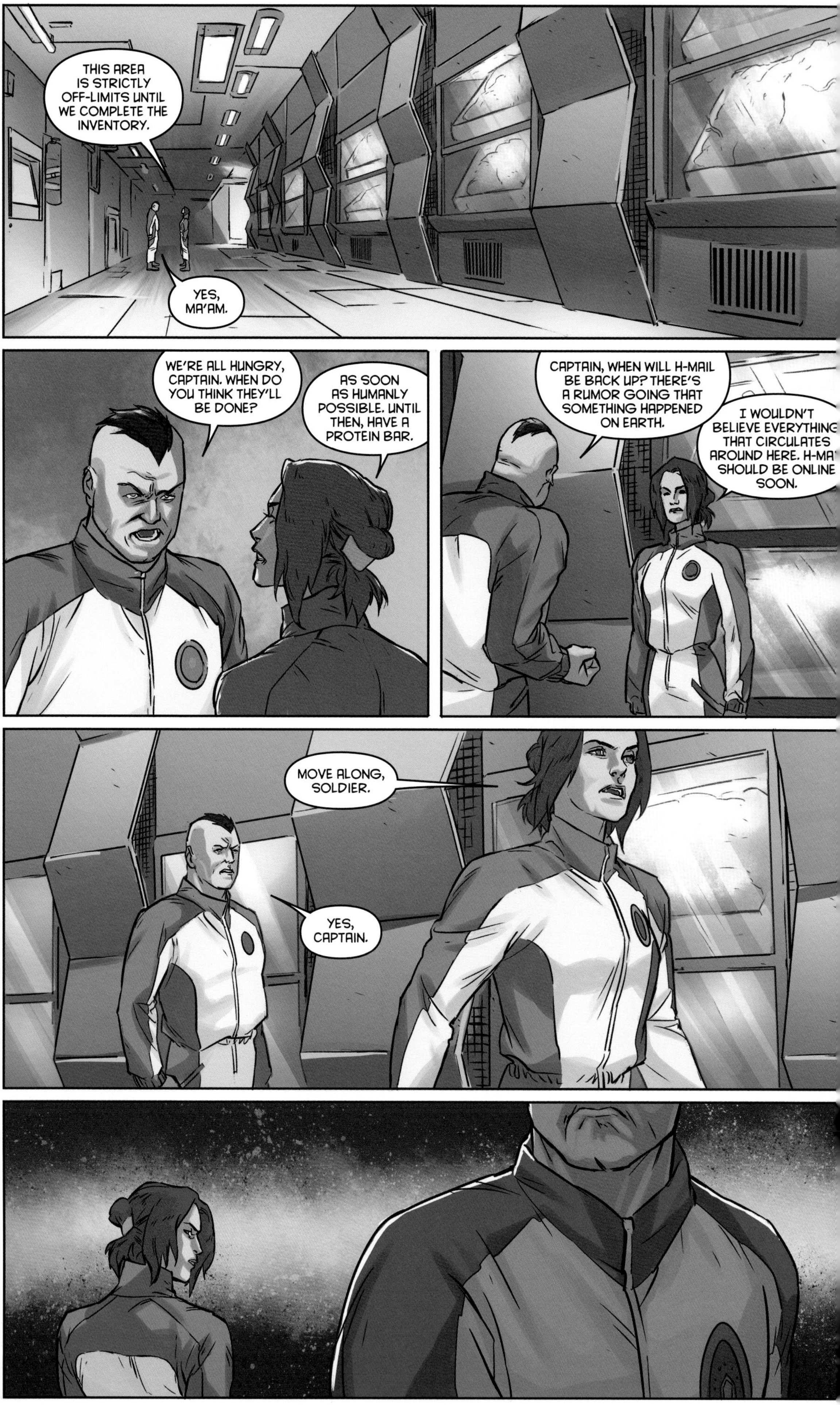

THIS AREA IS STRICTLY OFF-LIMITS UNTIL WE COMPLETE THE INVENTORY.
YES, MA'AM.
WE'RE ALL HUNGRY, CAPTAIN. WHEN DO YOU THINK THEY'LL BE DONE?
AS SOON AS HUMANLY POSSIBLE. UNTIL THEN, HAVE A PROTEIN BAR.
CAPTAIN, WHEN WILL H-MAIL BE BACK UP? THERE'S A RUMOR GOING THAT SOMETHING HAPPENED ON EARTH.
I WOULDN'T BELIEVE EVERYTHING THAT CIRCULATES AROUND HERE. H-MA SHOULD BE ONLINE SOON.
MOVE ALONG, SOLDIER.
YES, CAPTAIN.

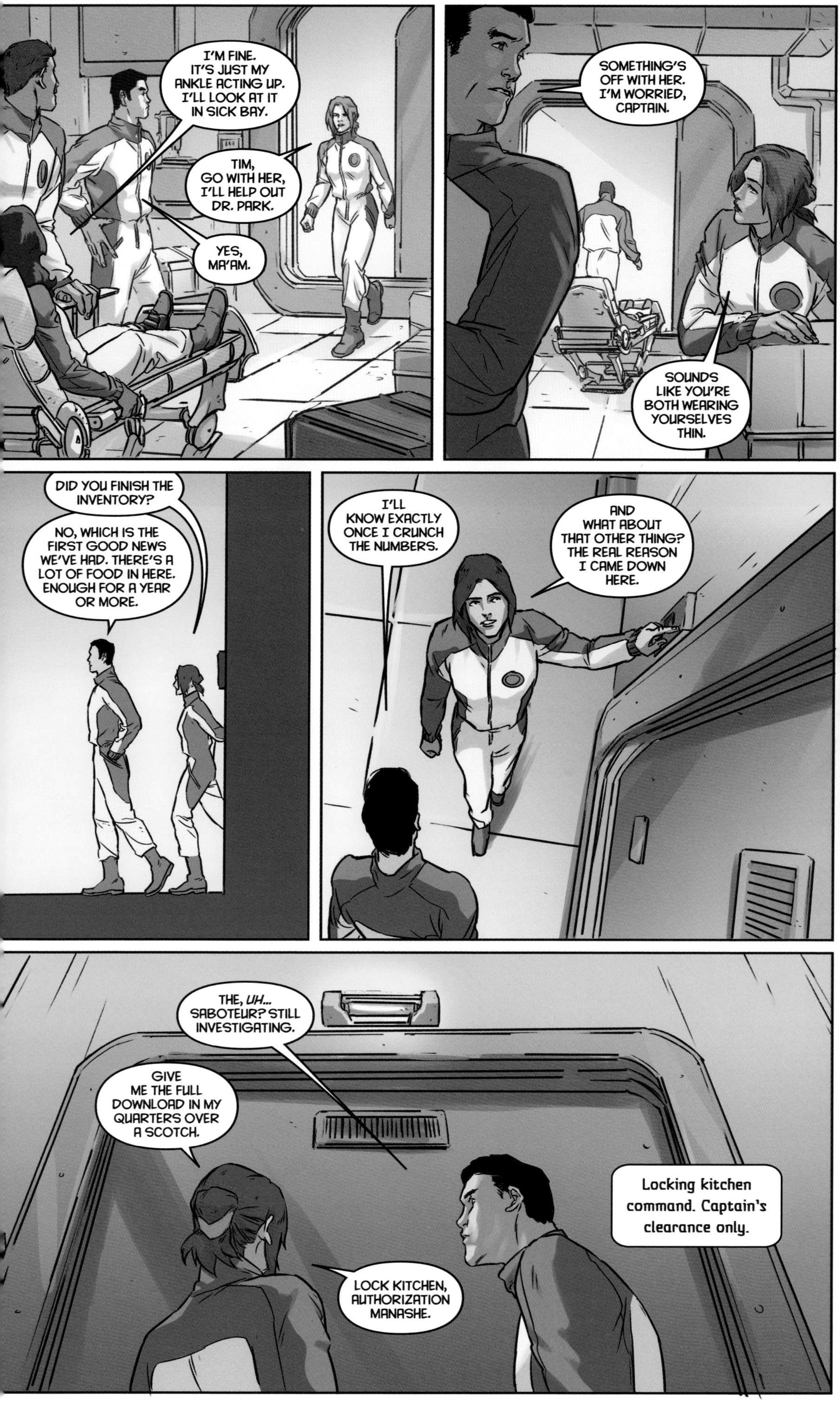
I'M FINE. IT'S JUST MY ANKLE ACTING UP. I'LL LOOK AT IT IN SICK BAY.
TIM, GO WITH HER, I'LL HELP OUT DR. PARK.
YES, MA'AM.
SOMETHING'S OFF WITH HER. I'M WORRIED, CAPTAIN.
SOUNDS LIKE YOU'RE BOTH WEARING YOURSELVES THIN.
DID YOU FINISH THE INVENTORY?
NO, WHICH IS THE FIRST GOOD NEWS WE'VE HAD. THERE'S A LOT OF FOOD IN HERE. ENOUGH FOR A YEAR OR MORE.
I'LL KNOW EXACTLY ONCE I CRUNCH THE NUMBERS.
AND WHAT ABOUT THAT OTHER THING? THE REAL REASON I CAME DOWN HERE.
THE, *UH*... SABOTEUR? STILL INVESTIGATING.
GIVE ME THE FULL DOWNLOAD IN MY QUARTERS OVER A SCOTCH.
Locking kitchen command. Captain's clearance only.
LOCK KITCHEN, AUTHORIZATION MANASHE.

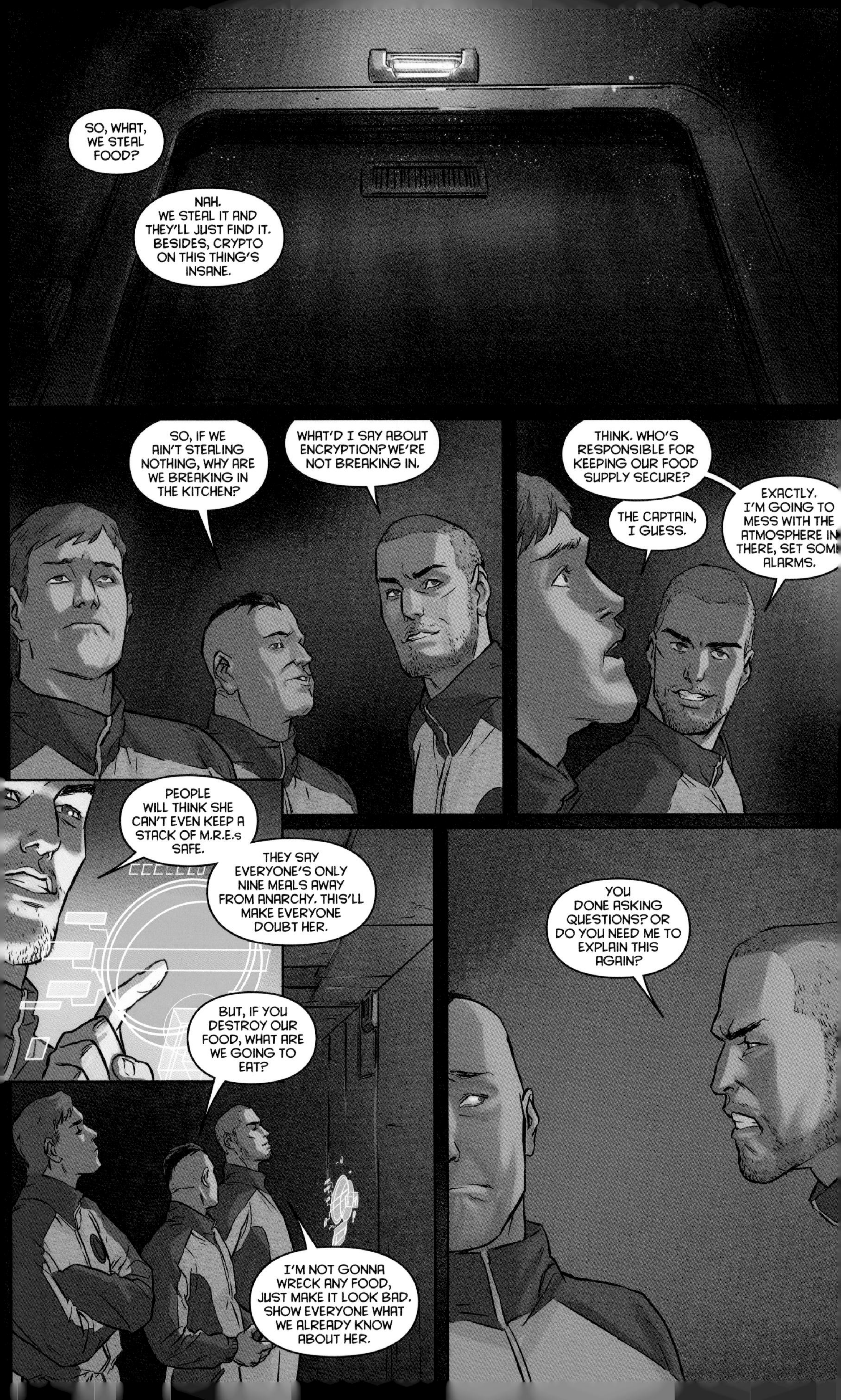
SO, WHAT, WE STEAL FOOD?
NAH. WE STEAL IT AND THEY'LL JUST FIND IT. BESIDES, CRYPTO ON THIS THING'S INSANE.
SO, IF WE AIN'T STEALING NOTHING, WHY ARE WE BREAKING IN THE KITCHEN?
WHAT'D I SAY ABOUT ENCRYPTION? WE'RE NOT BREAKING IN.
THINK. WHO'S RESPONSIBLE FOR KEEPING OUR FOOD SUPPLY SECURE?
THE CAPTAIN, I GUESS.
EXACTLY. I'M GOING TO MESS WITH THE ATMOSPHERE IN THERE, SET SOM ALARMS.
PEOPLE WILL THINK SHE CAN'T EVEN KEEP A STACK OF M.R.E.s SAFE.
THEY SAY EVERYONE'S ONLY NINE MEALS AWAY FROM ANARCHY. THIS'LL MAKE EVERYONE DOUBT HER.
BUT, IF YOU DESTROY OUR FOOD, WHAT ARE WE GOING TO EAT?
I'M NOT GONNA WRECK ANY FOOD, JUST MAKE IT LOOK BAD. SHOW EVERYONE WHAT WE ALREADY KNOW ABOUT HER.
YOU DONE ASKING QUESTIONS? OR DO YOU NEED ME TO EXPLAIN THIS AGAIN?

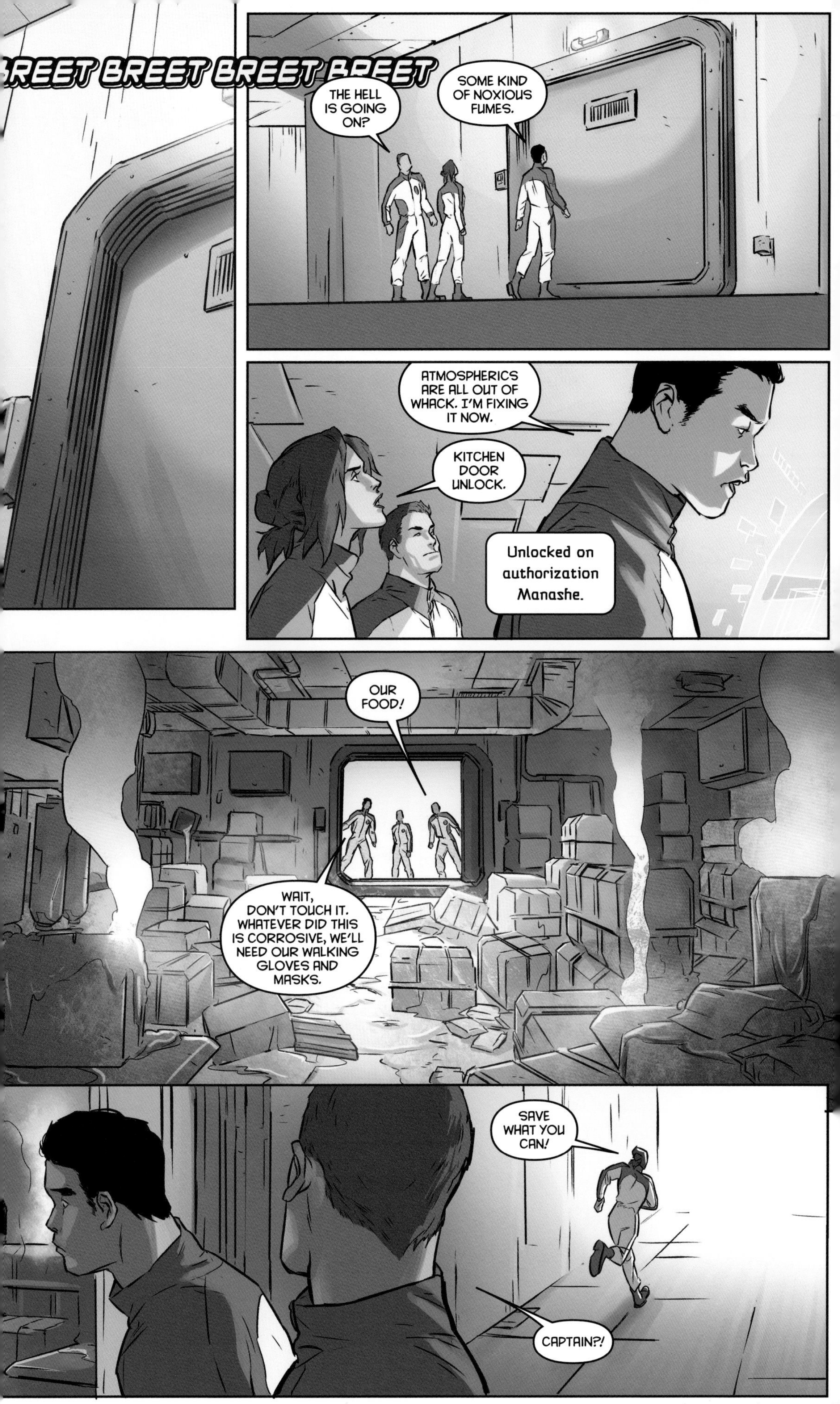
BREET BREET BREET BREET
THE HELL IS GOING ON?
SOME KIND OF NOXIOUS FUMES.
ATMOSPHERICS ARE ALL OUT OF WHACK. I'M FIXING IT NOW.
KITCHEN DOOR UNLOCK.
Unlocked on authorization Manashe.
OUR FOOD!
WAIT, DON'T TOUCH IT. WHATEVER DID THIS IS CORROSIVE, WE'LL NEED OUR WALKING GLOVES AND MASKS.
SAVE WHAT YOU CAN!
CAPTAIN?!

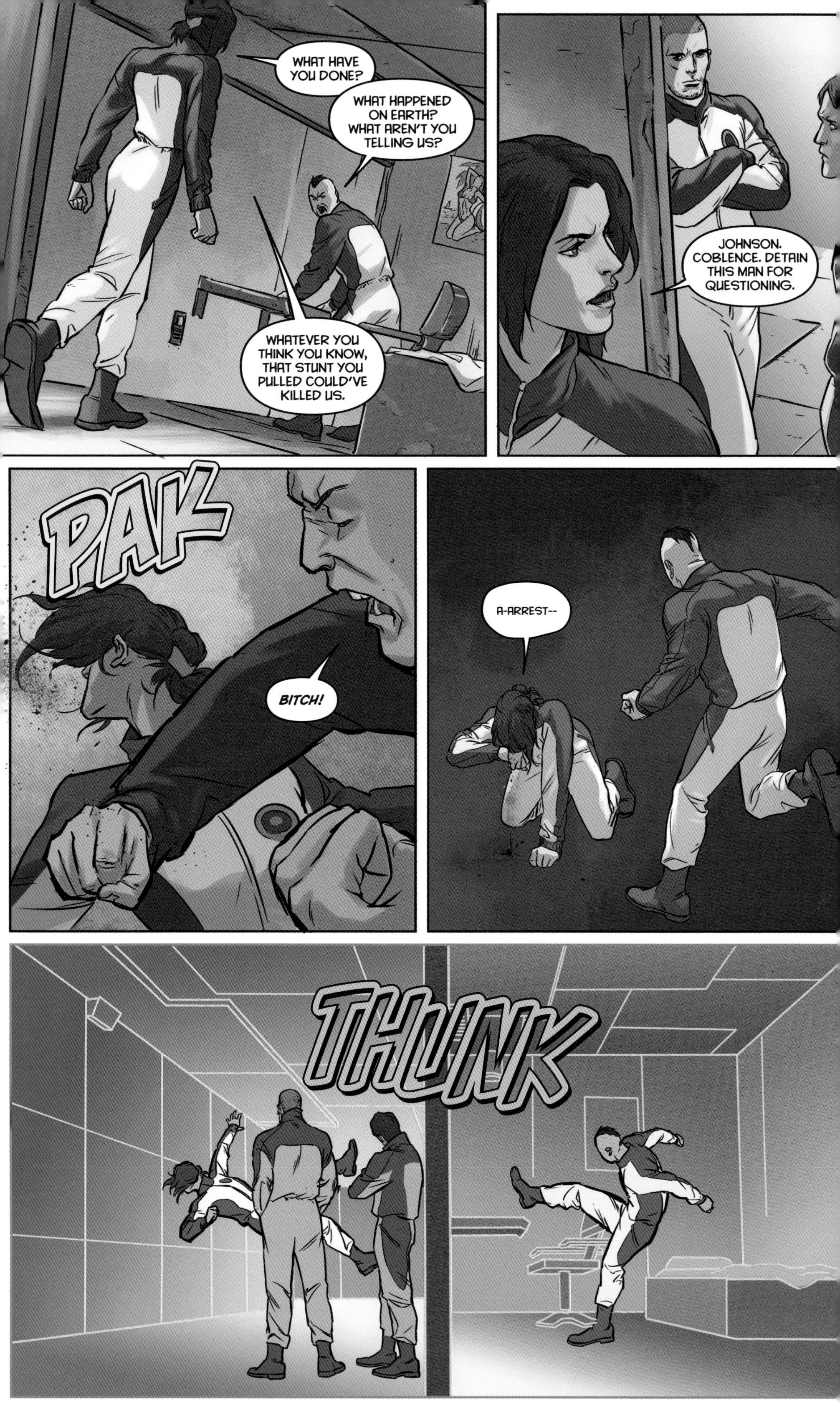
WHAT HAVE YOU DONE?
WHAT HAPPENED ON EARTH? WHAT AREN'T YOU TELLING US?
WHATEVER YOU THINK YOU KNOW, THAT STUNT YOU PULLED COULD'VE KILLED US.
JOHNSON. COBLENCE. DETAIN THIS MAN FOR QUESTIONING.
PAK
BITCH!
A-ARREST--
THUNK

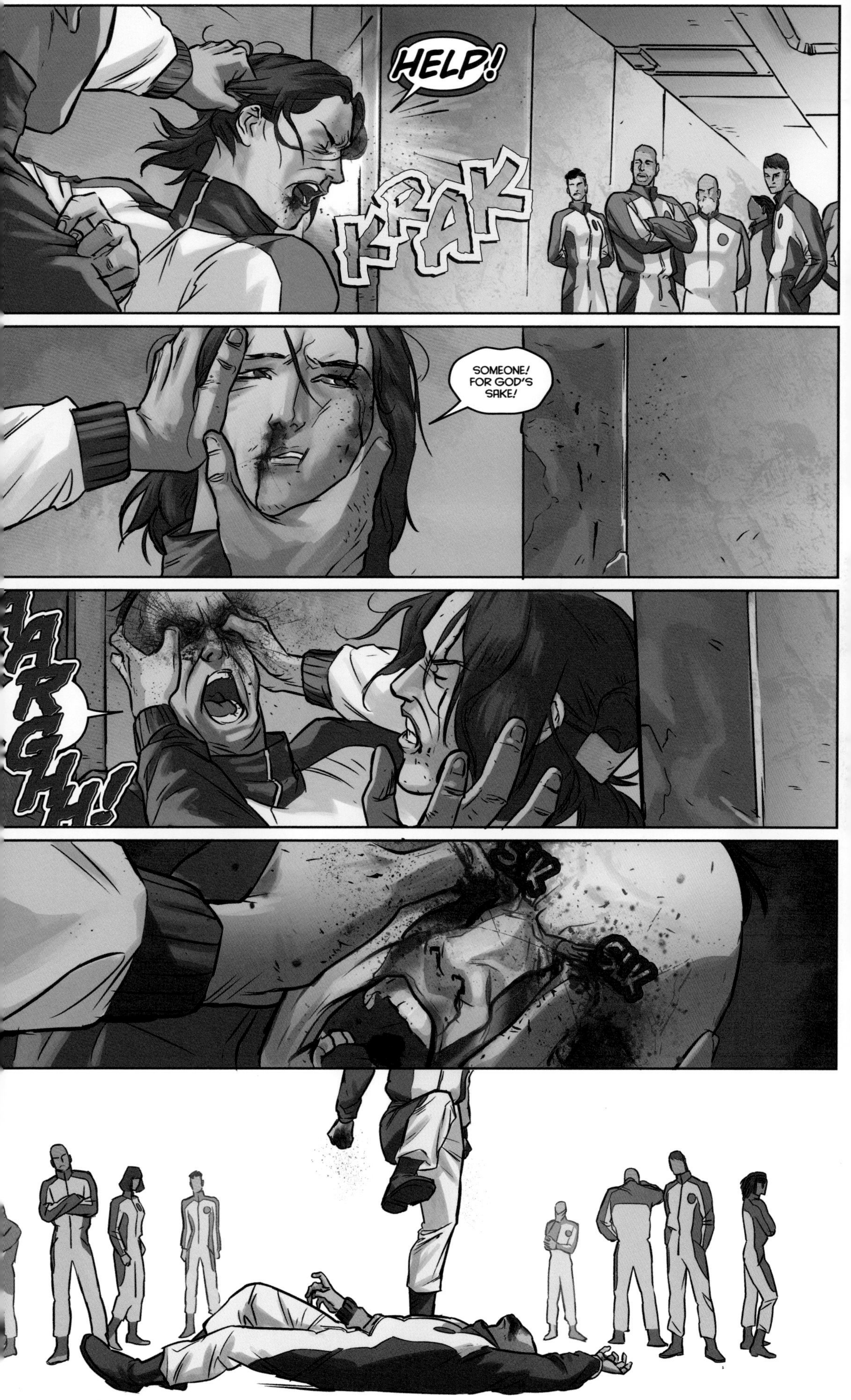
HELP!
KRAK
SOMEONE! FOR GOD'S SAKE!
ARGH!
SK
CH

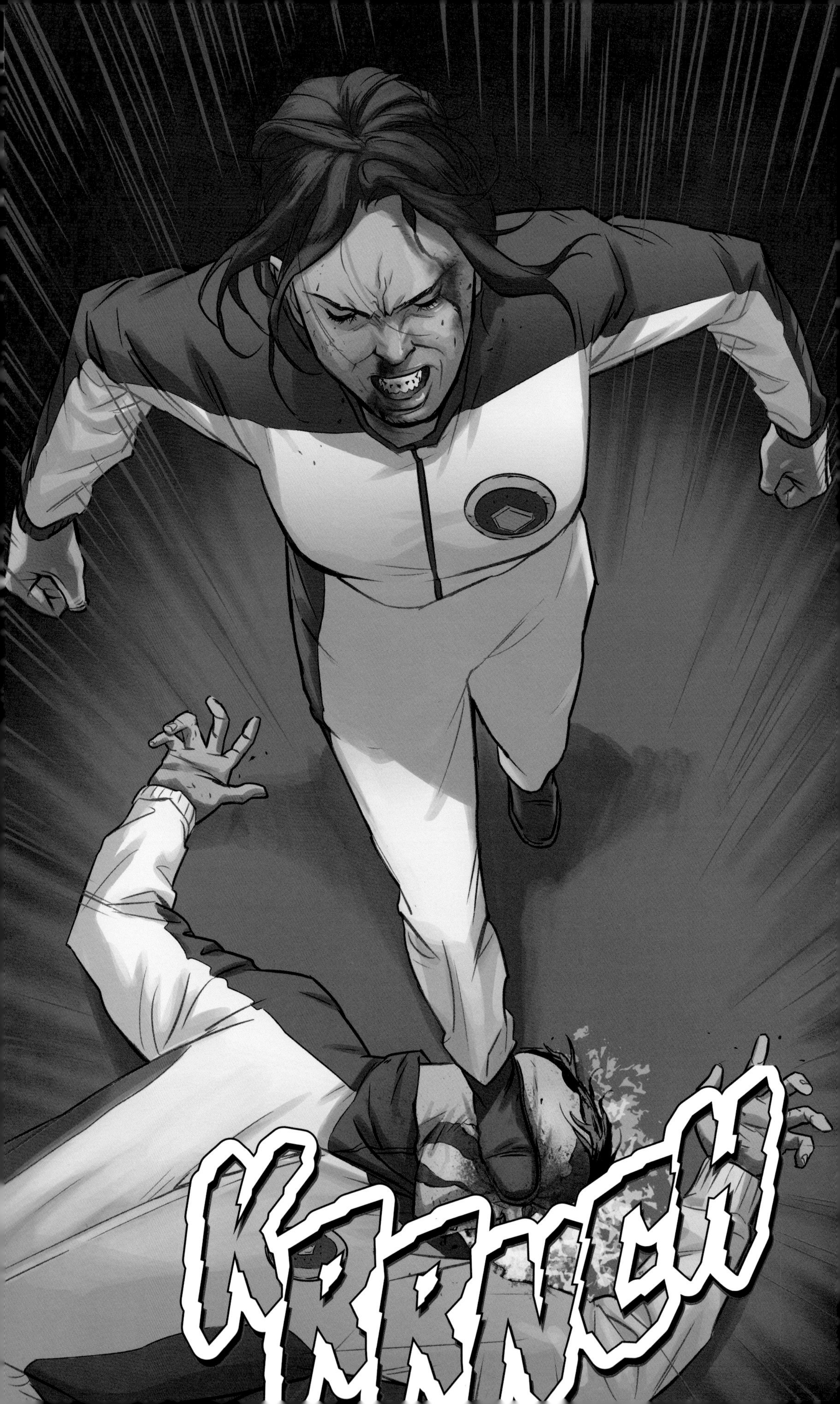
KRRNCH

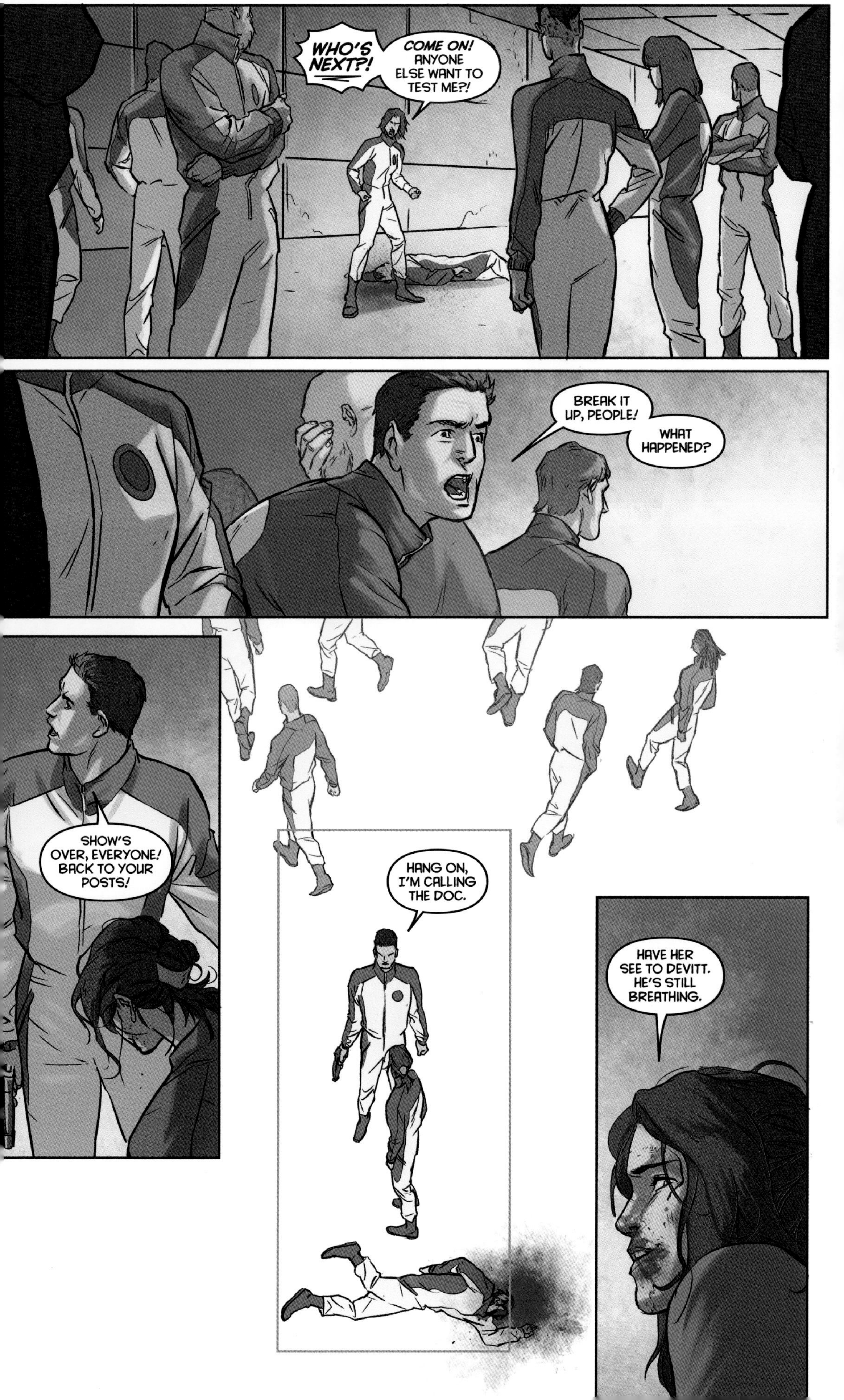
WHO'S NEXT?!
COME ON! ANYONE ELSE WANT TO TEST ME?!
BREAK IT UP, PEOPLE!
WHAT HAPPENED?
SHOW'S OVER, EVERYONE! BACK TO YOUR POSTS!
HANG ON, I'M CALLING THE DOC.
HAVE HER SEE TO DEVITT. HE'S STILL BREATHING.

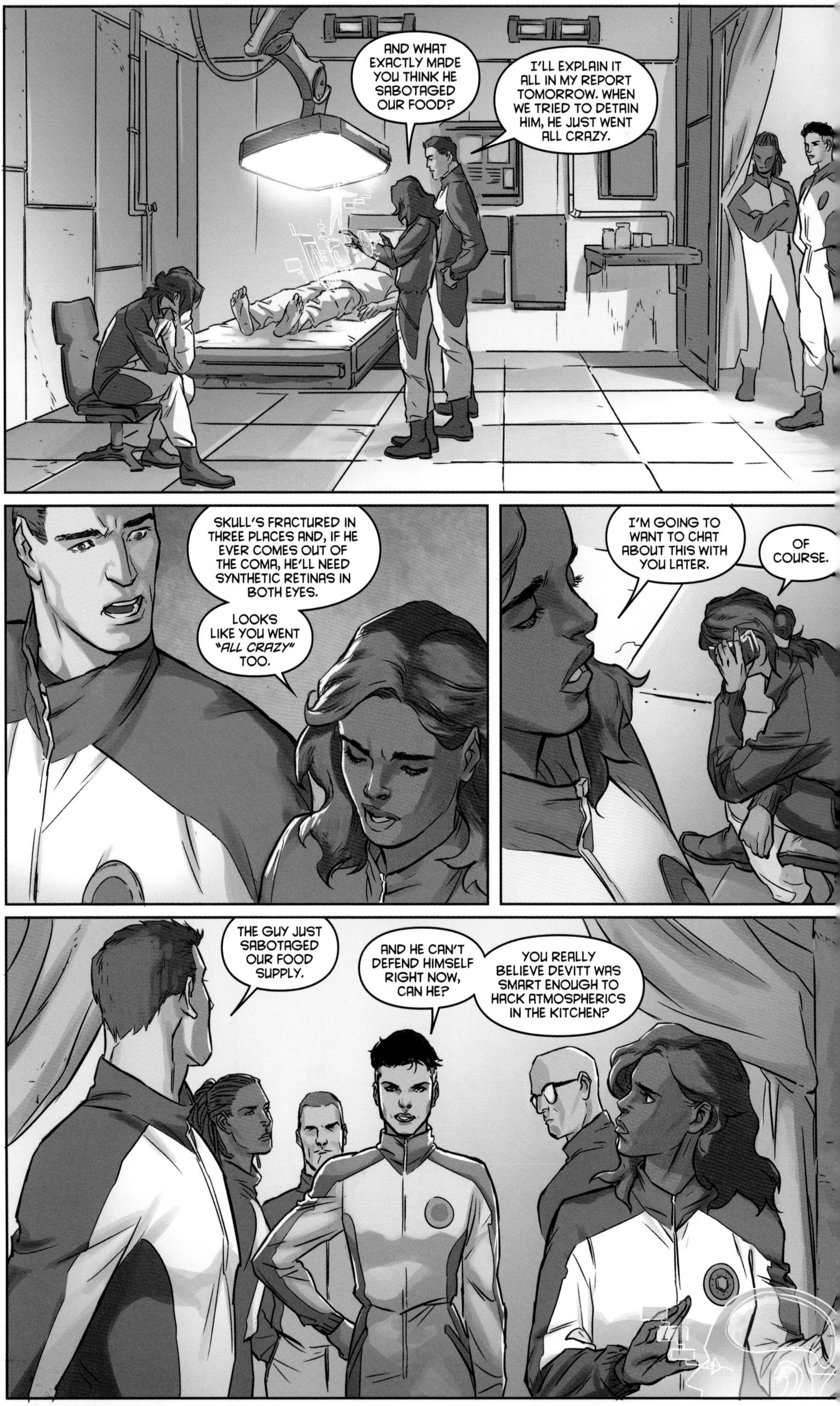
AND WHAT EXACTLY MADE YOU THINK HE SABOTAGED OUR FOOD?
I'LL EXPLAIN IT ALL IN MY REPORT TOMORROW. WHEN WE TRIED TO DETAIN HIM, HE JUST WENT ALL CRAZY.
SKULL'S FRACTURED IN THREE PLACES AND, IF HE EVER COMES OUT OF THE COMA, HE'LL NEED SYNTHETIC RETINAS IN BOTH EYES.
LOOKS LIKE YOU WENT "ALL CRAZY" TOO.
I'M GOING TO WANT TO CHAT ABOUT THIS WITH YOU LATER.
OF COURSE.
THE GUY JUST SABOTAGED OUR FOOD SUPPLY.
AND HE CAN'T DEFEND HIMSELF RIGHT NOW, CAN HE?
YOU REALLY BELIEVE DEVITT WAS SMART ENOUGH TO HACK ATMOSPHERICS IN THE KITCHEN?

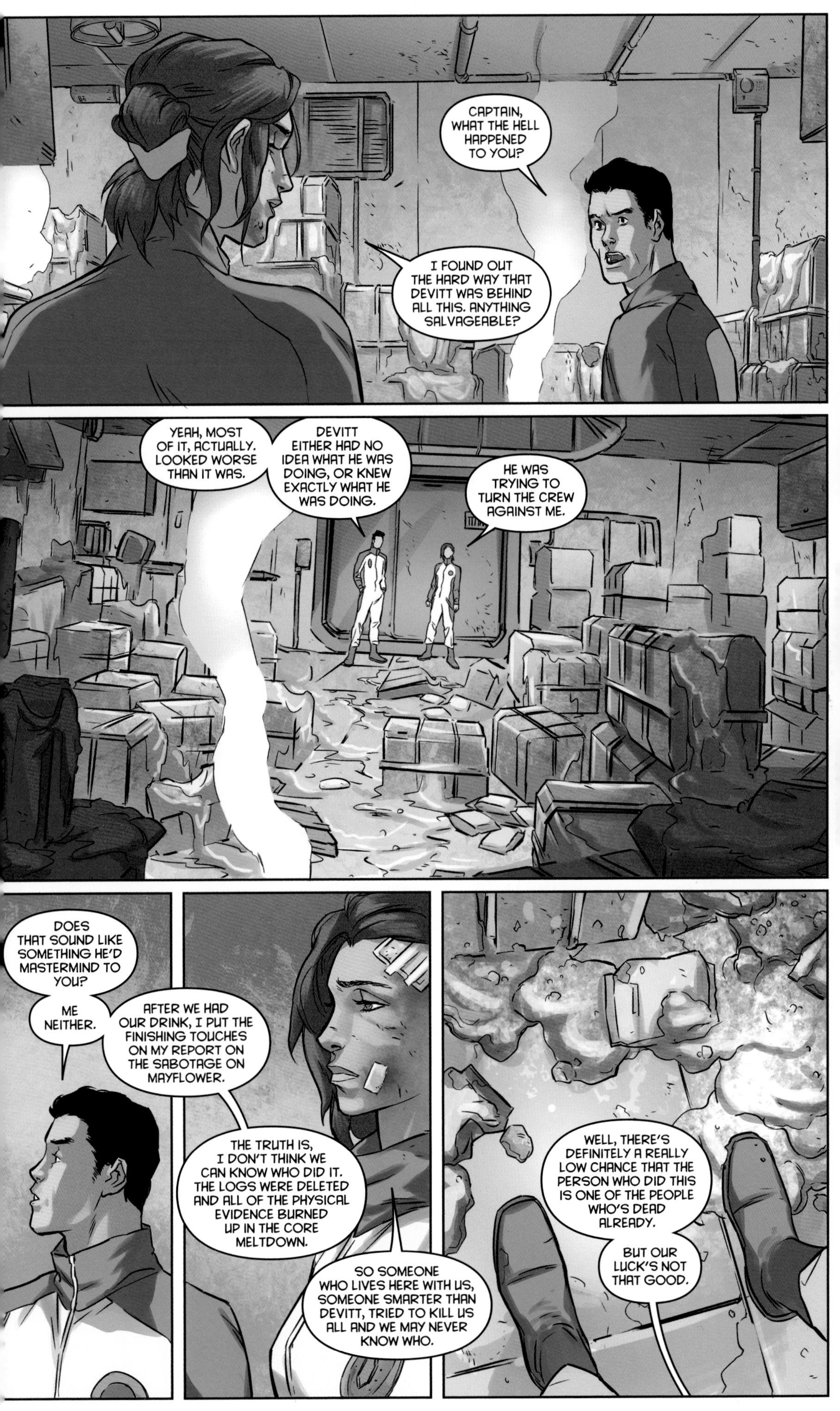

CAPTAIN, WHAT THE HELL HAPPENED TO YOU?
I FOUND OUT THE HARD WAY THAT DEVITT WAS BEHIND ALL THIS. ANYTHING SALVAGEABLE?
YEAH, MOST OF IT, ACTUALLY. LOOKED WORSE THAN IT WAS.
DEVITT EITHER HAD NO IDEA WHAT HE WAS DOING, OR KNEW EXACTLY WHAT HE WAS DOING.
HE WAS TRYING TO TURN THE CREW AGAINST ME.
DOES THAT SOUND LIKE SOMETHING HE'D MASTERMIND TO YOU?
ME NEITHER.
AFTER WE HAD OUR DRINK, I PUT THE FINISHING TOUCHES ON MY REPORT ON THE SABOTAGE ON MAYFLOWER.
THE TRUTH IS, I DON'T THINK WE CAN KNOW WHO DID IT. THE LOGS WERE DELETED AND ALL OF THE PHYSICAL EVIDENCE BURNED UP IN THE CORE MELTDOWN.
SO SOMEONE WHO LIVES HERE WITH US, SOMEONE SMARTER THAN DEVITT, TRIED TO KILL US ALL AND WE MAY NEVER KNOW WHO.
WELL, THERE'S DEFINITELY A REALLY LOW CHANCE THAT THE PERSON WHO DID THIS IS ONE OF THE PEOPLE WHO'S DEAD ALREADY.
BUT OUR LUCK'S NOT THAT GOOD.

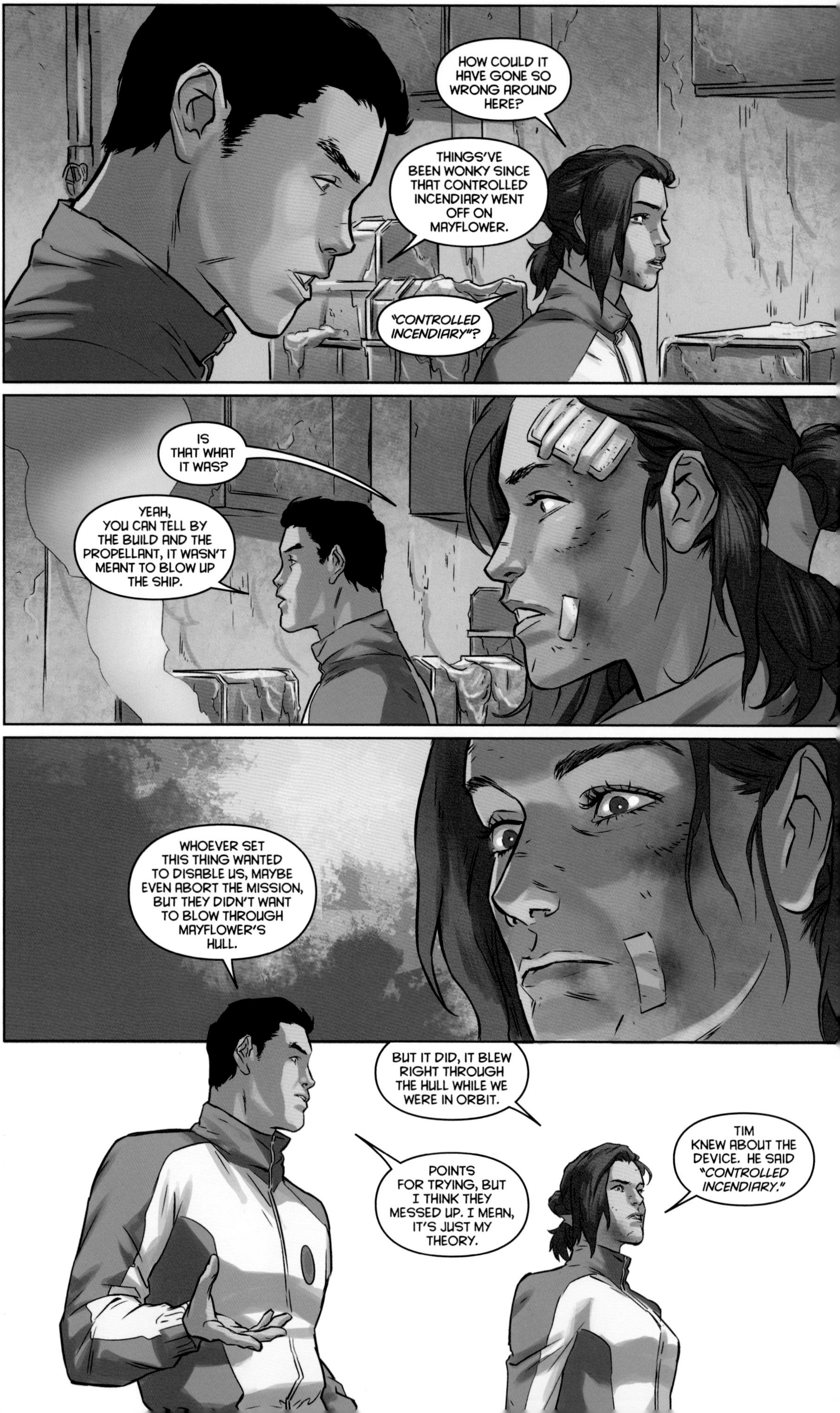
HOW COULD IT HAVE GONE SO WRONG AROUND HERE?
THINGS'VE BEEN WONKY SINCE THAT CONTROLLED INCENDIARY WENT OFF ON MAYFLOWER.
"CONTROLLED INCENDIARY"?
IS THAT WHAT IT WAS?
YEAH, YOU CAN TELL BY THE BUILD AND THE PROPELLANT, IT WASN'T MEANT TO BLOW UP THE SHIP.
WHOEVER SET THIS THING WANTED TO DISABLE US, MAYBE EVEN ABORT THE MISSION, BUT THEY DIDN'T WANT TO BLOW THROUGH MAYFLOWER'S HULL.
BUT IT DID, IT BLEW RIGHT THROUGH THE HULL WHILE WE WERE IN ORBIT.
POINTS FOR TRYING, BUT I THINK THEY MESSED UP. I MEAN, IT'S JUST MY THEORY.
TIM KNEW ABOUT THE DEVICE. HE SAID "CONTROLLED INCENDIARY."

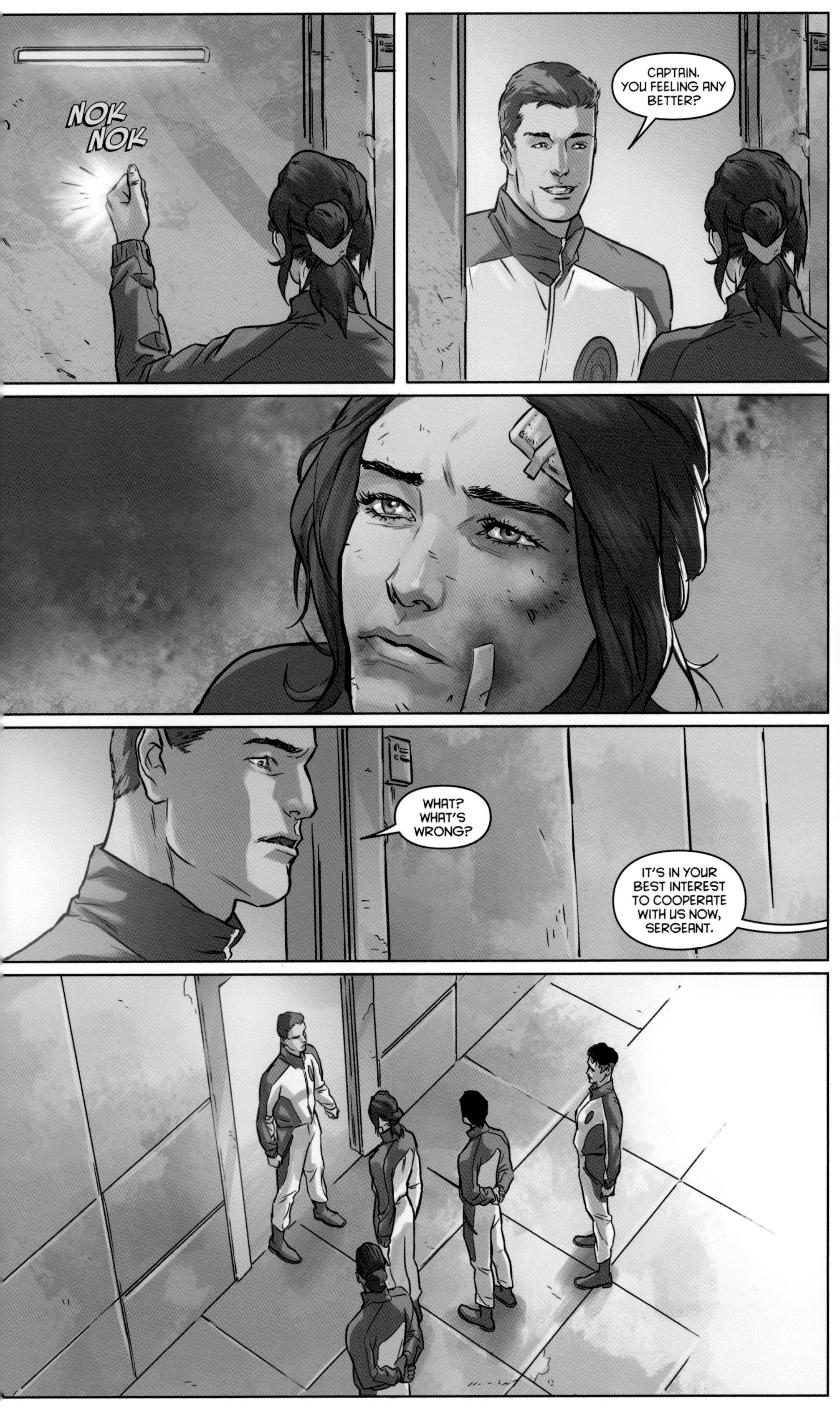
NOK NOK
CAPTAIN. YOU FEELING ANY BETTER?
WHAT? WHAT'S WRONG?
IT'S IN YOUR BEST INTEREST TO COOPERATE WITH US NOW, SERGEANT.

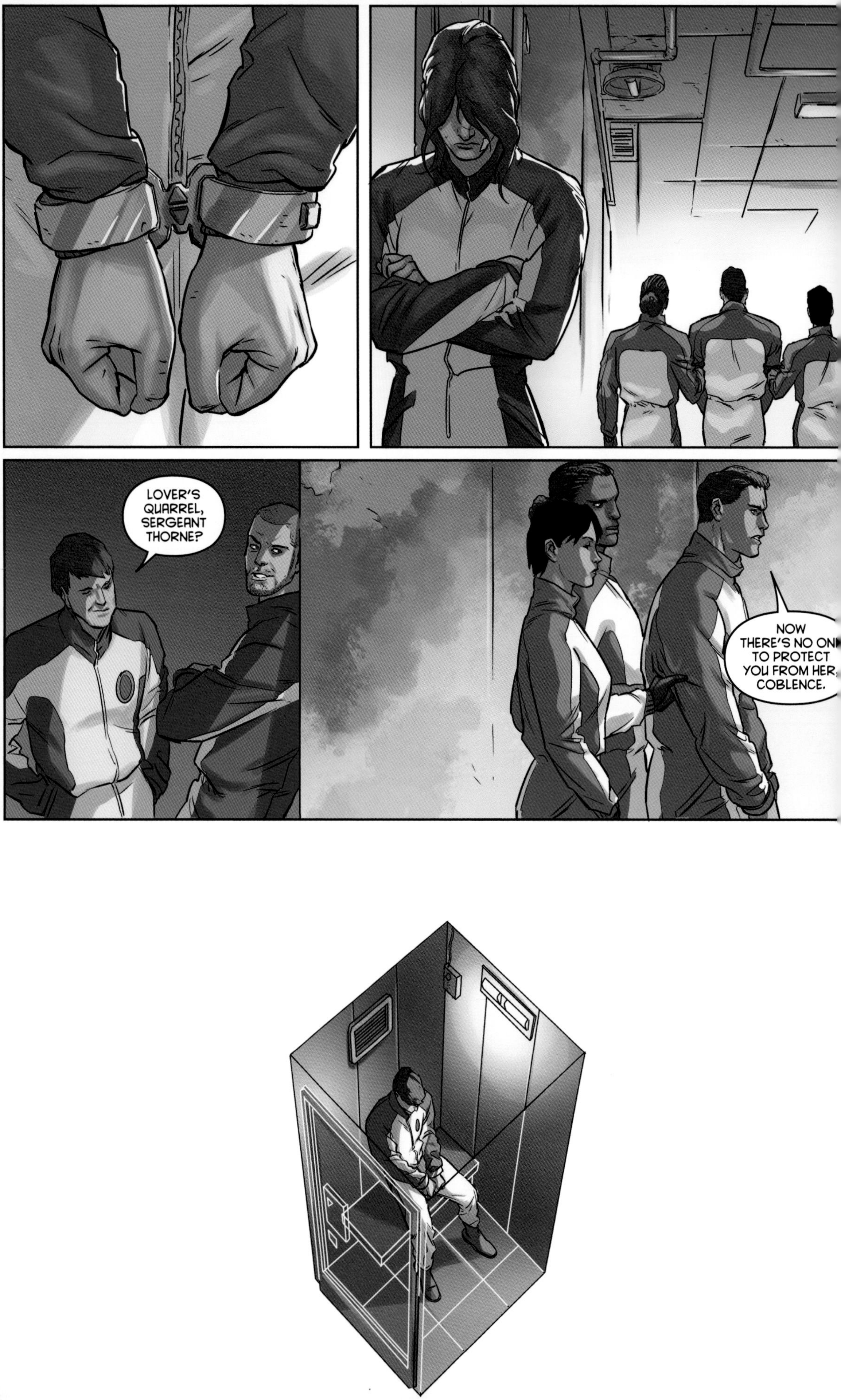
LOVER'S QUARREL, SERGEANT THORNE?
NOW THERE'S NO ON TO PROTECT YOU FROM HER, COBLENCE.

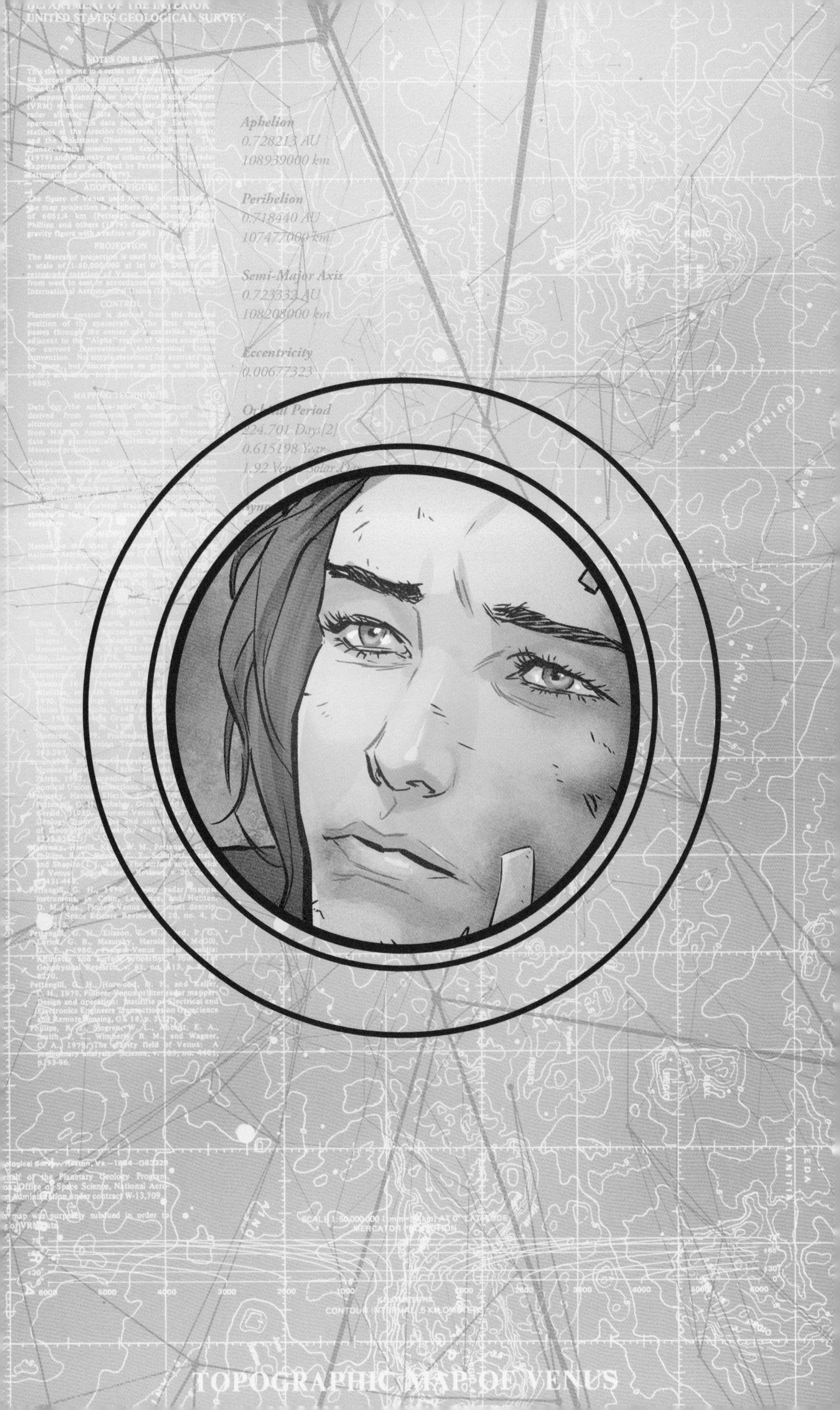
UNITED STATES GEOLOGICAL SURVEY
Aphelion
0.728213 AU
108939000 km
Peribelion
0.718440 AU
Semi-Major Axis
0.723332 AU
108208000 km
Eccentricity
0.00677323
224.701 Days[2]
0.615198 Year
GUINEVERE
TOPOGRAPHIC MAP OF VENUS

CHAPTER **FOUR**

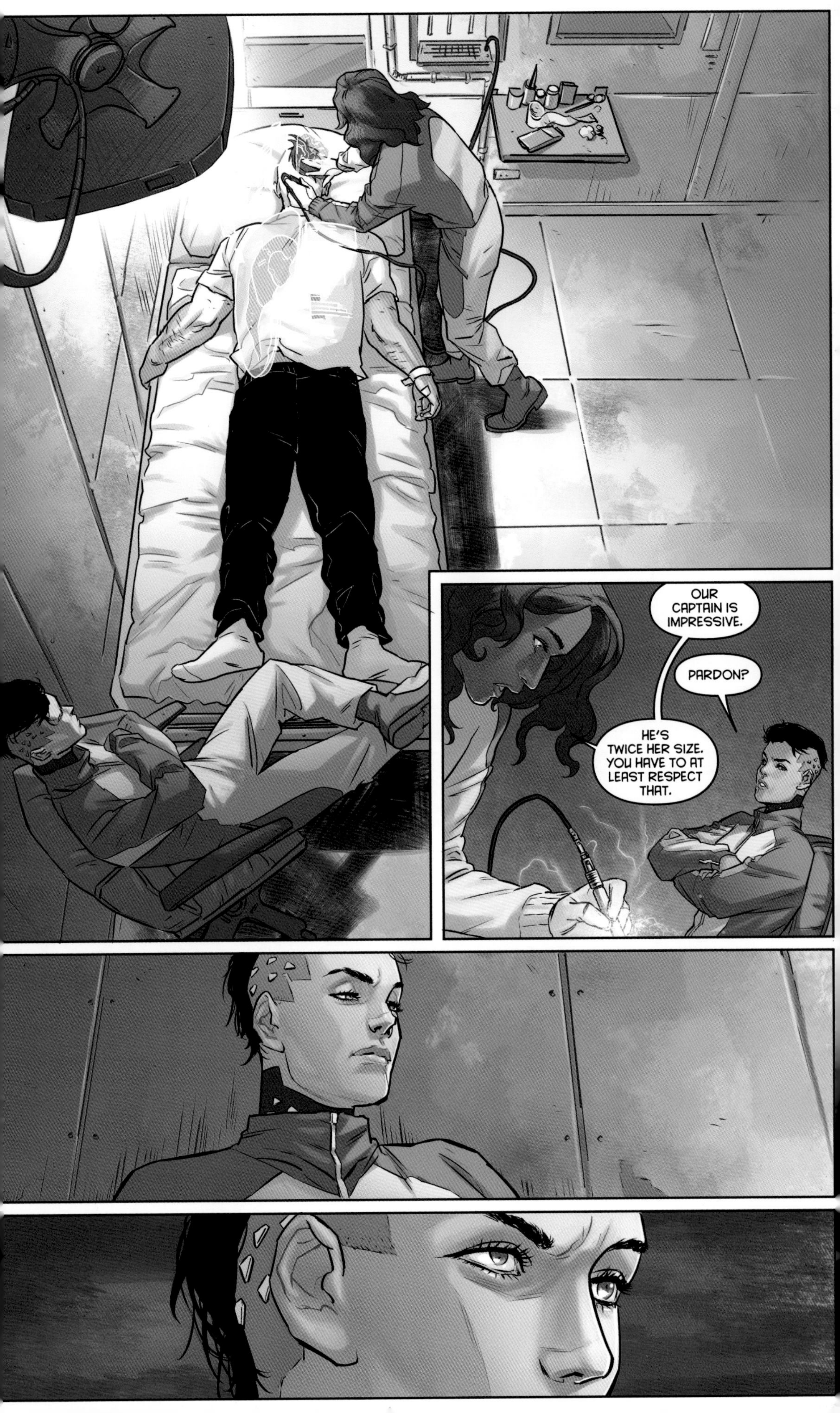
OUR CAPTAIN IS IMPRESSIVE.
PARDON?
HE'S TWICE HER SIZE. YOU HAVE TO AT LEAST RESPECT THAT.

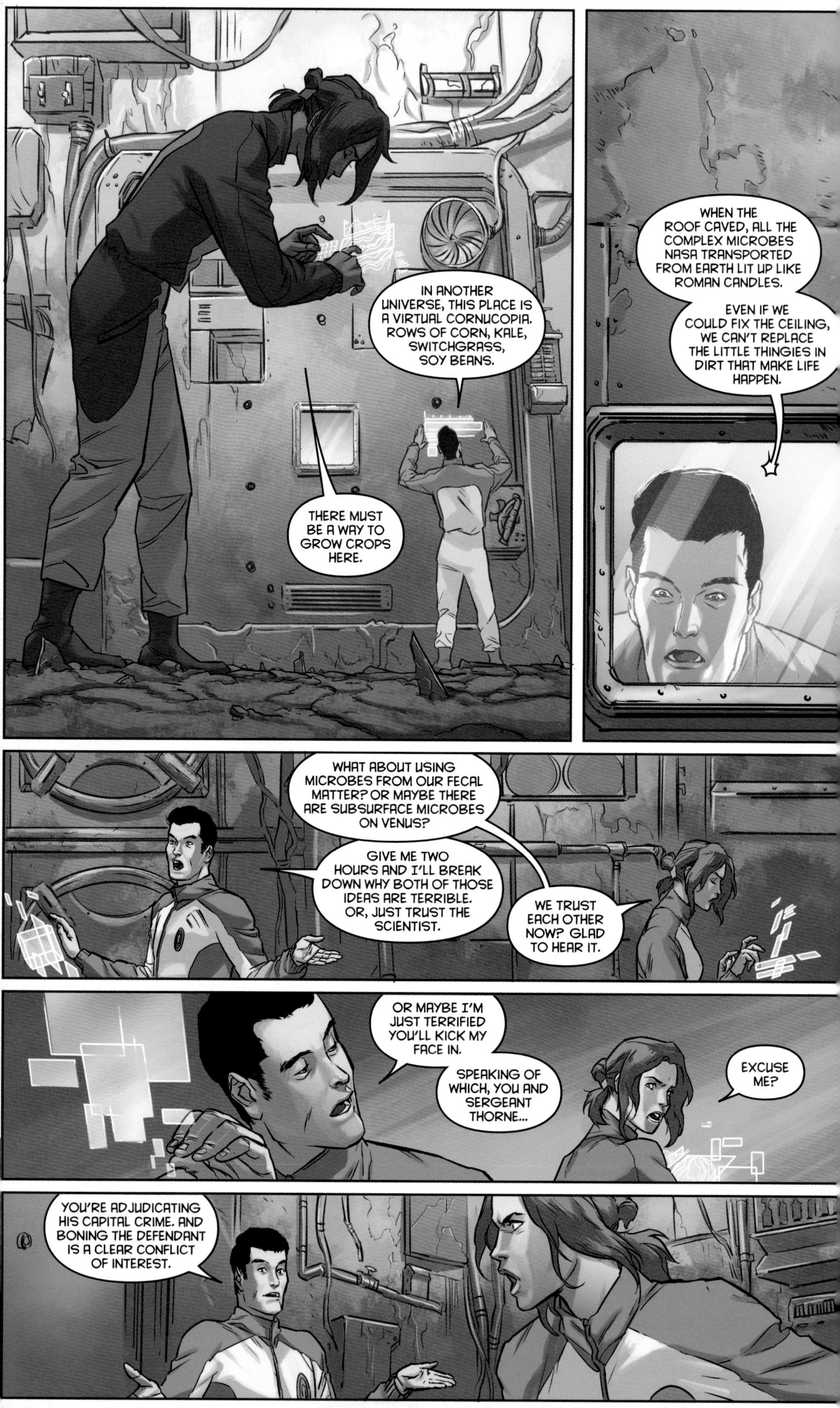
IN ANOTHER UNIVERSE, THIS PLACE IS A VIRTUAL CORNUCOPIA. ROWS OF CORN, KALE, SWITCHGRASS, SOY BEANS.
THERE MUST BE A WAY TO GROW CROPS HERE.
WHEN THE ROOF CAVED, ALL THE COMPLEX MICROBES NASA TRANSPORTED FROM EARTH LIT UP LIKE ROMAN CANDLES.
EVEN IF WE COULD FIX THE CEILING, WE CAN'T REPLACE THE LITTLE THINGIES IN DIRT THAT MAKE LIFE HAPPEN.
WHAT ABOUT USING MICROBES FROM OUR FECAL MATTER? OR MAYBE THERE ARE SUBSURFACE MICROBES ON VENUS?
GIVE ME TWO HOURS AND I'LL BREAK DOWN WHY BOTH OF THOSE IDEAS ARE TERRIBLE. OR, JUST TRUST THE SCIENTIST.
WE TRUST EACH OTHER NOW? GLAD TO HEAR IT.
OR MAYBE I'M JUST TERRIFIED YOU'LL KICK MY FACE IN.
SPEAKING OF WHICH, YOU AND SERGEANT THORNE...
EXCUSE ME?
YOU'RE ADJUDICATING HIS CAPITAL CRIME. AND BONING THE DEFENDANT IS A CLEAR CONFLICT OF INTEREST.

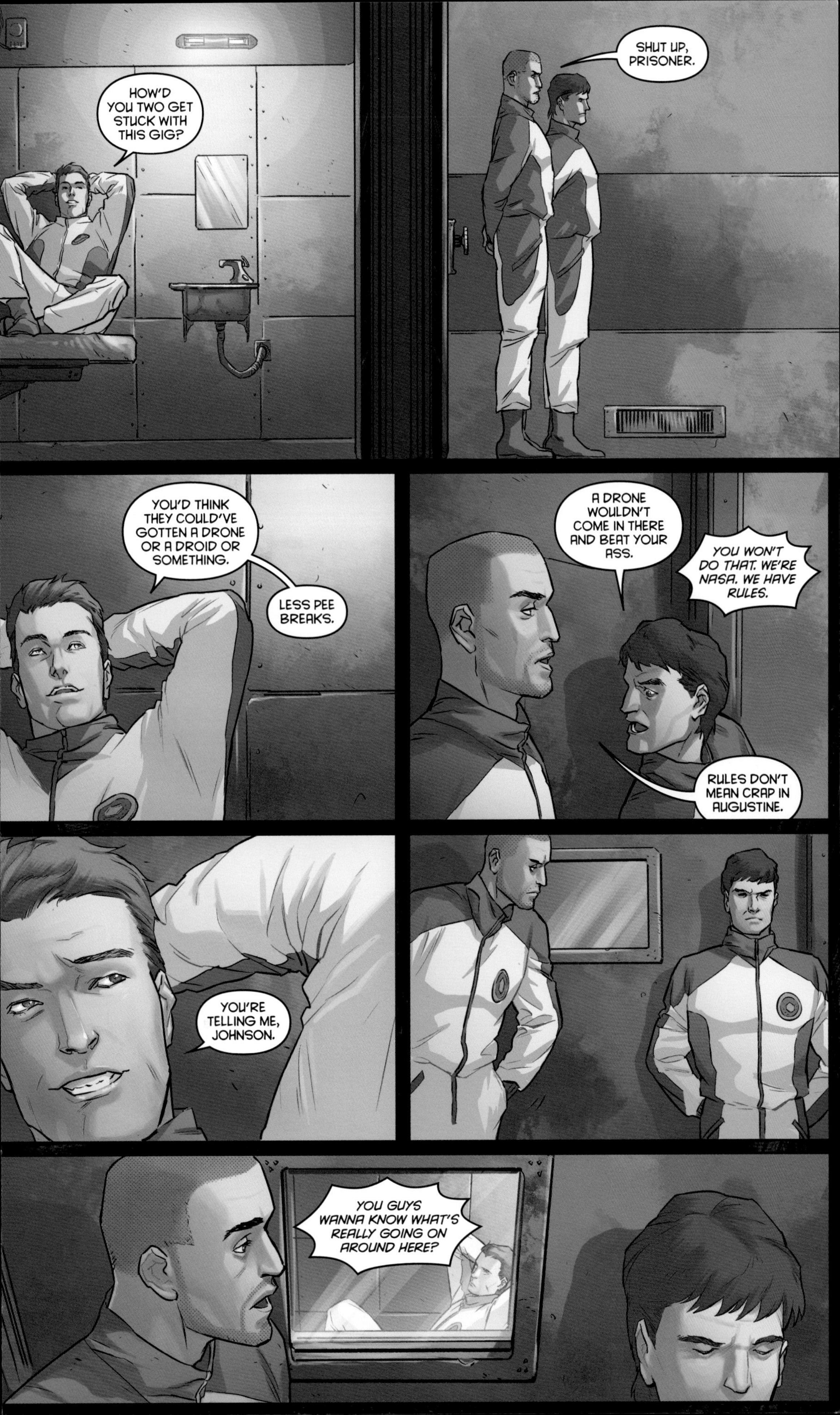
HOW'D YOU TWO GET STUCK WITH THIS GIG?
SHUT UP, PRISONER.
YOU'D THINK THEY COULD'VE GOTTEN A DRONE OR A DROID OR SOMETHING.
LESS PEE BREAKS.
A DRONE WOULDN'T COME IN THERE AND BEAT YOUR ASS.
YOU WON'T DO THAT. WE'RE NASA. WE HAVE RULES.
RULES DON'T MEAN CRAP IN AUGUSTINE.
YOU'RE TELLING ME, JOHNSON.
YOU GUYS WANNA KNOW WHAT'S REALLY GOING ON AROUND HERE?

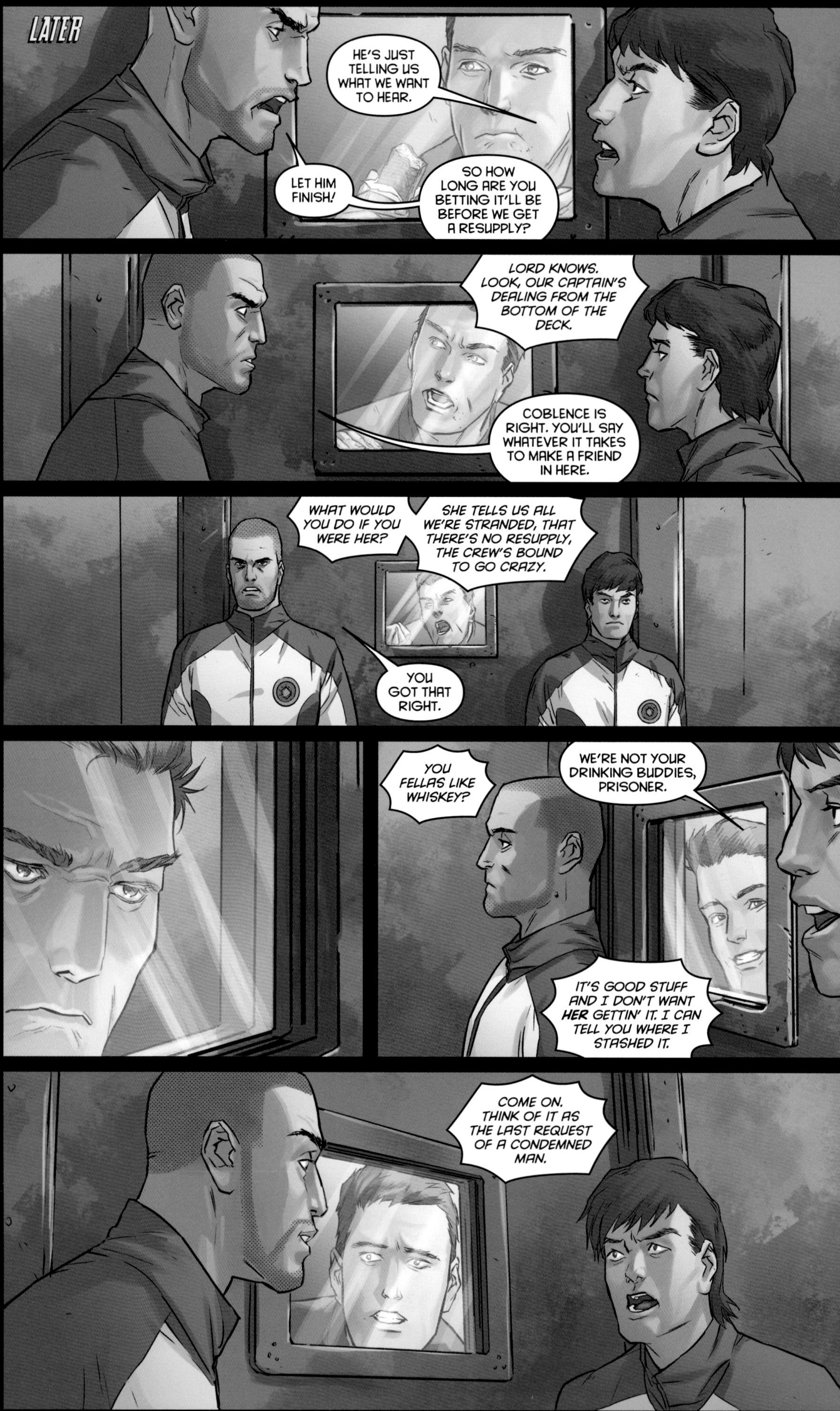
LATER
HE'S JUST TELLING US WHAT WE WANT TO HEAR.
LET HIM FINISH!
SO HOW LONG ARE YOU BETTING IT'LL BE BEFORE WE GET A RESUPPLY?
LORD KNOWS. LOOK, OUR CAPTAIN'S DEALING FROM THE BOTTOM OF THE DECK.
COBLENCE IS RIGHT. YOU'LL SAY WHATEVER IT TAKES TO MAKE A FRIEND IN HERE.
WHAT WOULD YOU DO IF YOU WERE HER?
SHE TELLS US ALL WE'RE STRANDED, THAT THERE'S NO RESUPPLY, THE CREW'S BOUND TO GO CRAZY.
YOU GOT THAT RIGHT.
YOU FELLAS LIKE WHISKEY?
WE'RE NOT YOUR DRINKING BUDDIES, PRISONER.
IT'S GOOD STUFF AND I DON'T WANT HER GETTIN' IT. I CAN TELL YOU WHERE I STASHED IT.
COME ON. THINK OF IT AS THE LAST REQUEST OF A CONDEMNED MAN.

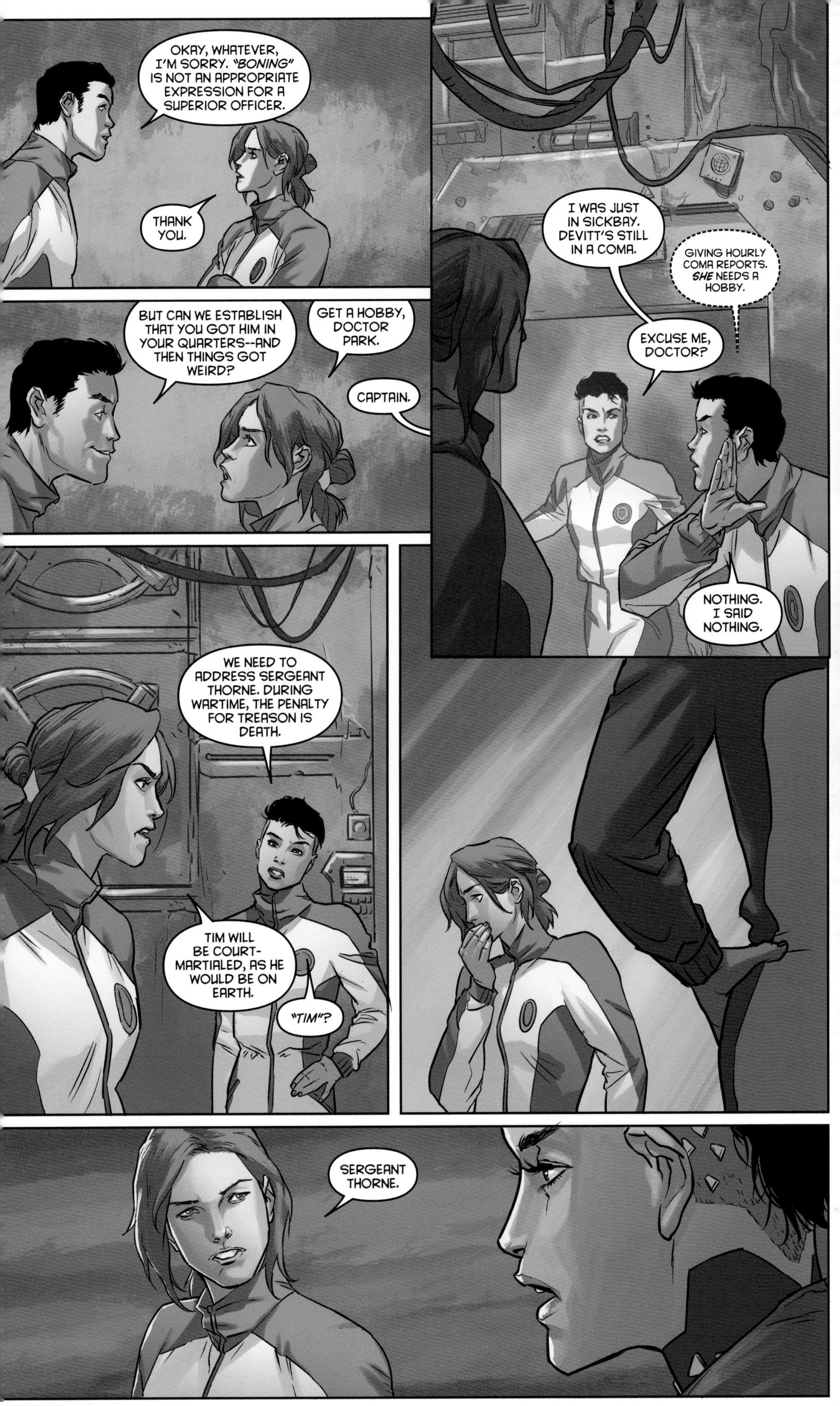
OKAY, WHATEVER, I'M SORRY. "BONING" IS NOT AN APPROPRIATE EXPRESSION FOR A SUPERIOR OFFICER.
THANK YOU.
BUT CAN WE ESTABLISH THAT YOU GOT HIM IN YOUR QUARTERS--AND THEN THINGS GOT WEIRD?
GET A HOBBY, DOCTOR PARK.
CAPTAIN.
I WAS JUST IN SICKBAY. DEVITT'S STILL IN A COMA.
GIVING HOURLY COMA REPORTS. SHE NEEDS A HOBBY.
EXCUSE ME, DOCTOR?
NOTHING. I SAID NOTHING.
WE NEED TO ADDRESS SERGEANT THORNE. DURING WARTIME, THE PENALTY FOR TREASON IS DEATH.
TIM WILL BE COURT-MARTIALED, AS HE WOULD BE ON EARTH.
"TIM"?
SERGEANT THORNE.

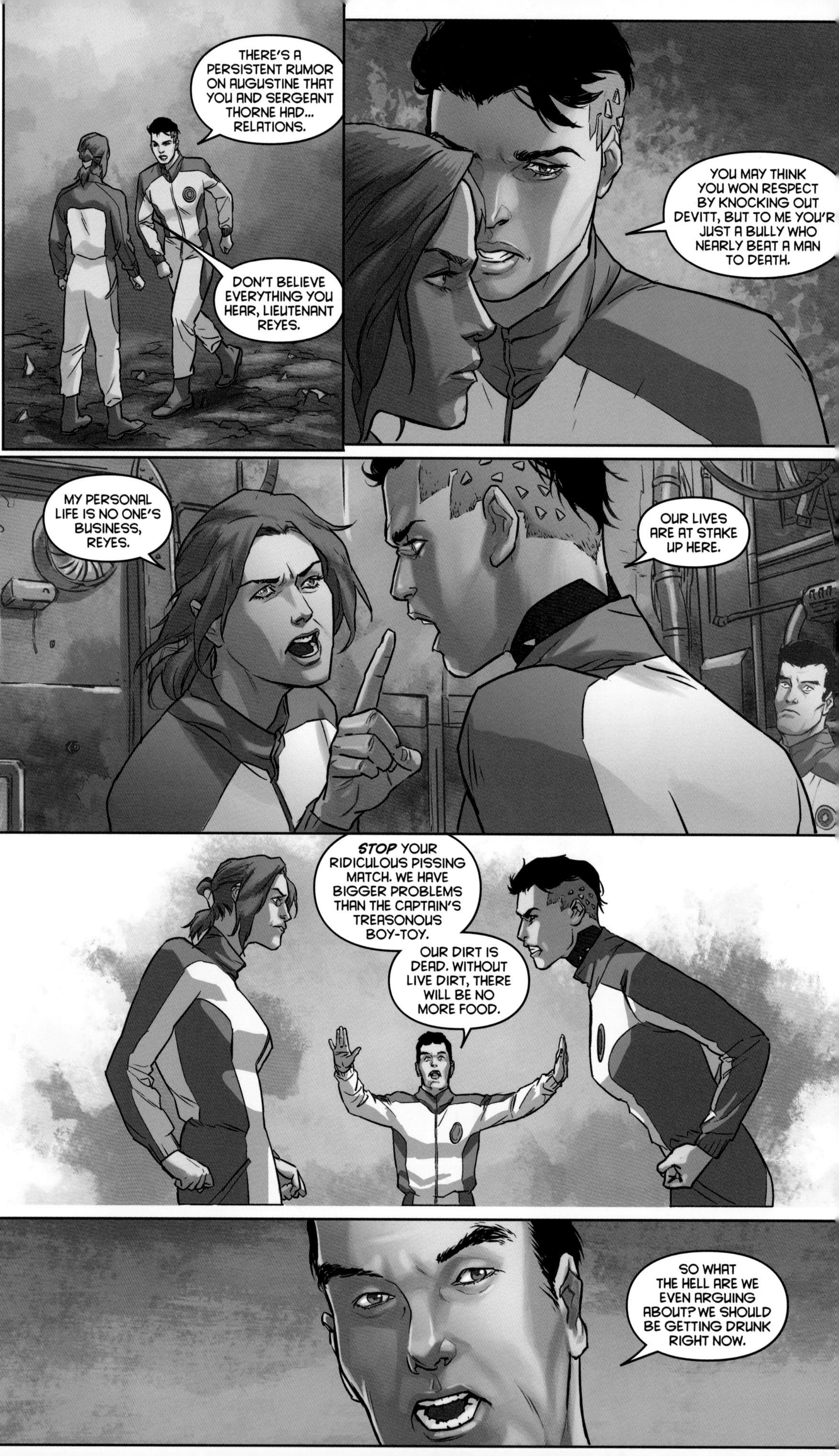
THERE'S A PERSISTENT RUMOR ON AUGUSTINE THAT YOU AND SERGEANT THORNE HAD... RELATIONS.
DON'T BELIEVE EVERYTHING YOU HEAR, LIEUTENANT REYES.
YOU MAY THINK YOU WON RESPECT BY KNOCKING OUT DEVITT, BUT TO ME YOU'R JUST A BULLY WHO NEARLY BEAT A MAN TO DEATH.
MY PERSONAL LIFE IS NO ONE'S BUSINESS, REYES.
OUR LIVES ARE AT STAKE UP HERE.
STOP YOUR RIDICULOUS PISSING MATCH. WE HAVE BIGGER PROBLEMS THAN THE CAPTAIN'S TREASONOUS BOY-TOY.
OUR DIRT IS DEAD. WITHOUT LIVE DIRT, THERE WILL BE NO MORE FOOD.
SO WHAT THE HELL ARE WE EVEN ARGUING ABOUT? WE SHOULD BE GETTING DRUNK RIGHT NOW.

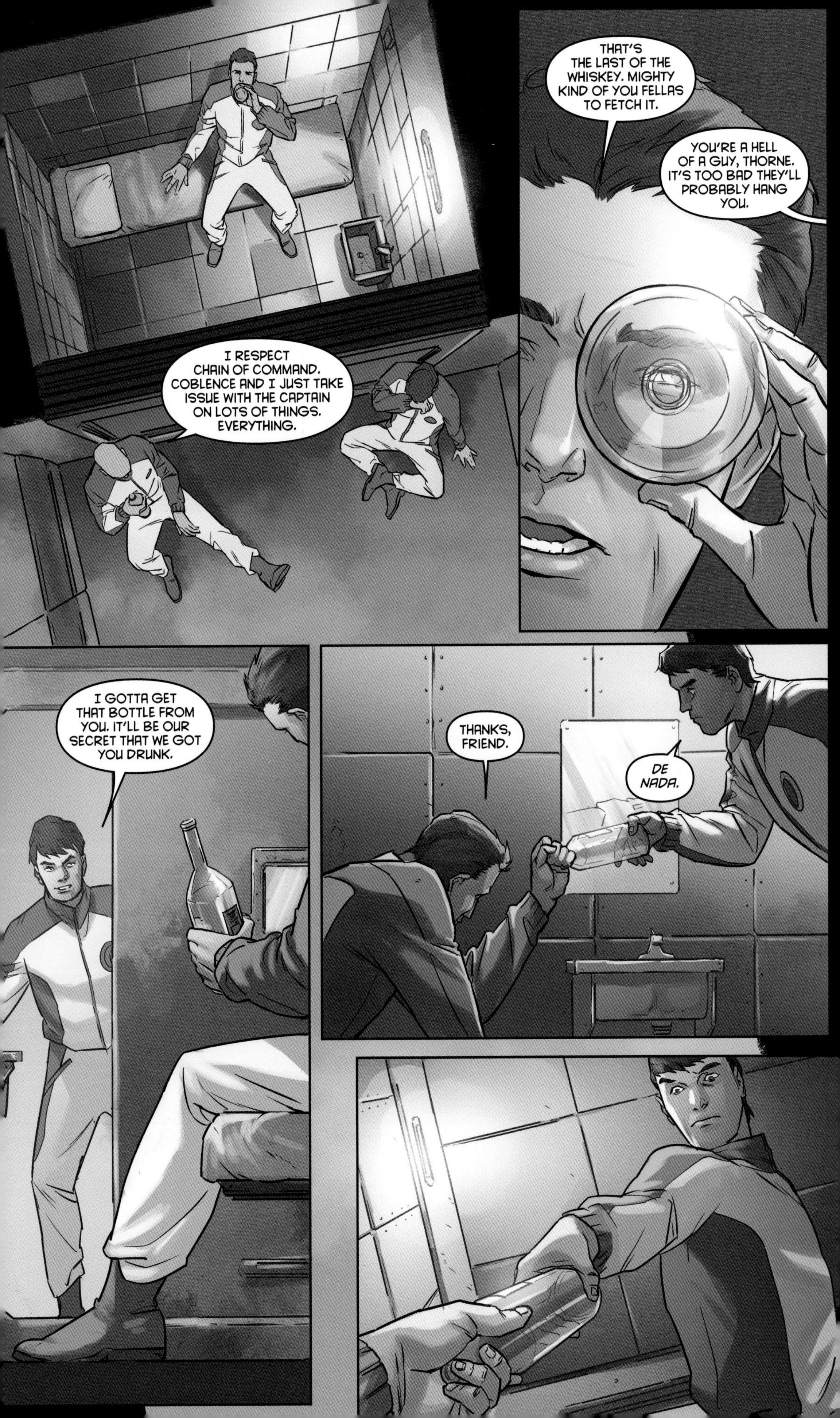
I RESPECT CHAIN OF COMMAND. COBLENCE AND I JUST TAKE ISSUE WITH THE CAPTAIN ON LOTS OF THINGS. EVERYTHING.
THAT'S THE LAST OF THE WHISKEY. MIGHTY KIND OF YOU FELLAS TO FETCH IT.
YOU'RE A HELL OF A GUY, THORNE. IT'S TOO BAD THEY'LL PROBABLY HANG YOU.
I GOTTA GET THAT BOTTLE FROM YOU. IT'LL BE OUR SECRET THAT WE GOT YOU DRUNK.
THANKS, FRIEND.
DE NADA.

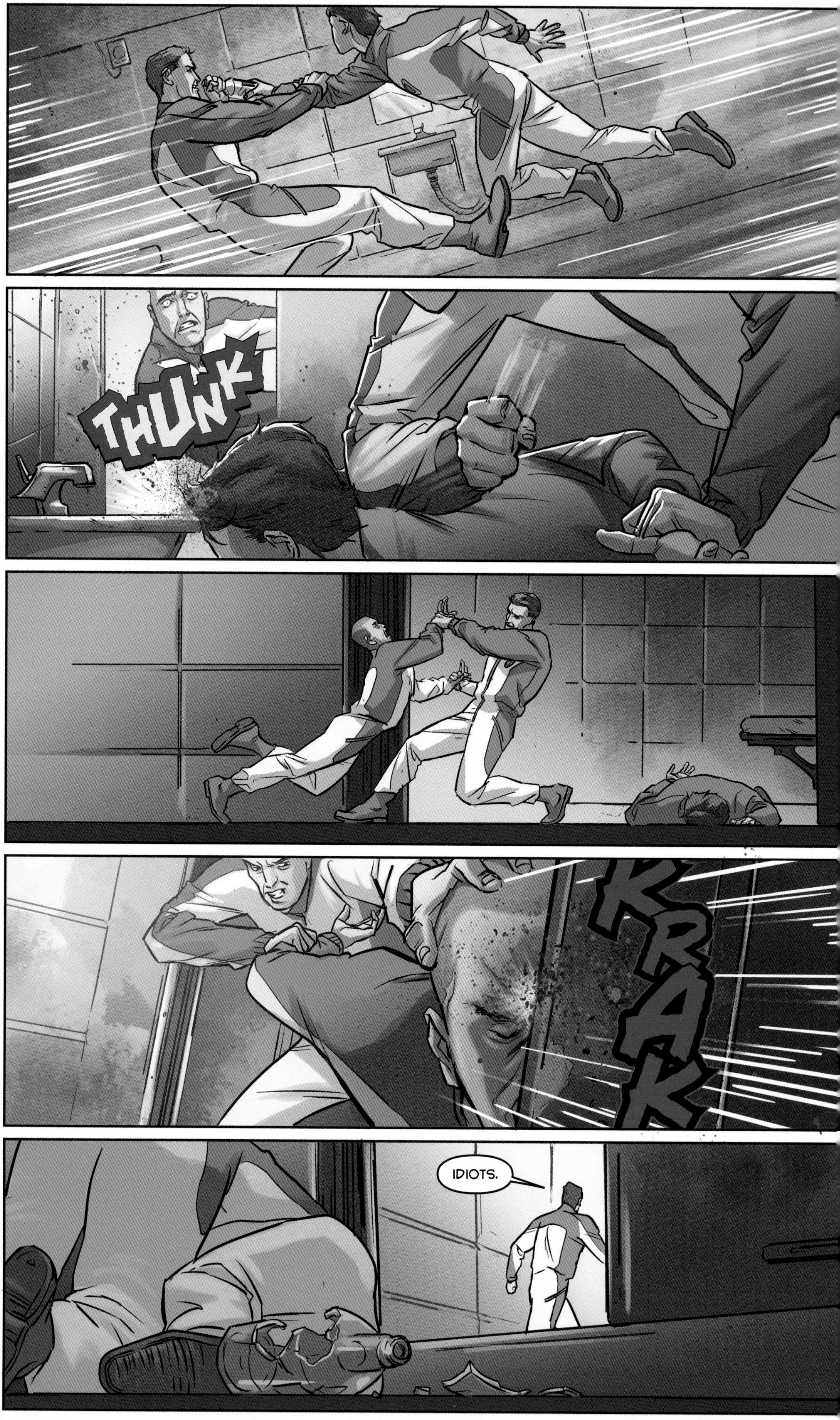
THUNK
KRAK
IDIOTS.

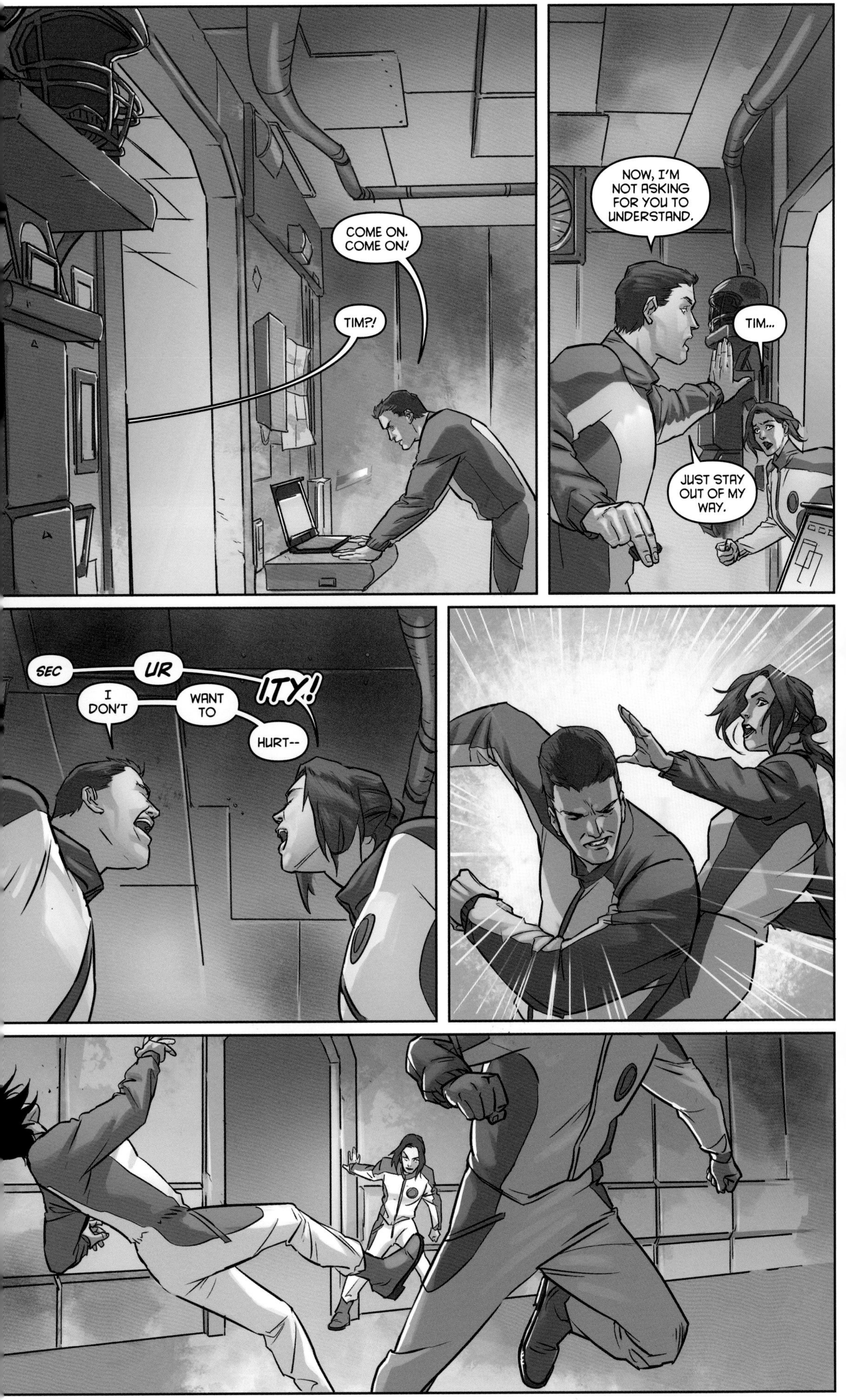
COME ON.
COME ON!
TIM?!
NOW, I'M NOT ASKING FOR YOU TO UNDERSTAND.
TIM...
JUST STAY OUT OF MY WAY.
SEC
UR
ITY!
I DON'T
WANT TO
HURT--

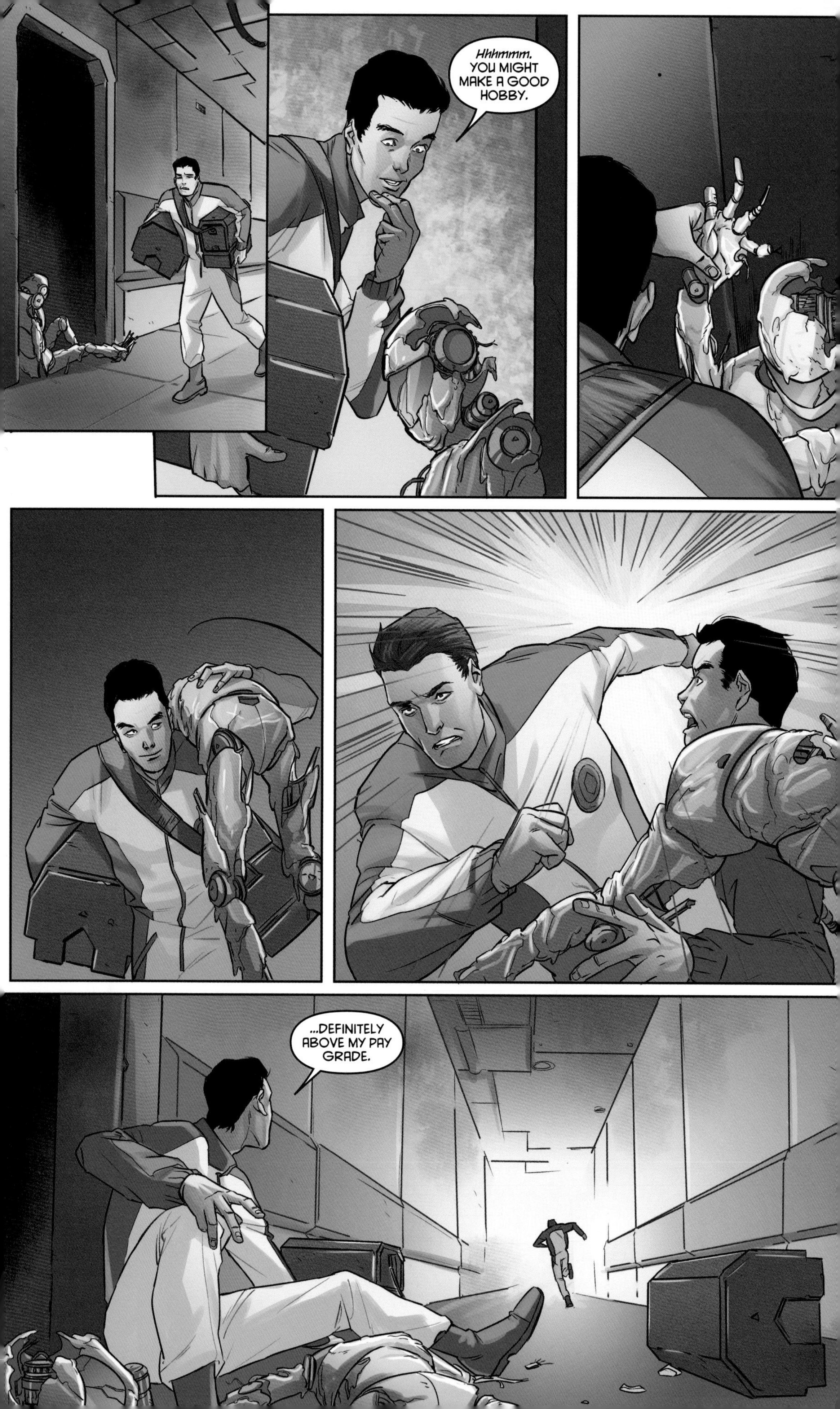
Hhhmmm. YOU MIGHT MAKE A GOOD HOBBY.
...DEFINITELY ABOVE MY PAY GRADE.

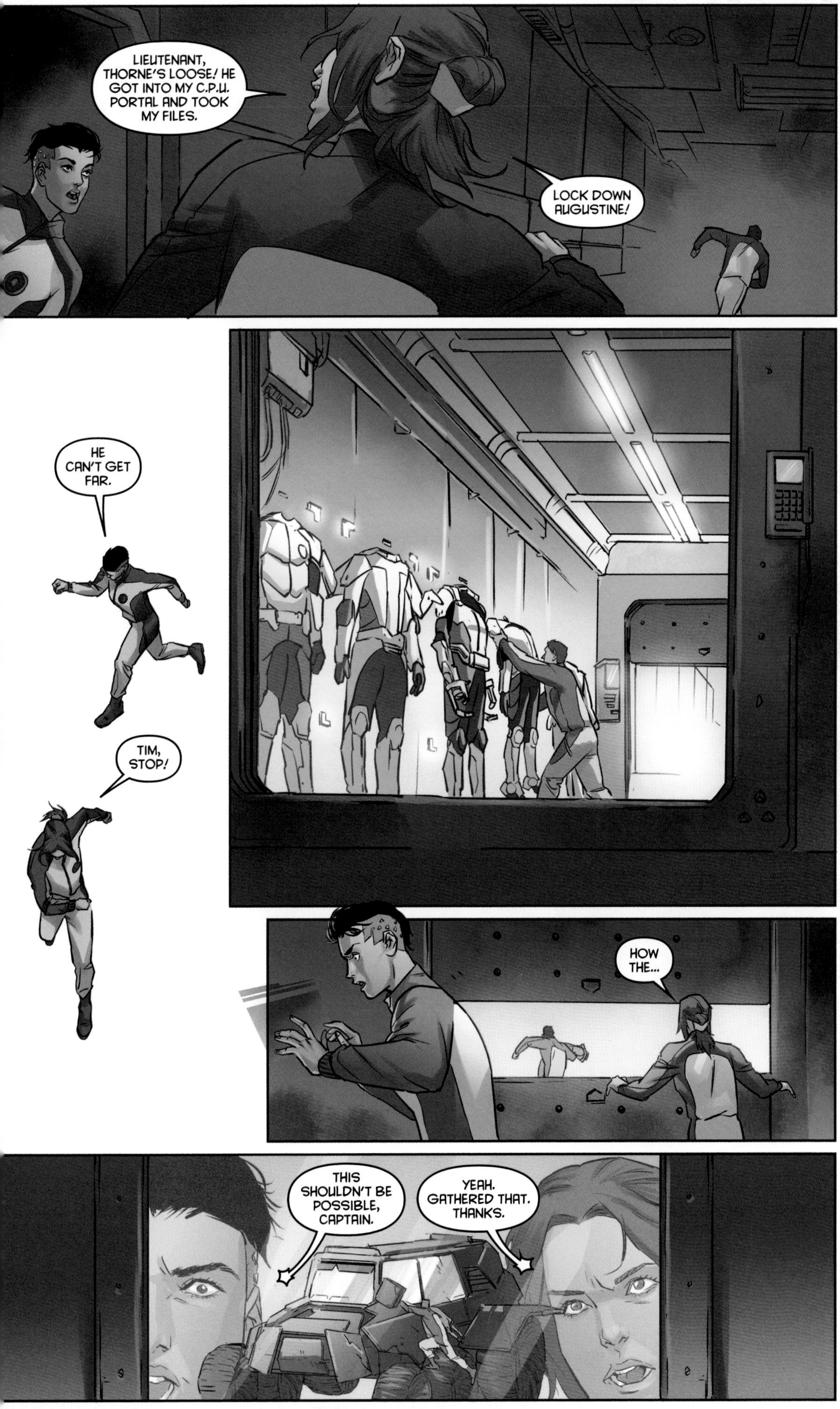
LIEUTENANT, THORNE'S LOOSE! HE GOT INTO MY C.P.U. PORTAL AND TOOK MY FILES.
LOCK DOWN AUGUSTINE!
HE CAN'T GET FAR.
TIM, STOP!
HOW THE...
THIS SHOULDN'T BE POSSIBLE, CAPTAIN.
YEAH. GATHERED THAT. THANKS.

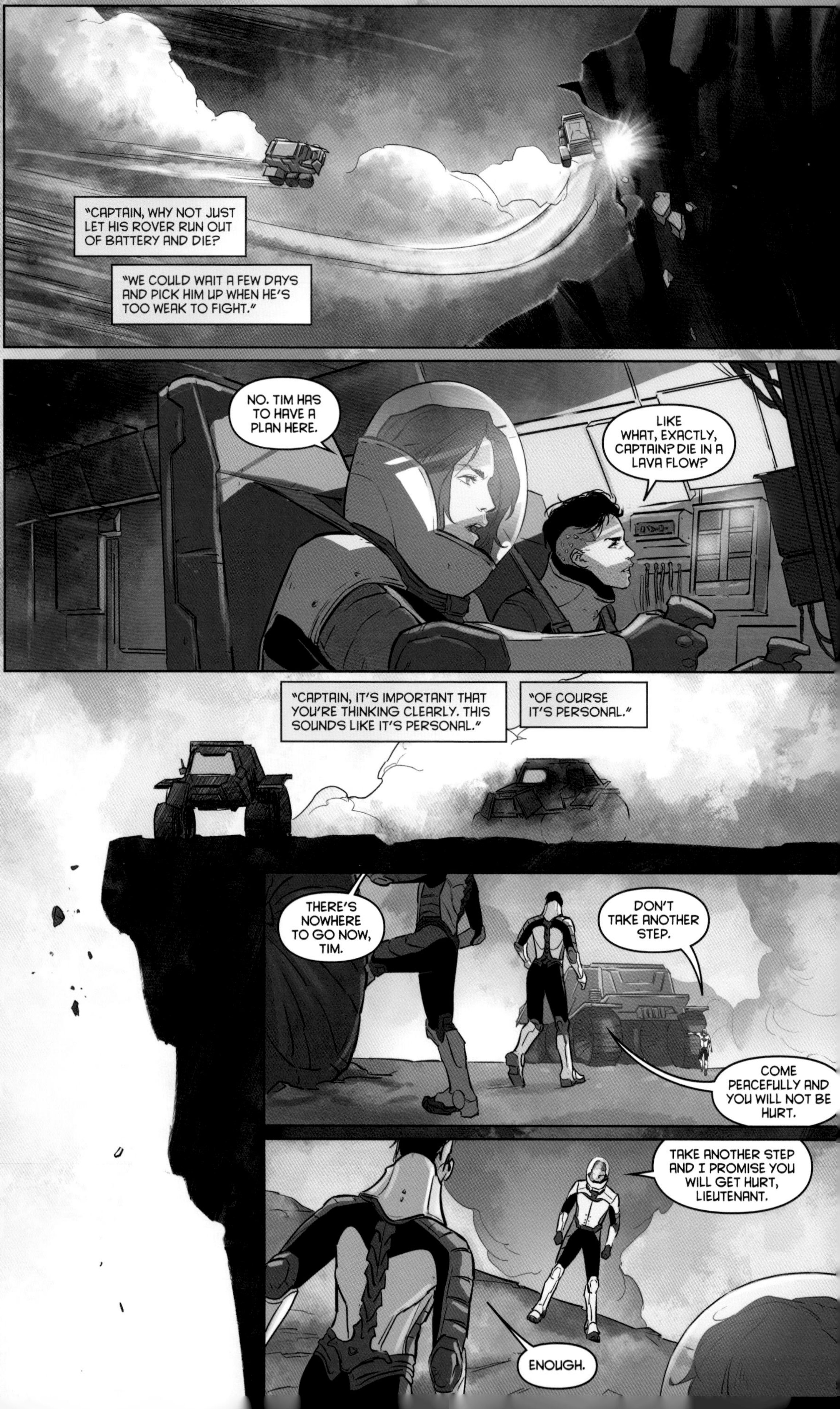
"CAPTAIN, WHY NOT JUST LET HIS ROVER RUN OUT OF BATTERY AND DIE?
"WE COULD WAIT A FEW DAYS AND PICK HIM UP WHEN HE'S TOO WEAK TO FIGHT."
NO. TIM HAS TO HAVE A PLAN HERE.
LIKE WHAT, EXACTLY, CAPTAIN? DIE IN A LAVA FLOW?
"CAPTAIN, IT'S IMPORTANT THAT YOU'RE THINKING CLEARLY. THIS SOUNDS LIKE IT'S PERSONAL."
"OF COURSE IT'S PERSONAL."
THERE'S NOWHERE TO GO NOW, TIM.
DON'T TAKE ANOTHER STEP.
COME PEACEFULLY AND YOU WILL NOT BE HURT.
TAKE ANOTHER STEP AND I PROMISE YOU WILL GET HURT, LIEUTENANT.
ENOUGH.

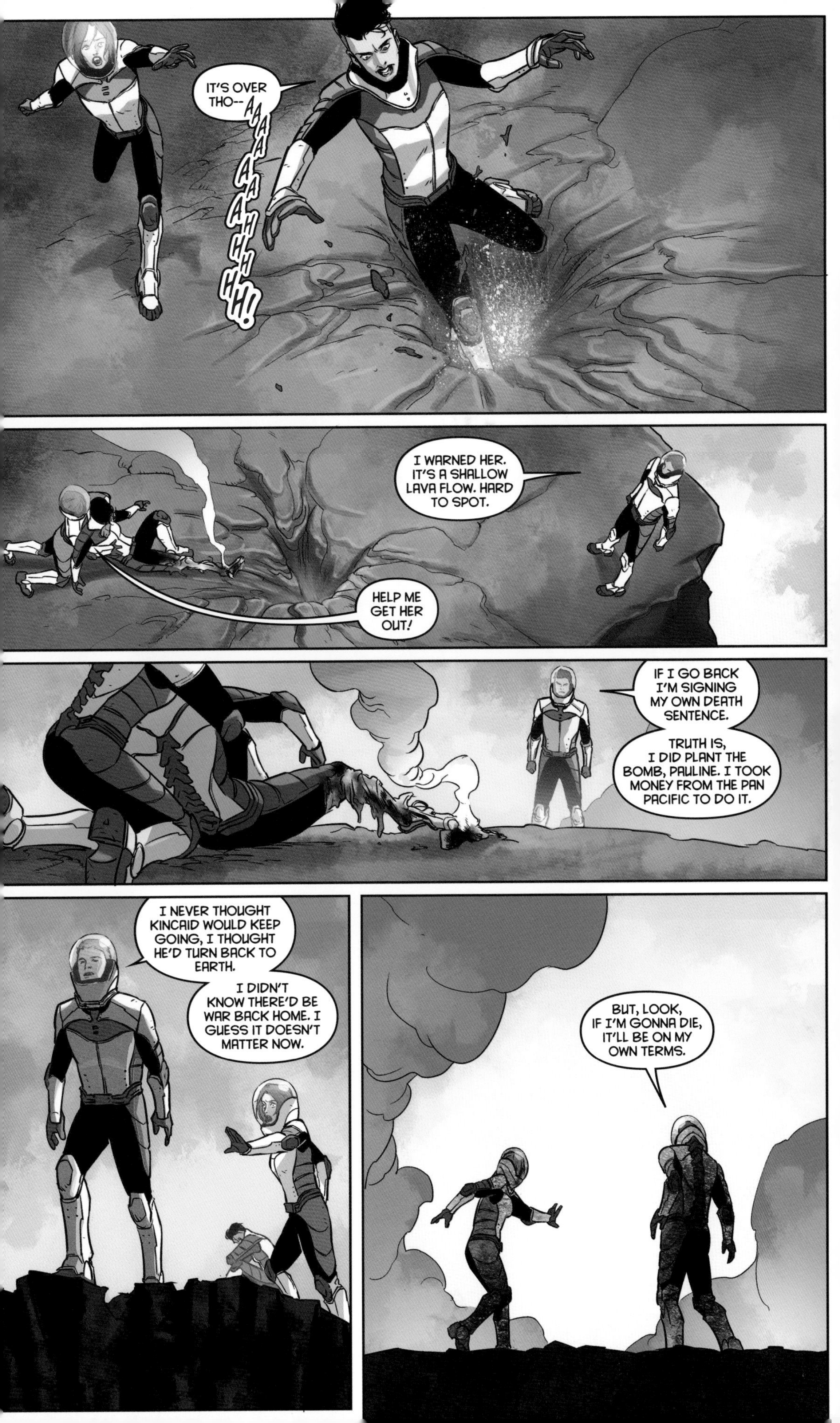
IT'S OVER THO--AAAAAAAHHHHH!
I WARNED HER. IT'S A SHALLOW LAVA FLOW. HARD TO SPOT.
HELP ME GET HER OUT!
IF I GO BACK I'M SIGNING MY OWN DEATH SENTENCE.
TRUTH IS, I DID PLANT THE BOMB, PAULINE. I TOOK MONEY FROM THE PAN PACIFIC TO DO IT.
I NEVER THOUGHT KINCAID WOULD KEEP GOING, I THOUGHT HE'D TURN BACK TO EARTH.
I DIDN'T KNOW THERE'D BE WAR BACK HOME. I GUESS IT DOESN'T MATTER NOW.
BUT, LOOK, IF I'M GONNA DIE, IT'LL BE ON MY OWN TERMS.

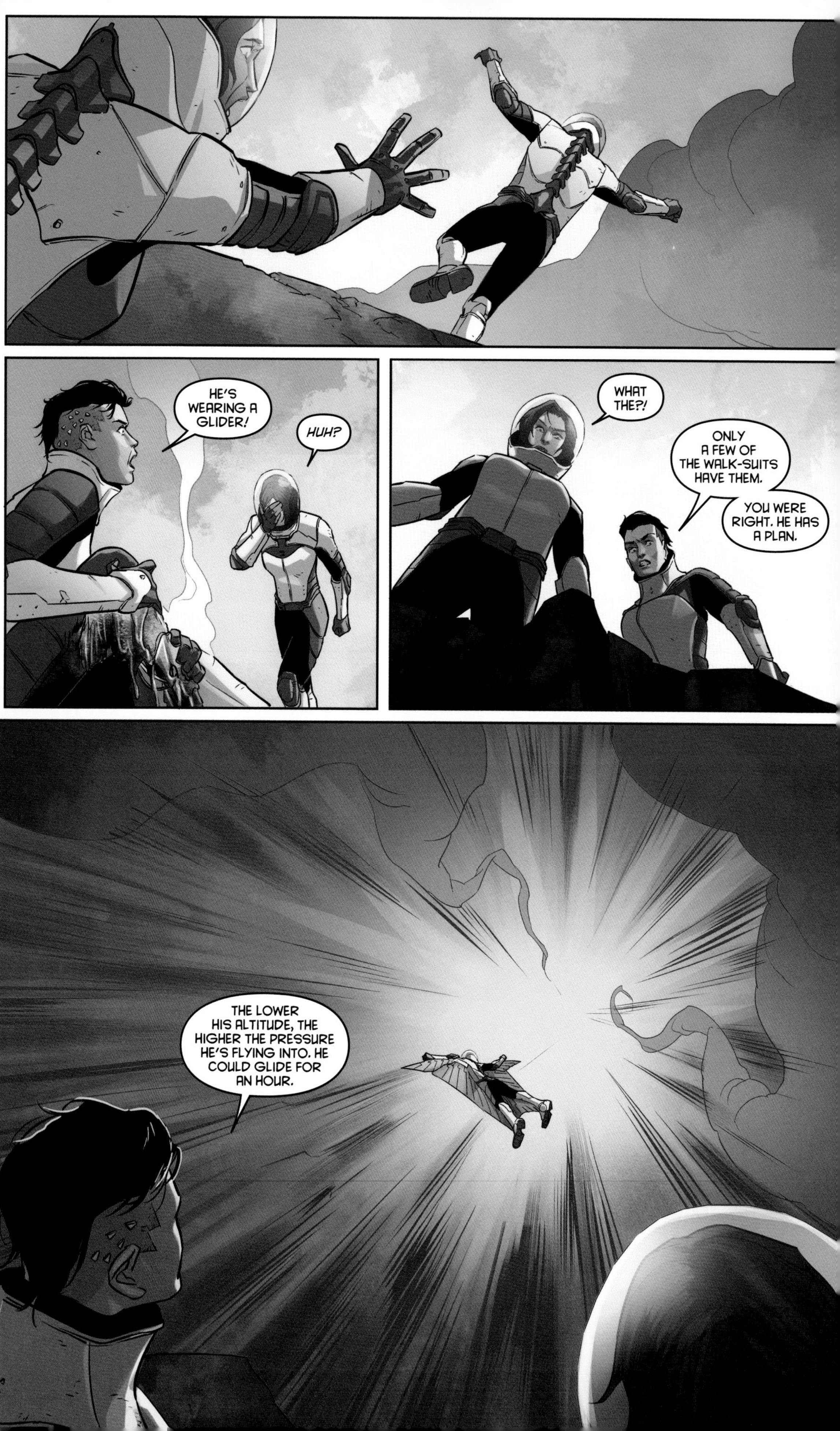
HE'S WEARING A GLIDER!
HUH?
WHAT THE?!
ONLY A FEW OF THE WALK-SUITS HAVE THEM.
YOU WERE RIGHT. HE HAS A PLAN.
THE LOWER HIS ALTITUDE, THE HIGHER THE PRESSURE HE'S FLYING INTO. HE COULD GLIDE FOR AN HOUR.

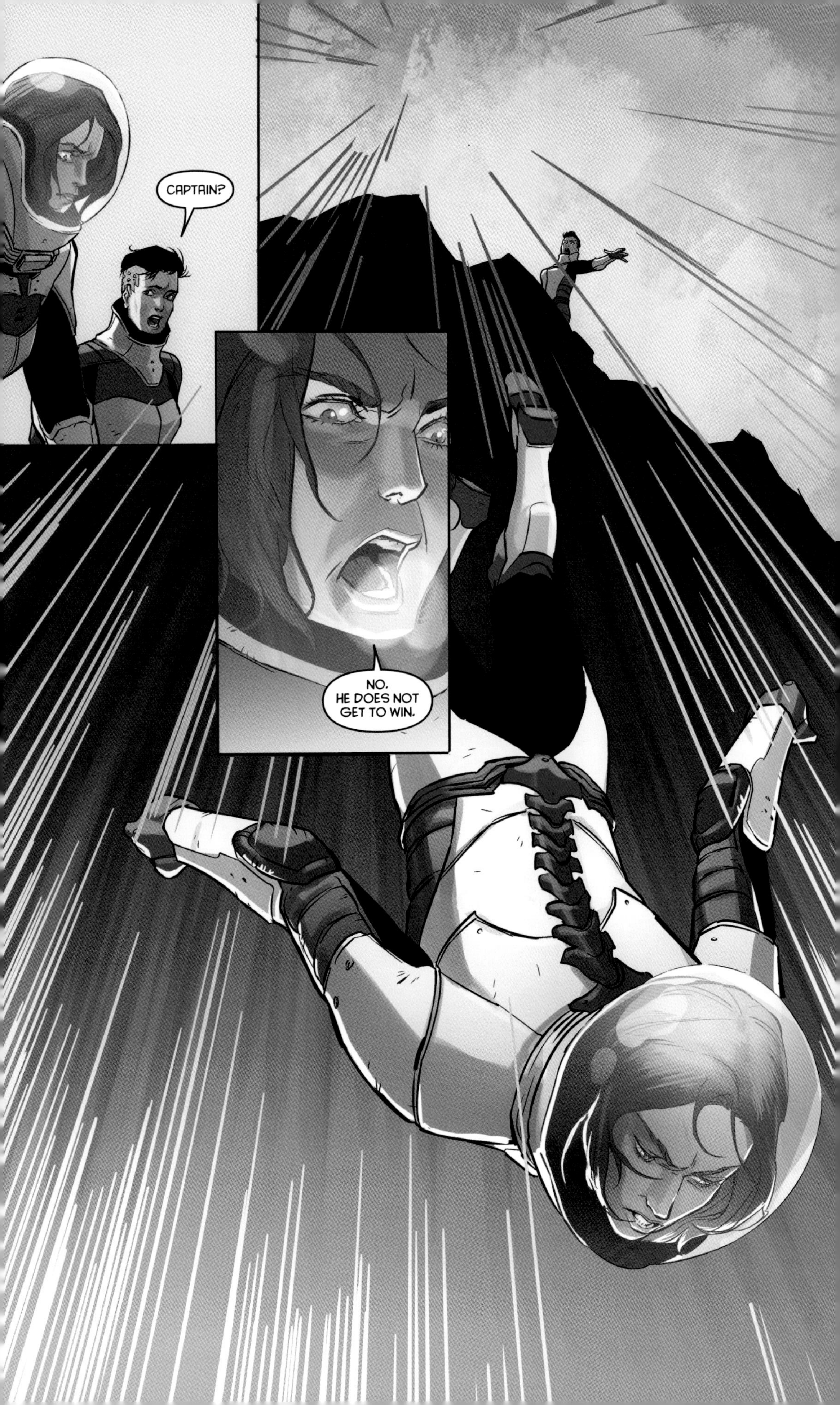
CAPTAIN?
NO. HE DOES NOT GET TO WIN.

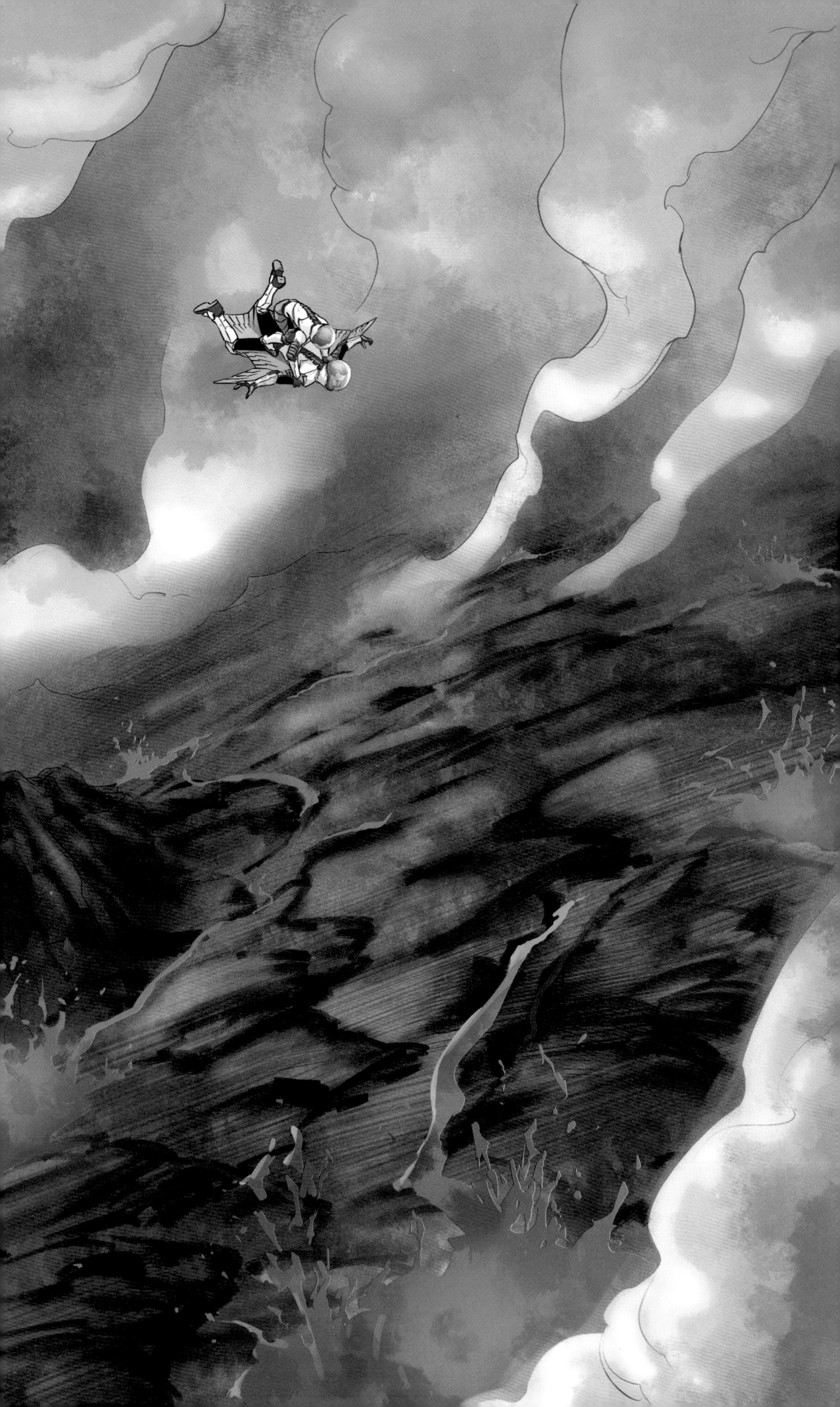

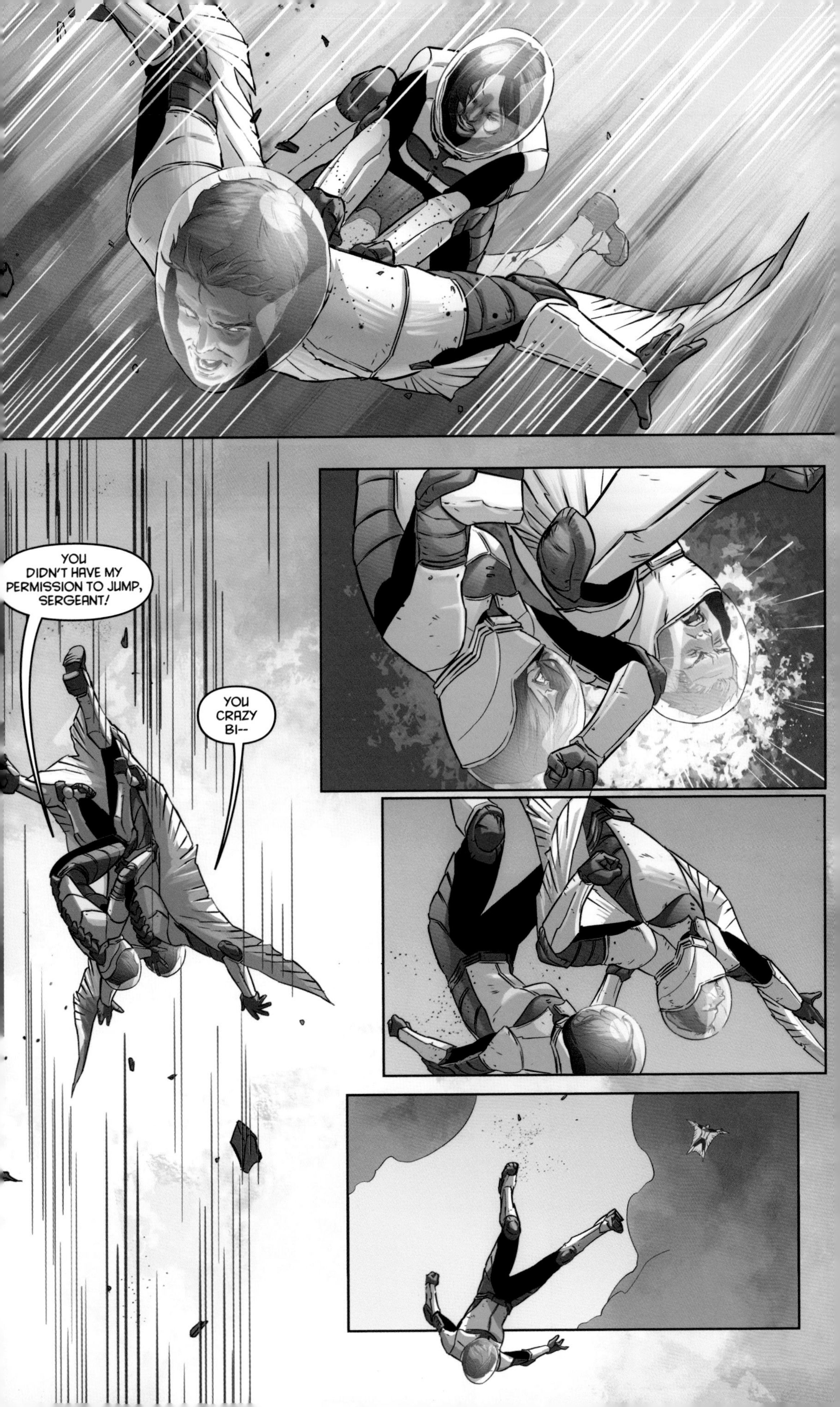
YOU DIDN'T HAVE MY PERMISSION TO JUMP, SERGEANT!
YOU CRAZY BI--

REYES--

THIS THING'S NOT BUILT FOR TWO. WE'RE GOING TO HIT THE DECK HARD.

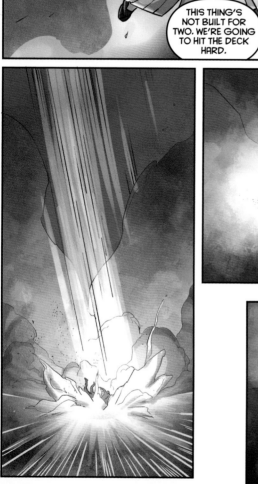

THAT WAS STUPID.

I GOT MY FILES BACK.

THERE GOES YOUR CHANCE TO MAKE CAPTAIN TODAY.

DAY'S NOT OVER YET.

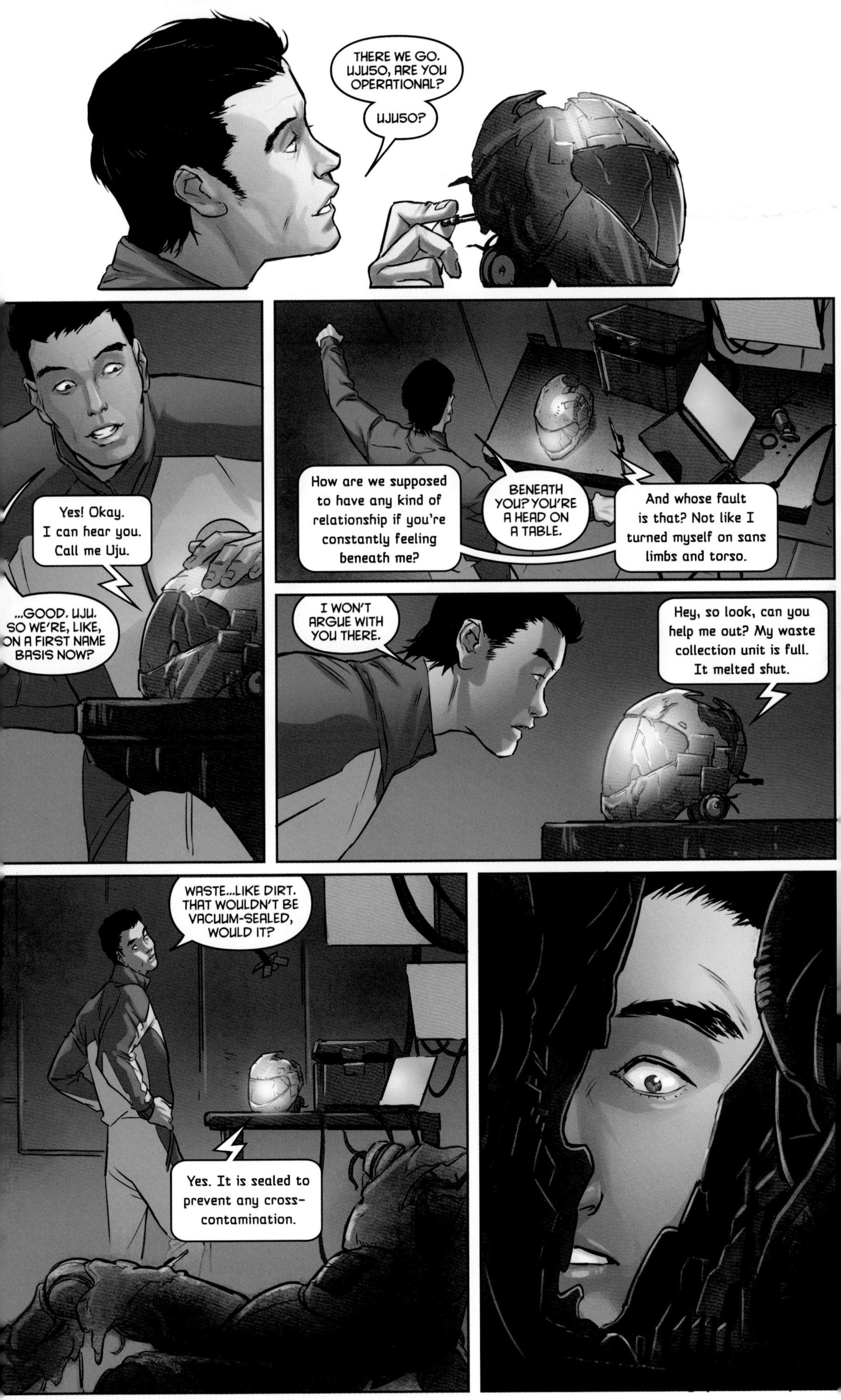

THERE WE GO. UJUSO, ARE YOU OPERATIONAL?
UJUSO?
Yes! Okay. I can hear you. Call me Uju.
...GOOD. UJU. SO WE'RE, LIKE, ON A FIRST NAME BASIS NOW?
How are we supposed to have any kind of relationship if you're constantly feeling beneath me?
BENEATH YOU? YOU'RE A HEAD ON A TABLE.
And whose fault is that? Not like I turned myself on sans limbs and torso.
I WON'T ARGUE WITH YOU THERE.
Hey, so look, can you help me out? My waste collection unit is full. It melted shut.
WASTE...LIKE DIRT. THAT WOULDN'T BE VACUUM-SEALED, WOULD IT?
Yes. It is sealed to prevent any cross-contamination.

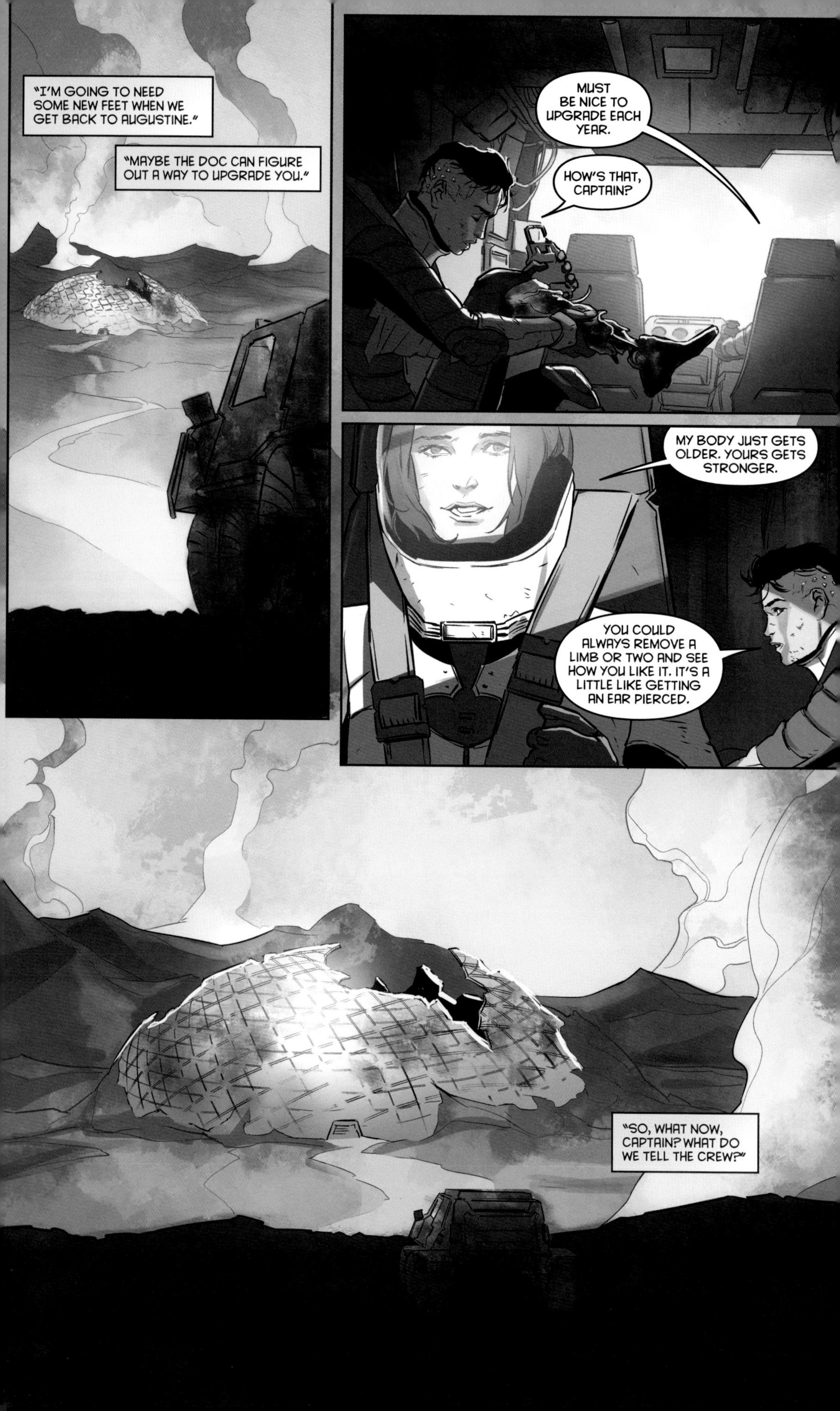
"I'M GOING TO NEED SOME NEW FEET WHEN WE GET BACK TO AUGUSTINE."
"MAYBE THE DOC CAN FIGURE OUT A WAY TO UPGRADE YOU."
MUST BE NICE TO UPGRADE EACH YEAR.
HOW'S THAT, CAPTAIN?
MY BODY JUST GETS OLDER. YOURS GETS STRONGER.
YOU COULD ALWAYS REMOVE A LIMB OR TWO AND SEE HOW YOU LIKE IT. IT'S A LITTLE LIKE GETTING AN EAR PIERCED.
"SO, WHAT NOW, CAPTAIN? WHAT DO WE TELL THE CREW?"

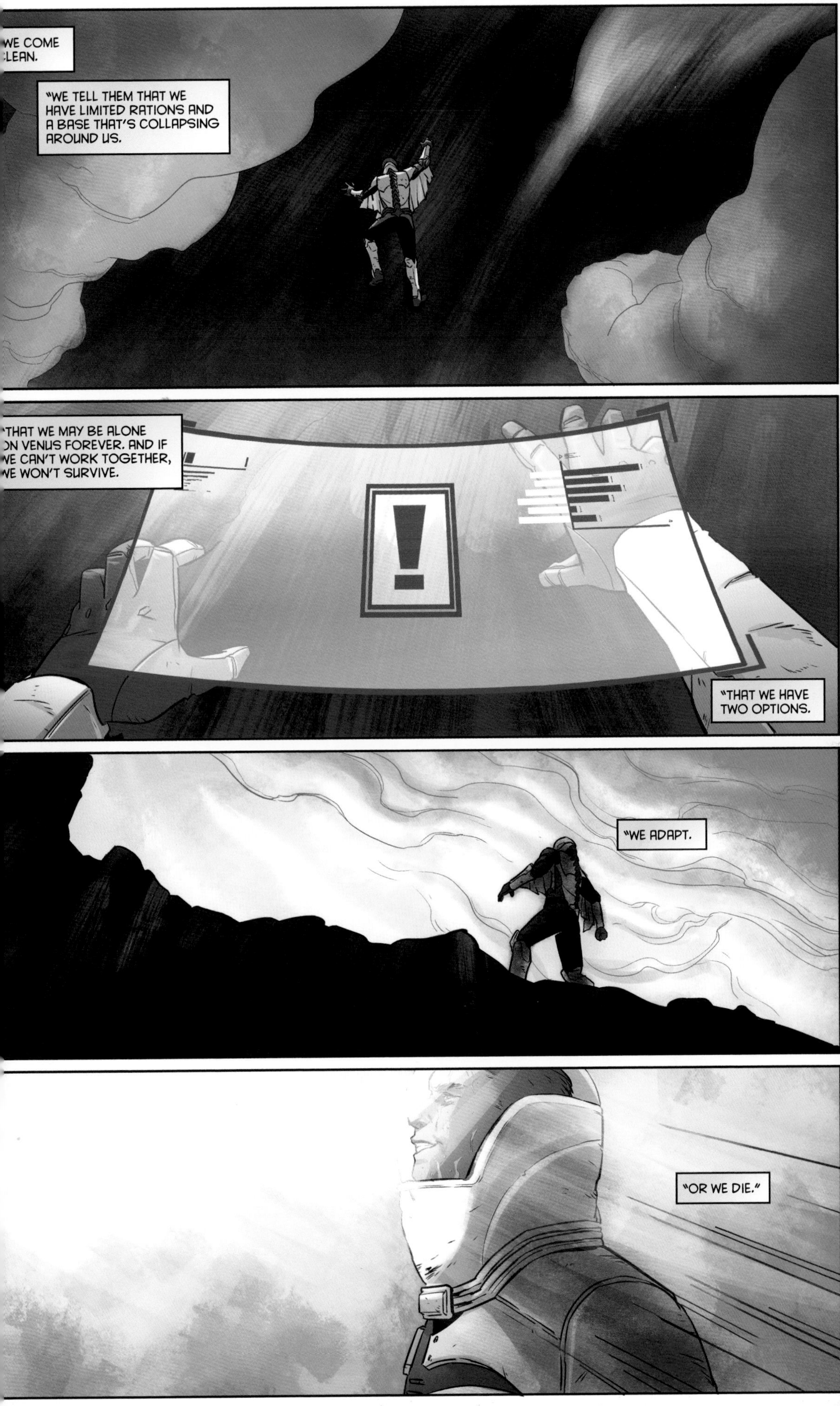

WE COME
CLEAN.
"WE TELL THEM THAT WE HAVE LIMITED RATIONS AND A BASE THAT'S COLLAPSING AROUND US.
"THAT WE MAY BE ALONE ON VENUS FOREVER. AND IF WE CAN'T WORK TOGETHER, WE WON'T SURVIVE.
"THAT WE HAVE TWO OPTIONS.
"WE ADAPT.
"OR WE DIE."

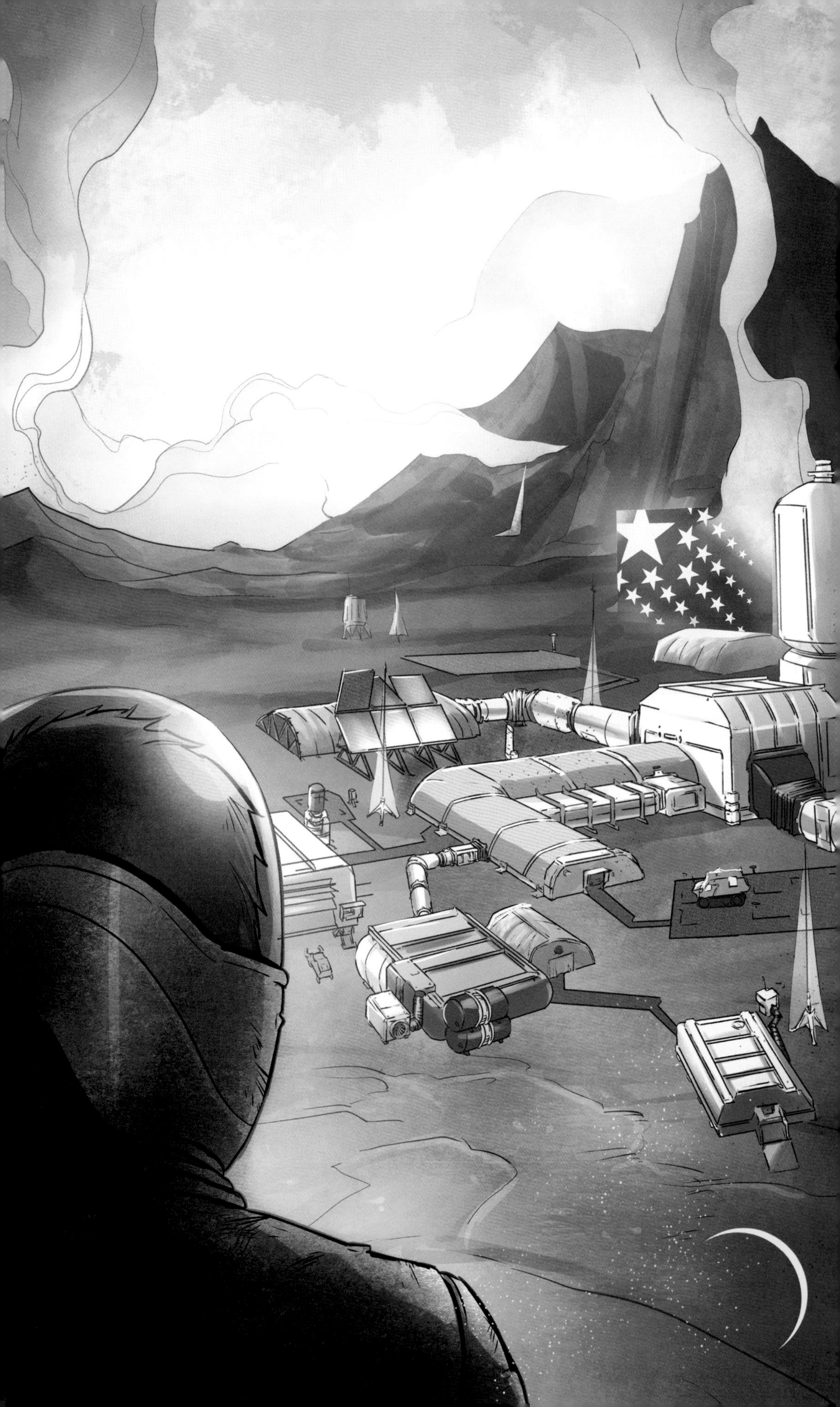

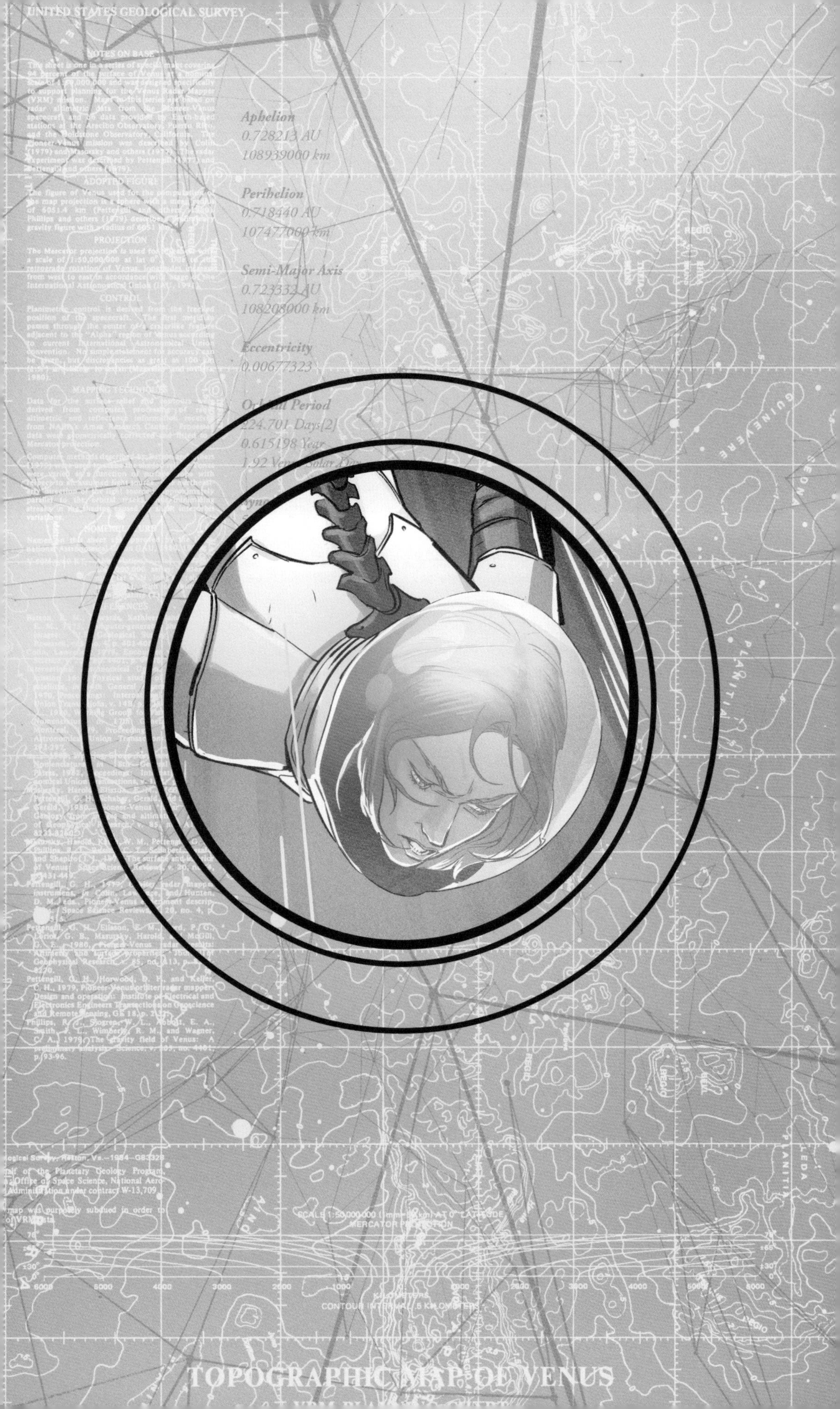
UNITED STATES GEOLOGICAL SURVEY
Aphelion
0.728213 AU
108939000 km
Perihelion
0.718440 AU
107477000 km
Semi-Major Axis
0.723332 AU
108208000 km
Eccentricity
0.00677323
224.701 Days[2]
0.615198 Year
TOPOGRAPHIC MAP OF VENUS

A NEW FRONTIER

Venus is virtually an unexplored world. There have been few Venus orbiter missions and even fewer landers... lasting only a few hours on its hellish surface. With surface temperatures of 880 degrees F, a surface pressure 90 times as great as sea level on Earth, and sulfuric acid rain, it is by far the most difficult of the terrestrial planets to explore... and colonize.

But humans are a curious lot. We need to explore, to discover, and to eventually master. Exploration is how we discover our place in the universe. However, before these forays into the unknown can be attempted, we first have to dream about them. Consider humans' quest to land on the Moon. Humans had dreamed about it for centuries. It wasn't until the Apollo Program that it became a reality. So, if humanity is to expand off of this small blue world, it is vital that we first imagine living on those other worlds. From there we need to develop the technologies needed to keep our frail bodies alive in those harsh and alien environments... and then to just do it. So stories of exploration and living on other worlds are the first step needed to make those quests a reality.

One such future reality is making other worlds habitable for humans. In science fiction the term is terraforming: changing the conditions on another world so that humans can live on it. But we first must ask, "Is terraforming possible?" The way I answer this is, does it violate a law of nature? If it does, it's not possible. If it doesn't then it is, we just don't know how to accomplish it. As an example, can we go faster than the speed of light? No. That would violate our understanding of relativity. Can a human being live to be 400 years old? ... Yes. It does not violate a law of nature. We just don't know how to do it. Our limited understanding does not allow us to develop the needed technologies to perform such a feat... but it is possible. And so is terraforming. We just don't know how to do it.

One day we will colonize other worlds, and we have already begun. The International Space Station is our first step. We are learning how to live off of the Earth. The next step will be to colonize the Moon, which will be done in our lifetime. Then we migrate into the vast dark ocean of interplanetary space. But to make this a reality, we need the support of people and governments to recognize the value of it and to marshal the resources needed to make it happen. In the 1960s Wernher von Braun was asked what it would take to send humans to the Moon. He simply said, "The will to do so." The "will" is the desire, the resources, the technology, and the human spirit to make it happen.

Comic books are one vehicle for dreaming about tomorrow. In comics, we don't have to worry about all of the technical details for designing one possible future, we can just transport our imaginations to those far-off worlds. Comics are how we begin to dream about tomorrow. It's how we begin to get excited about walking on Mars, seeing Saturn's majestic rings up close, and, yes, developing a basecamp on Maxwell Montes, the highest point on the surface of Venus. The more places in this and other solar systems we can think about and read about, the more likely they will become a reality.

Space exploration is all about discovery. We learn about ourselves and about our place in the Solar System. Discoveries are happening all the time, all around the globe in all different technical areas. Areas as diverse as measuring the residual heat from the birth of the universe, to finding the Higgs Boson, to one day soon detecting life on Earth-like planets around other stars. I do not know what discovery will be made next. The only thing I can say is that the more we learn, the more there is to learn. So, let's go on a journey of discovery to Venus. If not in reality then let's start with our imagination. Let's dream about it and make it one step closer to becoming a reality.

RANDII R. WESSEN
A-Team Lead Study Architect
Jet Propulsion Laboratory

ART & SCIENCE

The arts and entertainment are driven by imagination, and what better place to turn to fuel our imaginations than exploring other worlds? Science is also driven by imagination, and we get the best of both worlds when a writer puts science in the service of art.

Science-fiction, in general, and space exploration in particular, have long played a central role in film and television—and, of course, comics. One of the first popular movies was Georges Méliès's *A Trip to the Moon*, featuring the iconic scene where a rocket ship crashes into one of the eyes on the Moon's face. The tradition continues: of the top ten highest-grossing movies of all time, a healthy eight of them center on science-fiction or fantasy themes.

It's not hard to see why. Humans are natural-born adventurers, seeking out new vistas to explore and conquer, and space is the primary frontier remaining to be explored. We've seen the first tentative beginnings of the process, with humans reaching the Moon and robotic satellites flung across the reaches of the Solar System. The next step is a doozy: Mars and Venus, our nearest planetary neighbors, are enormously more difficult to visit than even the Moon. But we will get there. It's what human beings do.

Rick Loverd gives us a compelling picture of what those future missions might look like, finding inspiration in the science of today to imagine the futuristic world of the Mayflower mission. That world is equal parts strange and familiar. The ship is powered by a stellerator fusion reactor and the base camp on Venus controlled by an AI. There are drones and rovers, space suits and synthetic biology—all the advanced technologies one would need to colonize a harsh environment like the surface of Venus, all of which have their roots in the technology of today.

Even the details of the (now partially-terraformed) planet itself are drawn from real-world science, right down to the landscape littered with black rocks and lava flows. And who can forget the image of hailstones rife with sulfuric acid falling at half-speed though the Venusian atmosphere? That's the power of melding art and science.

The environments of outer space and other worlds are so exotic and dangerous, so literally alien, that they provide extraordinary settings for tales of exploration and adventure. But it's the human beings at the center of those stories that we identify with. Science-fiction provides new and fun ways to put our heroes through their paces, to test their humanity in ways our ancestors couldn't have imagined. The crew members of the Mayflower are first and foremost fallible human beings. There is conflict, grief, fear, and self-doubt, but also courage and camaraderie as they struggle to survive in the face of near-impossible odds.

The essence of an exciting story is a journey. It may be metaphorical, as our heroes try something new and are transformed thereby, but there's nothing like a good old-fashioned literal journey to get the juices flowing.

If science informs fiction, fiction certainly returns the favor. Everyone is familiar with the list of technological advances that were prefigured in fiction, from rocket ships to smartphones. But more importantly, fiction provides inspiration. Ask some scientists, and you are sure to find that many of them were initially hooked by science-fiction and fantasy when they were children. The two fields stem from a common source: human curiosity and a quest to explore the unknown.

A great comic book, like a great film or novel, allows us to put ourselves in new environments before it becomes literally possible. It's a simulation of reality: not only of the technological challenges, but of the human dilemmas that explorers will inevitably face. Fiction is our first view into the future.

JENNIFER OUELLETTE
Senior Science Editor, Gizmodo

EARTH'S EVIL TWIN

When you first look at Venus's stats, it's easy to think it's Earth's twin.

After all, it's nearly the same size, with a diameter of 12,014 km (95% Earth's). It has about 82% the mass of Earth, giving it almost the same density as our home planet, which in turn implies it's made of very nearly the same material: iron, rock, and so on.

But when you look more closely, things get ugly fast. Venus is so hostile an environment that it would make the devil jealous. The atmosphere is incredibly thick, with a surface pressure 90 *times higher* than Earth's. The air is almost entirely carbon dioxide, which generates a ridiculous greenhouse effect. The surface temperature is a sweltering 460° C (860° F). The clouds there aren't made of water vapor like ours... they're composed of sulfuric acid.

Yes, seriously. Venus isn't Earth's twin. It's Earth's *evil* twin.

You can see why colonists would want to terraform Venus before planting a flag. Going there now is an exercise in seeing how long it takes to die.

That's not really a joke; in the 1960s and '70s the Soviet Union sent a series of probes to the surface of Venus, and none lasted much more than two hours, destroyed by the hellish conditions.

It's an interesting problem: not so much if your landing craft will survive (it won't, at least not for long), but what will kill it first.

In the upper atmosphere, conditions are pretty similar to Earth at the same altitude. The temperature is quite cold, well below the freezing point of water, until you drop to about 60 km above the surface. There, the temperature is right about 0° C, and the pressure roughly 10% Earth at sea level.

Sounds nice, but then, you're right in the middle of the cloud deck. The *concentrated sulfuric acid* cloud deck. It's best not to stay long.

As you descend, the temperature screams up. You get a moment of pause; at 50 km conditions are almost clement. The air is roughly room temperature, and the pressure is about the same as sea level on Earth. But it won't last long. Descend 10 more klicks and the temperature is well above the boiling point of water, and the pressure is four times sea level — like being 40 meters under water on Earth. By the time you're 10 km above the surface, the pressure is now 50 atmospheres, like being in a submarine half a kilometer underwater. The temperature is high enough to melt lead. Most metals will start to soften.

By the time you hit the surface, well, unless your spaceship is built like a tank, you're in trouble. Those Soviet probes were hardened, so overbuilt that they barely had room under their armor for scientific instruments, and even then they lasted for less time than it takes to watch your typical superhero movie.

Terraforming Venus is a monumental task, one that it's not at all clear how to do. But in the end, it's probably a heck of a lot easier than trying to colonize Venus the way it is. You *could* build floating structures that stay at that 50 km-or-so sweet spot. But then, sulfuric acid. The best protection from *that* is tungsten and lead, which are resistant, but may be kinda heavy.

Venus is a rough town.

The irony of all this — above and beyond Venus looking so Earth-like on paper — is that the planet is one of the most beautiful objects in the sky. The cloud cover makes it so reflective that it's the third brightest natural object in the sky (after the Sun and Moon), and usually best visible in the twilight sky, when the horizon is still deep blue from lingering daylight. The contrast of brilliant Venus and the sky around it is striking, enhancing that beauty.

But then, the contrast between Venus and Earth is also striking. Perhaps, though, that enhances the appreciation we have of the beauty of our own planet. For now, at least, it's the only one we've got.

PHIL PLAIT
Author of Slate's Bad Astronomy Blog
Astronomer, Public Speaker, Science Evangelizer, and Author

UNLIKELY HOME

We don't want to grow up to be like Venus. Any apocalyptic scenario you can imagine on Earth pales in comparison to the nicest day on Venus; over 800 degrees Fahrenheit, with a surface pressure nearly 100 times that of the Earth, topped by a decent chance of sulfuric acid rain. Our sister planet is no place to call home. She even rotates the wrong way – the Sun rises in the west and sets in the east.

But once upon a time Venus might have been a more habitable world. A world perhaps even with oceans of liquid water flanked by beautiful volcanoes. The story of Venus is the story of a planet set on a path of peril by too much carbon dioxide – a so-called runaway greenhouse.

Could we rewind the clock on Venus? Could she be returned to a state of existence where we might someday call her home? Unlikely. Very unlikely. In fact, let me just say that it will probably, almost certainly, never happen. Period.

But by taking us on a fantastical journey into a future where humans inhabit and work to change Venus, Rick lays out a parable that hits much closer to home: how will humanity handle the crisis of climate change? How far will we let our planet go down the path of peril? What actions might we take to control the greenhouse effect? This is the great challenge we face in the decades and century to come. It's a challenge that may entail great engineering feats to suck the carbon dioxide out of our skies, to control the cycles of wind and rain, to harness the power of the Sun while also tending to the delicate balance of the intricate ecosystems that make our planet such a beautiful place for life. What our planet looks like one hundred years from now, two hundred years from now...one thousand years from now... is in part being determined by our actions today. How will we proceed? What kind of planet do we want to grow up to be?

K. P. HAND, PH.D.
Deputy Chief Scientist for Solar System Exploration
NASA Jet Propulsion Laboratory

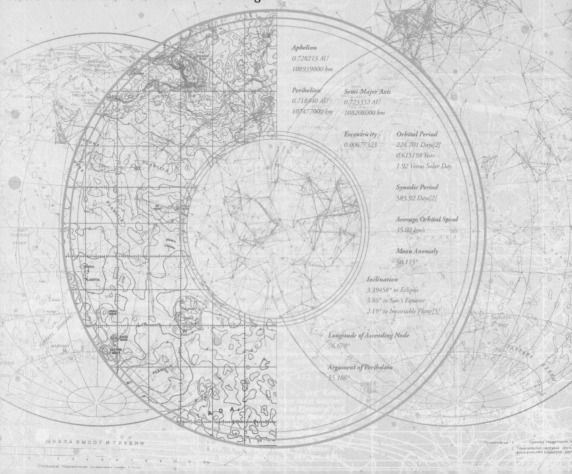

Aphelion
0.728213 AU
108939000 km

Perihelion
0.718440 AU
107477000 km

Semi-Major Axis
0.723332 AU
108208000 km

Eccentricity
0.006772323

Orbital Period
224.701 Days[2]
0.615198 Years
1.92 Venus Solar Day

Synodic Period
583.92 Days[2]

Average Orbital Speed
35.02 km/s

Mean Anomaly
50.115°

Inclination
3.39458° to Ecliptic
3.86° to Sun's Equator
2.19° to Invariable Plane[3]

Longitude of Ascending Node
76.678°

Argument of Perihelion
55.186°

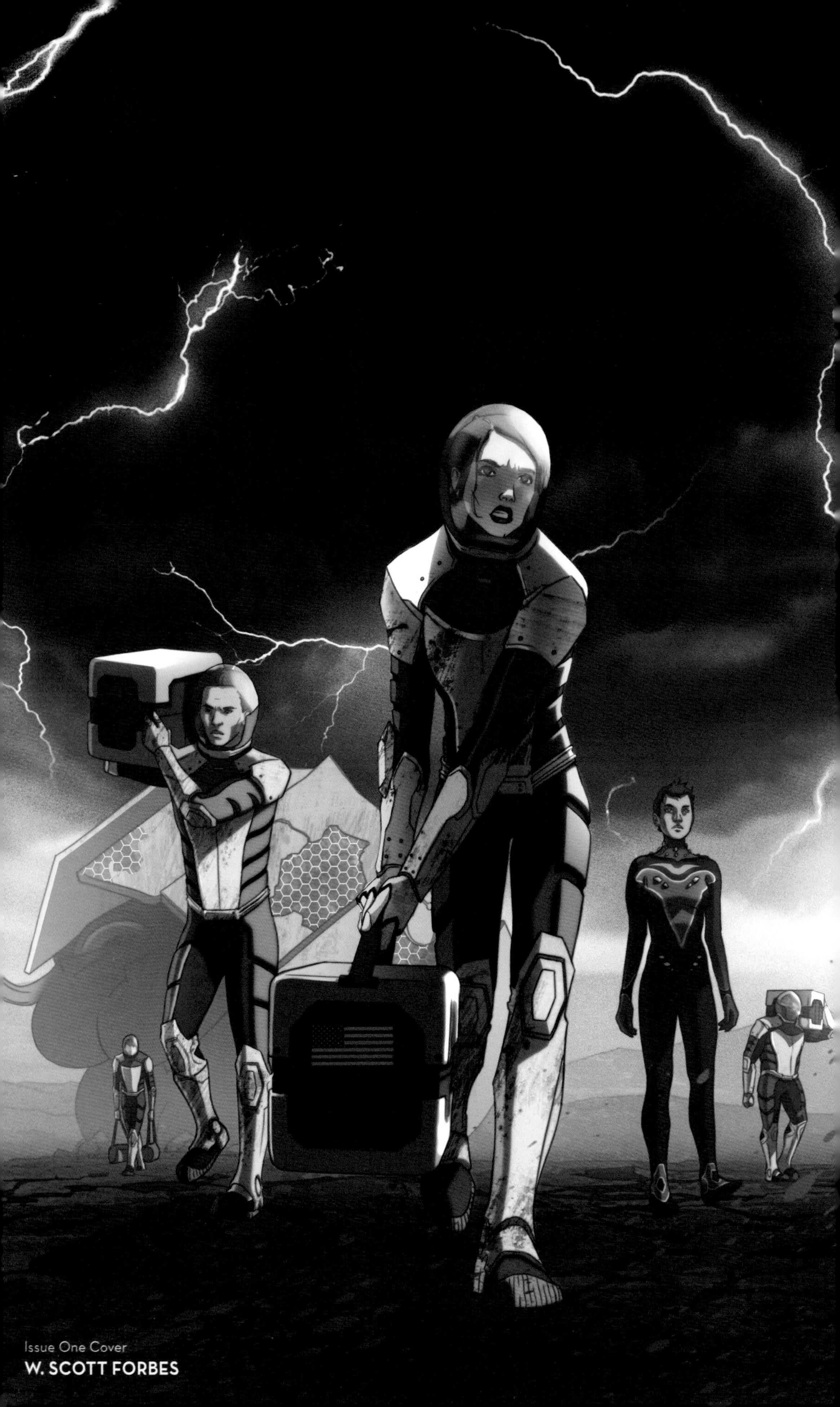

Issue One Cover
W. SCOTT FORBES

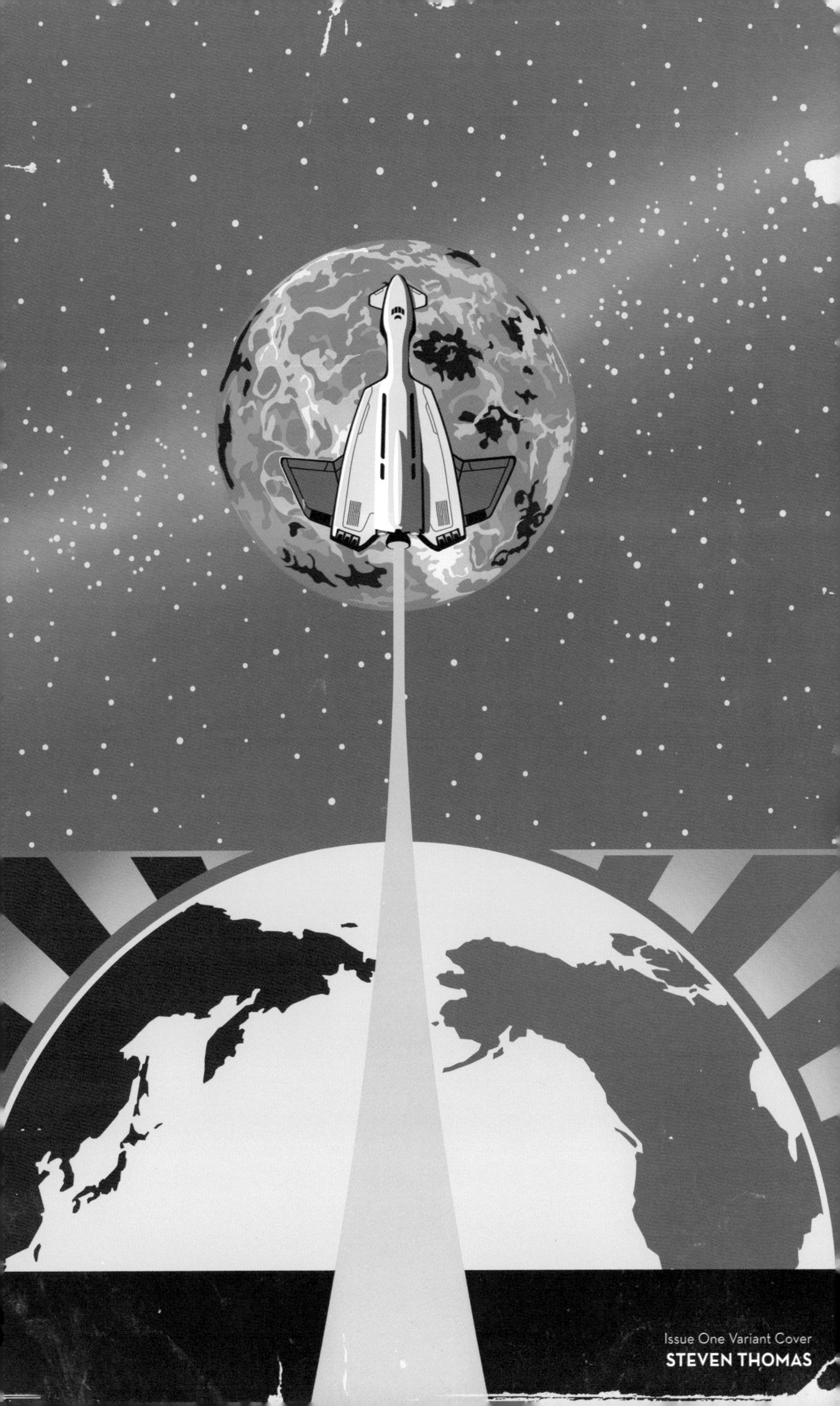

Issue One Variant Cover
STEVEN THOMAS

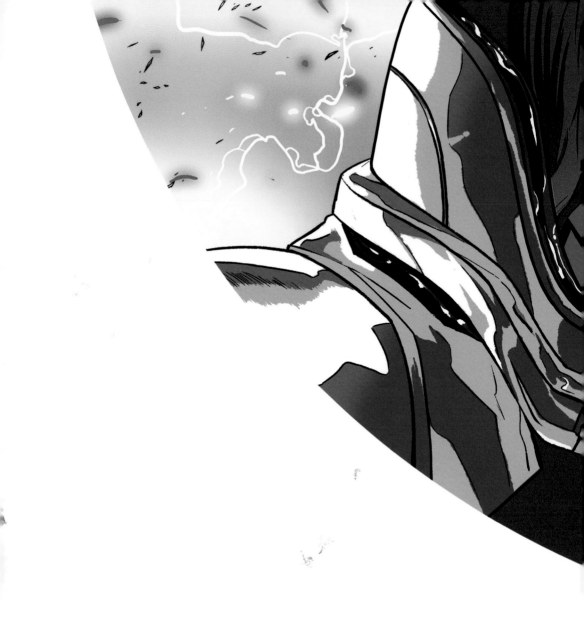

Issue One BOOM! Ten Years Variant Cover
FELIPE SMITH

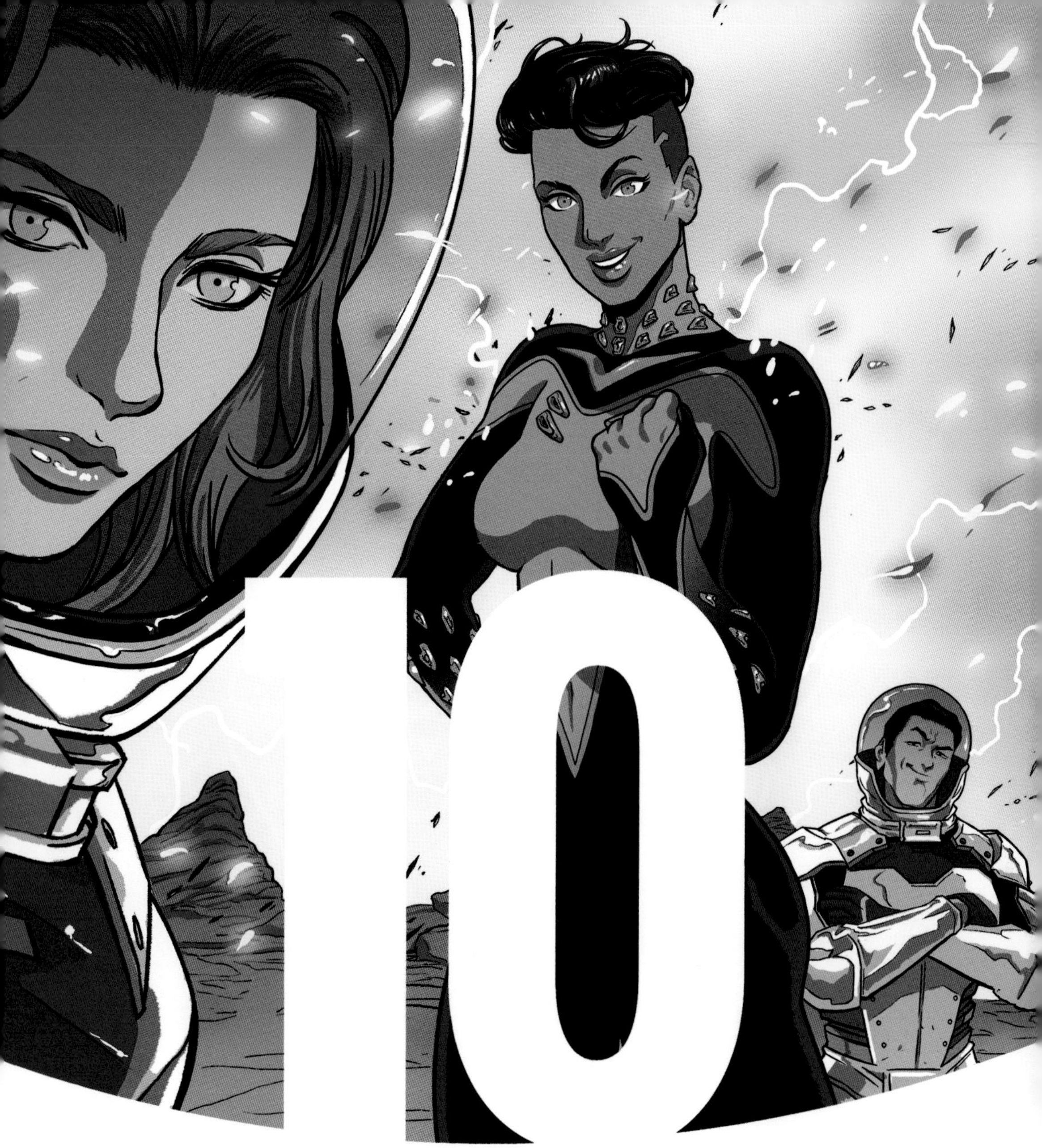
10

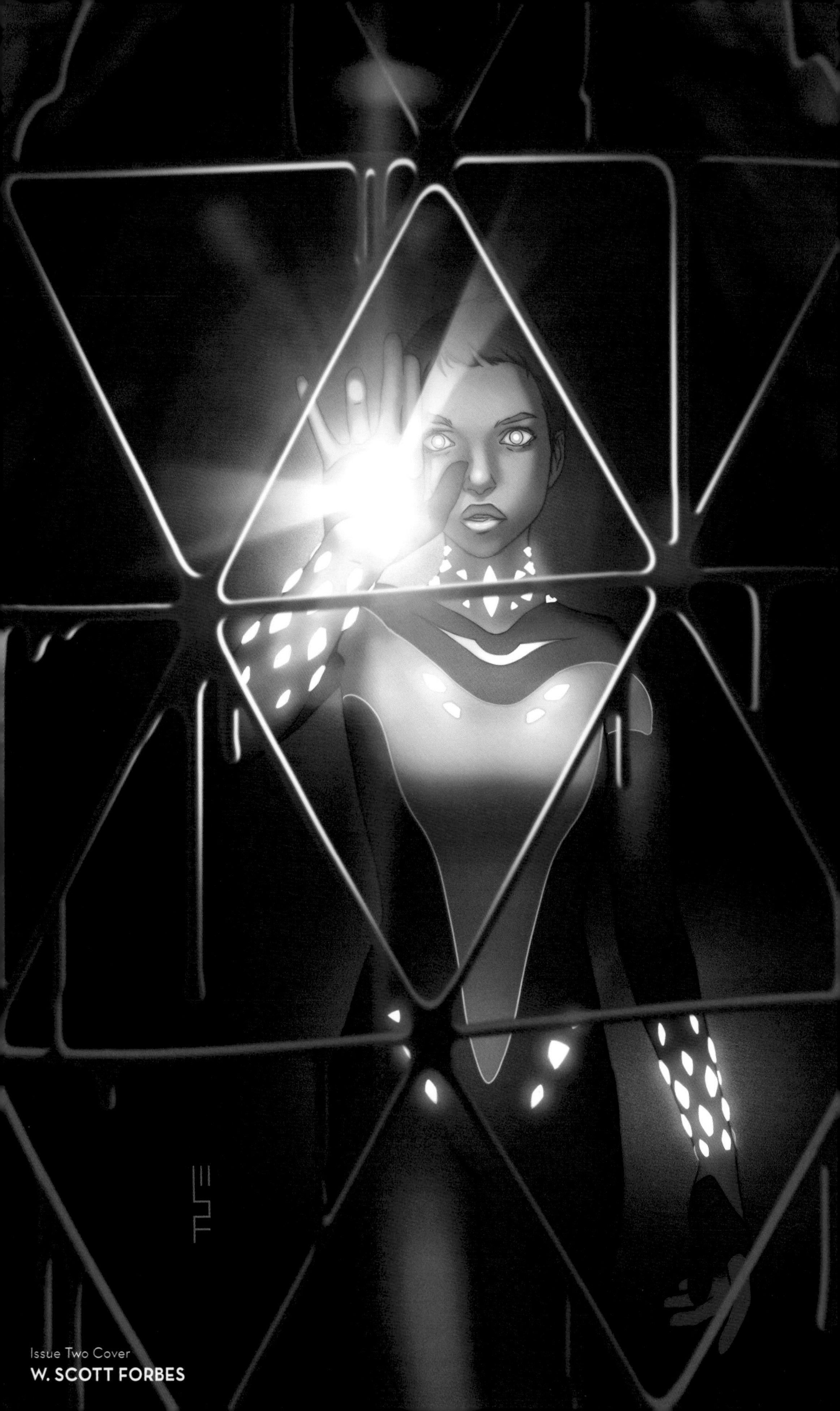

Issue Two Cover
W. SCOTT FORBES

Issue Three Cover
W. SCOTT FORBES

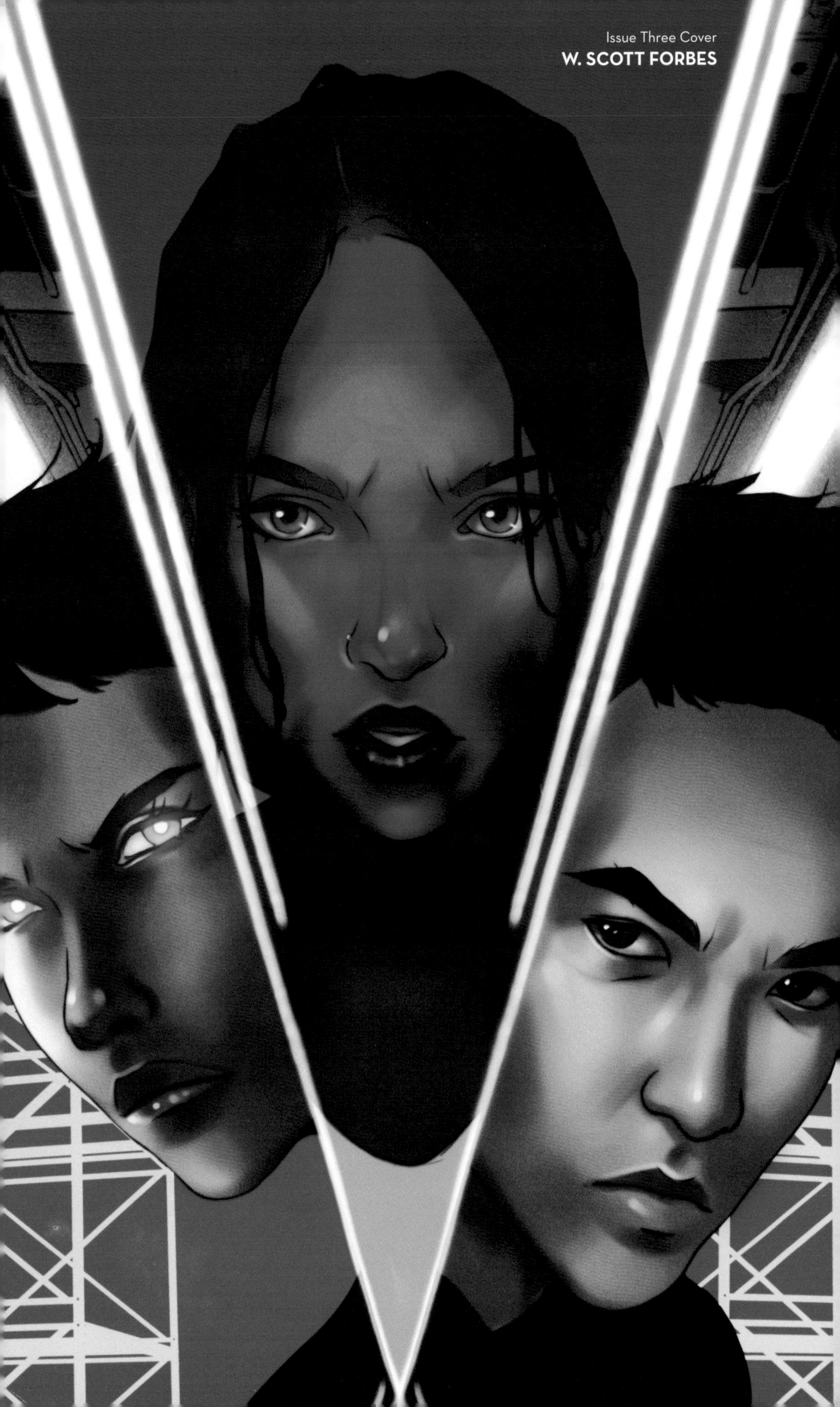

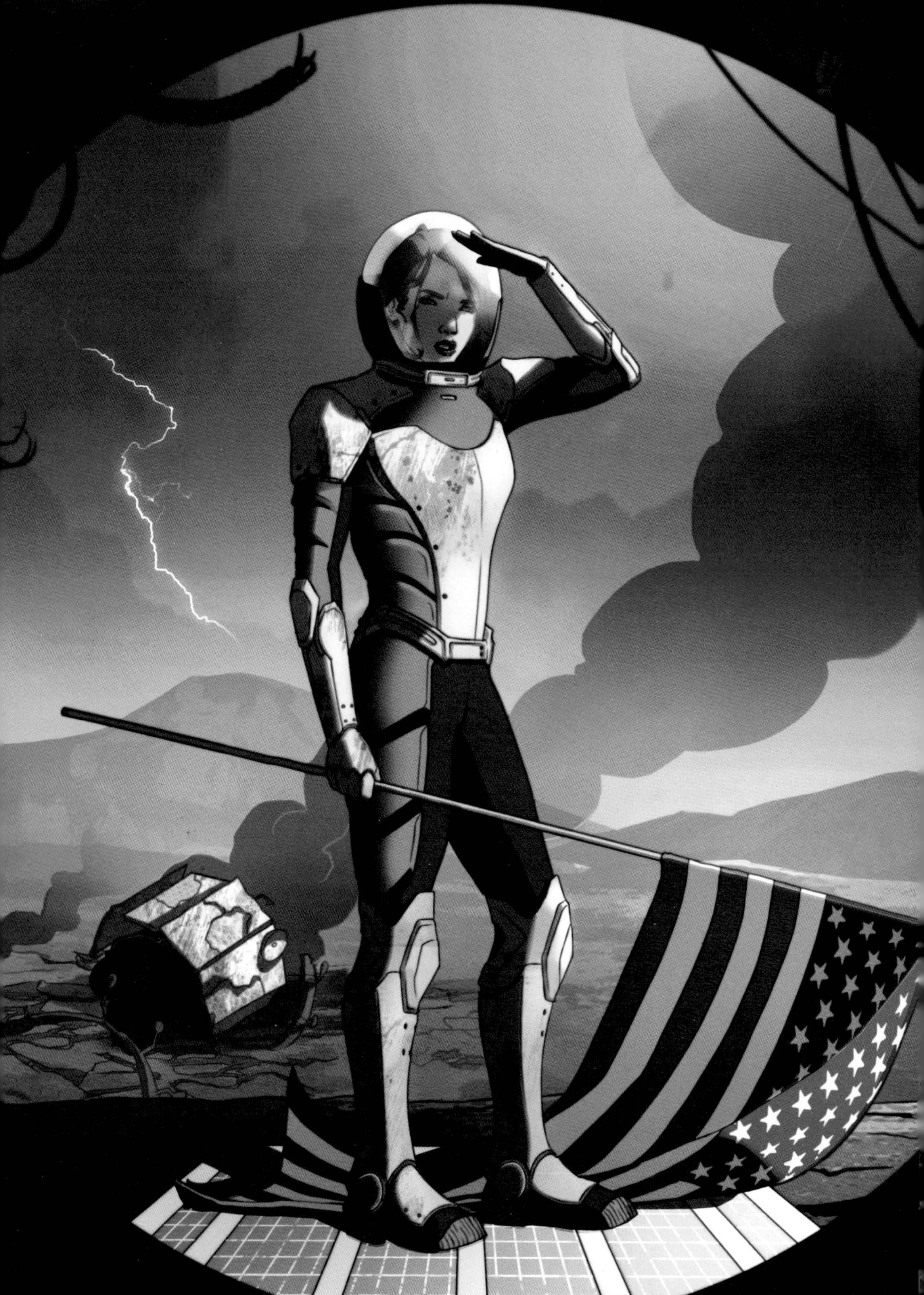

Issue Four Cover
W. SCOTT FORBES